# Cultural Perspectives
# on Child Development

# Cultural Perspectives on Child Development

Edited by

## Daniel A. Wagner
University of Pennsylvania

## Harold W. Stevenson
University of Michigan

W. H. Freeman and Company
San Francisco

*Project Editor:* Judith Wilson

*Copy Editor:* Michael Miller

*Designer:* Valerie Swanson

*Production Coordinators:* Valerie Swanson and William Murdock

*Illustration Coordinator:* Cheryl Nufer

*Artist:* Katherine Monahan

*Compositor:* Graphic Typesetting Service

*Printer and Binder:* The Maple-Vail Book Manufacturing Group

**Library of Congress Cataloging in Publication Data**
Main entry under title:

Cultural perspectives on child development.

(A Series of books in psychology)
Bibliography: p.
Includes index.
1. Child psychology—Cross-cultural studies.
2. Cognition in children—Cross-cultural studies.
I. Wagner, Daniel A., 1946–    . II. Stevenson, Harold
William, 1924–    . III. Series.
BF721.C76        155.4        81-9884
ISBN 0-7167-1289-X            AACR2
ISBN 0-7167-1290-3 (pbk.)

Printed in the United States of America

9  8  7  6  5  4  3  2  1  0    MP    0  8  9  8  7  6  5  4  3  2

# Contents

# Preface

Child development research has expanded vigorously during the past few decades. Knowledge about children has increased, new kinds of questions are being asked, and new areas of study are developing, including the exciting field of cross-cultural research.

Much of what we were able to say about children in the past was based on information gathered only from white middle-class Western children. Cross-cultural studies have helped to remedy this deficiency by providing information about child development in diverse cultures and in a variety of settings. Indeed, we cannot consider child development in its broad context unless we know how children grow and develop in environments and cultures different from those in which much of our research has already been conducted. Although anthropologists and some psychologists tried for many years to impress this point upon us, only recently has the field of child development become international in scope and less ethnocentric in its theories and research.

There are many indications of the field's vitality. A *Handbook of Cross-Cultural Psychology* is being published in several volumes (Triandis, 1980 *et seq.*), and a *Handbook of Cross-Cultural Human Development* (Munroe, Munroe, and Whiting, 1981) is now available. Several textbooks and books of readings in cross-cultural aspects of child development have appeared, such as those by Dasen, 1977; Munroe and Munroe, 1975; and Werner, 1979.

With all these volumes, why then should there be a need for another book? There are several reasons. Handbooks are encyclopedic, and textbooks typically contain only brief summaries of studies. Students find it rewarding to supplement these sources by reading about particular studies in more detail. Articles from professional journals are sometimes assigned for this purpose. However, journal articles are usually written for professionals who have sophisticated backgrounds in methodology, statistics, and theory.

We decided, therefore, to ask a number of leading researchers to write original chapters that would introduce their research to a nonprofessional audience. We requested that they try to provide a context for their research and present their ideas in a manner that would be readily understandable. Authors were asked to concentrate on a single study or a short series of studies, rather than attempt to describe larger segments of research. Research projects were chosen that dealt with varied research topics, children of differing ages, and research sites in diverse parts of the world.

We hope that this sample of cross-cultural studies will give readers an understanding of why cross-cultural studies are undertaken, a sensitivity to methodological problems, and an expanded concept of the development of the child. The following paragraphs offer a preview.

## THE CHAPTERS

The book begins with a chapter by Super and Harkness on emotional development during infancy and early childhood. They describe how emotional behavior is expressed during infancy and how it is regulated by the infant's caretakers and environment. Drawing on their experiences among the Kipsigis people of Kenya, Super and Harkness give us a vivid view of the ways in which universal elements of human emotional expression are molded by culture.

Lester and Brazelton and their colleagues (Chapter 2) have been working on the development of the newborn child in the United States and abroad. The Brazelton Neonatal Assessment Scale is widely used for studying the range and variation of behavior in normal, preterm, and "at-risk" babies. This research group, with well-trained observers, is providing a richer understanding of the baby's first contacts with the extra-uterine environment. In their chapter, Lester and Brazelton integrate research from several cultures in which studies on neonatal behavior were undertaken.

Blount (Chapter 3) is a sociolinguist and anthropologist who has been working with bilingual children. While many investigators of language development have focused on children's skills, Blount has brought our attention to the importance of parental speech in infants' efforts at communication. He describes prominent components of parental language that appear to be crucial for the acquisition of language skills and compares these for English- and Spanish-speaking parents.

The study of culture and perception is one of the older areas of research in cross-cultural psychology. Nevertheless, there has been little research on the acquisition of perceptual skills in different cultural settings. In Chapter 4, Jahoda and McGurk, using a set of ingenious experiments, explicate the process by which children learn to perceive the representation of objects and depth in pictures. The implications of the study go beyond the acquisition of perceptual skills in children, for they give us insights into the general operation of perception.

In Chapter 5 Wagner discusses the importance of ontogenetic or developmental research in formulating theories of cognition in the child and in the adult. In presenting research on the development of perception and memory among children in Morocco and Yucatan, Wagner delineates some of the necessary and sufficient factors required for understanding the socialization of cognition.

One of the largest research projects undertaken in child development outside the United States is the study by a group of researchers at INCAP (Institute for Nutrition in Central America and Panama) on the influences of nutritional supplementation on physical and cognitive development of rural children in Guatemala. This long-term project has added important information about the effects of moderate malnutrition and nutritional supplementation on cognitive and intellectual development. In Chapter 6, Townsend, Klein, Irwin, Owens, Yarbrough, and Engle provide an overview of the influence of nutritional status on the mental development of preschool children, a topic of practical and theoretical importance.

Piaget's research, originally conducted in Geneva, has become world famous. Since Piaget's first publications in the 1920s, many investigators have asked whether the phenomena reported by Piaget can be found in children in other parts of the world. Nyiti (Chapter 7) attempts to answer this question by investigating the performance of Canadian children from English-speaking and Micmac Indian families on Piaget's "conservation" tasks. After describing the general outline of Piaget's theory of stages, Nyiti shows how children may appear to lag behind others in their progression through the stages when the language and culture of the examiner differ from those of the child.

Ciborowski and Price-Williams (Chapter 8) continue the inquiry into the universality of Piagetian proposals by studying the phenomenon of "animism," the tendency to attribute "life" and "will" to objects, among Pidgin-speaking children in Hawaii. Conducting such studies turns out to be more difficult than might be expected: The presence of animism in children's thought depends on the language and culture of the children involved.

There has been a growing interest in the nature of cognitive development in nonschool settings. In the forefront of this field, Greenfield and Lave (Chapter 9) discuss their research in Mexico and Liberia. From this work they develop an innovative model for understanding informal education. This approach has important implications for those concerned with the relation between school, society, and intellectual development.

Schools were established as formal settings for transmitting information from one generation to another. But what other influences do they have on children's development? Can we show, for example, that children who attend school perform differently from nonschooled children on cognitive tasks that are not directly taught in school? Stevenson (Chapter 10) and his colleagues have been studying this question among the Quechua Indians of Peru, and he reports about part of a large study that has just been completed.

Holtzman (Chapter 11) and his colleagues have been engaged in the cross-cultural study of personality in Mexican and American children and adolescents. Holtzman's work uses standardized tests and inkblot techniques as well as formal interviews. This continuation of an early, popular approach to studies of culture and personality helps us understand commonalities and differences between groups of children of different cultures growing up in urban settings.

In Chapter 12, Edwards presents her work on the development of moral judgment among Kenyan children. Kohlberg's well-known stage theory of moral development is adopted as the research framework. By studying within-culture differences in moral reasoning, Edwards is able to propose nonuniversal alternatives to the theory. This work shows the power of the cross-cultural approach in testing theories in which some cultures are said to be "superior" to others.

A cultural perspective on human development is inevitable, and we hope that these chapters will help the reader to develop such a perspective. The reader will observe that a majority of chapters reflect a growing interest in the cognitive aspects of children's growth and development. We expect that the future will produce a greater diversity in both authorship and research topics as increasing numbers of investigators consider the interactive nature of culture and child development.

It is interesting to note that much of the research in the past 20 years was conducted among Third World cultures by Western investigators. We had hoped to be able to obtain more manuscripts from authors from the Third World, but we were unable to make such arrangements.

As we look back on the completed volume, we are aware of our good fortune in having been able to work with such an excellent group of collaborators. We are grateful to them for taking time from busy schedules to write these chapters.

*June 1981*

*Daniel A. Wagner*
*Harold W. Stevenson*

# Acknowledgments

Fieldwork and preparation of the chapter by Super and Harkness were supported in part by grants from the William T. Grant Foundation, the Carnegie Corporation of New York, the Spencer Foundation, and the National Institute of Mental Health (Grant MH-33281).

The work described in the chapter by Lester and Brazelton was supported by NIMH National Research Service Award No. IF32MH06062 and by the William T. Grant Foundation.

Support for the field work described in Wagner's chapter was provided primarily by the Social Science Research Council. The preparation of this paper was supported by funds from the National Institute of Mental Health while the author was a postdoctoral fellow at Harvard University.

The research of Townsend, Klein, Irwin, Owens, Yarbrough, and Engle was supported in part by the National Institute of Health (NICHD), Bethesda, Maryland (Contract No. NO1/DH-5-0640), and the National Science Foundation, Washington, D.C. (Grant Soc 77-01063, "Uniform Measures of Social Competence"), in collaboration with the Institute for Social Science Research, University of California at Los Angeles.

Nyiti's studies were supported by a faculty research grant at the College of Cape Breton, Sydney, Nova Scotia, Canada. Thanks are due to Brenda Stewart and Murdina Marshall for their assistance in collecting the data. We would also like the extend our thanks to school officials in Sydney and Eskasoni for granting admission to the schools and to parents for allowing their children to participate in this project.

The research work upon which the chapter by Ciborowski and Price-Williams are based was supported mainly by a grant from the Carnegie Corporation of New York. It was also supported in part by PHS Grant HD 04612, NICHD, Mental Retardation Center, in the School of Medicine, University of California at Los Angeles. The following students of anthropology graciously gave permission for the use of their field notes for the period of 1973 to 1976: Sandra Gaile, Jill Korbin, and Frank Newton.

The research by Stevenson was supported by the William T. Grant Foundation and the National Science Foundation (Grant 7611785).

# Cultural Perspectives
# on Child Development

# 1

# The Development of Affect in Infancy and Early Childhood

*Charles M. Super*
*Sara Harkness*

I had occasion twice in one week to meet passengers from ships at the ocean terminal in Sydney. One ship was the *Southern Cross*, from Southampton, and the other was the *Galileo Galilei* from Milan. In the one case the dockside was crowded with a throng of people, babies and grandparents, laughing, weeping, shouting. Men embraced and kissed; women shrieked and rushed into passionate greetings. There was tumultuous confusion. From the other ship the passengers passed sedately down the gangplank, in orderly groups; there were waves of hands and smiles, polite handshakes, and impassive greetings such as "How nice to see you again." (Nash, 1970, p. 428)

Group differences in publicly visible emotional behavior have been a source of amazement, amusement, and trouble since time immemorial, for they have a particularly personal aspect. Language differences do not share this personal quality, for they are experienced subjectively as a rupture in the medium of communication. Behind the odd sounds lie thoughts which, once translated, we assume we would understand. Emotional displays, however, seem to be the content of a communication, not its medium. Laughter, tears, and silence appear universal in meaning; we need no translator. But why are other people so cold or so boisterous? Have they no heart or no decency? Seeing the African laugh at a blind man's confusion, or the European tenderly waste scarce food on a dog, we "know" what the other is doing; we only ask how it is possible that a person could do such a thing.

## CULTURE AND PERSONALITY

Emotional states and expressions are among the behaviors related to culture. Partly regulated themselves by values and beliefs about reality, emotions work to support (or sometimes to subvert) social institutions such as marriage, warfare, charity, cooperative labor groups, and legal mechanisms for settlement of disputes. How is it that people from different cultures come to display different emotional behaviors in apparently similar circumstances? For several decades, it was thought that the study of infancy and early childhood in other cultures would provide an answer. People in other cultures behave differently, the theory said, partly because they have different personalities. They have different personalities because they were reared in a way very different from the way we were reared.

The relationship between personality and larger cultural dimensions is a recurring focus of theory and research in the social sciences. The field of "culture and personality" emerged within anthropology as Margaret Mead, Ruth Benedict, John Whiting, and other pioneers in the field recognized that anthropology could not fulfill the task of understanding culture without accounting for how culture operates through the individual. The anthropologist never sees a culture—only the things and behaviors produced by the members of a culture. The knowledge and skills, beliefs and values of the culture are held by individuals who acquired them in the past and will pass them on to the next generation. An important aspect of understanding how cultures work, therefore, is understanding how individuals learn to use their cultures.

In pursuing this inquiry, social scientists of the culture-and-personality era (roughly the 1930s to the 1950s) naturally looked to psychological theories of the time to help them understand child development. In many ways the interdisciplinary fit was a good one, for a prominent school of thought in psychology at the time was the new and promising field of psychoanalysis. Freud and those influenced by his ideas focused their

attention on the role of childhood experiences in shaping adult personality. The psychologists' work coincided with the theoretical needs of the
anthropologists.

In the 1950s and 1960s, by and large, both anthropology and psychology become more diverse in their theoretical focus, and the driving
unity behind "culture and personality" weakened. There are many reasons for this, some of them related to the natural history of scientific
fields as they explore paradigms of inquiry. More immediately, however,
there were three problems with the culture-and-personality school of
investigation that continued to frustrate a sense of resolution despite
considerable effort and progress. One was the challenge of more posi-
tivist kinds of investigation: the dissection, measurement, and quantitative analysis that were revolutionizing psychology, sociology, and other
fields. Qualitative methods of cultural analysis, like those of psychoanalysis, too often seemed inferior but were at the same time difficult to
supplement when dealing with such large and complex subjects as culture. Second, the approach depended on concepts such as "national
character" or "modal personality" for each culture, resulting from the
"typical" methods of child rearing. Many anthropologists came to think
that more allowance was needed for diversity within a culture. Finally,
the stature of psychoanalysis and learning theory, the grand schemes of
psychology that were used in the culture-and-personality approach, began to crumble within the field of psychology as they seemed to require
more and more detail to explain less and less.

The momentum of creative and exciting research on culture and personality stalled, in effect, somewhere in the 1950s, just as the experimental approach to studying American children's behavior started to
grow in both success and size. Cultural perspectives on infancy and early
childhood have not figured large in recent research and teaching in child
development, in part because of weaknesses in the ethnographic and
cross-cultural work, in part because of the enormous outpouring of experimental research, and in part because of ethnocentricity, an insen-
sitivity to cultural variation, by psychologists and the field of psychology
in general (see Harkness and Super, 1980; LeVine, 1980).


## THE NEW "INTERDISCIPLINE"

Today there is a new interest in revitalizing the interdisciplinary en-
deavor, for psychological anthropology (heir to culture and personality)
and comparative child development are emerging with new vigor in their
own fields, incorporating recent theoretical advances with traditional

strengths and reaching at the same time for the complementary powers of the sister disciplines. Cycles of progress, like cycles of fashion, have a way of building on the conceptual lines of a full generation before, restating the useful questions and concepts, abandoning hypotheses and viewpoints that proved disappointing, and trying out new ideas for theory and research.

Social and affective development appears to be a particularly promising domain for the new synthesis. The older culture-and-personality effort suffered from too broad and shallow a sweep, while traditional developmental approaches to this topic have been too insular. In our view, a satisfactory theory of social and affective development must eventually incorporate three elements: (1) a statement of the thrust of growth universal to our species, (2) a recognition of the expressive behavioral patterns encouraged by culturally regulated socialization for particular situations, and (3) an appreciation of the sequences of developmental events as they occur in the context of the full span of life.

In this essay we consider aspects of these three points from a comparative perspective. First, we present evidence of the universal emergence of some basic emotional displays, namely happy social play with caretakers and distress at their departure. Second, we illustrate the shaping of these universals into patterns of particular cultural significance. Third, we discuss the importance of the sequences of emotional learning within a culture in understanding the consequences of early affective socialization. Our examples are drawn from a variety of sources and locales, but in the second and third sections we describe in more detail the affective development of children in Kokwet, a Kipsigis community in rural Kenya.

## THE EMERGENCE OF EMOTIONAL DISPLAYS

The display of any behavior, or integrated complex of behaviors, rests on neuromotor competence. Mature, appropriate displays of emotional behavior involve not only the overt acts (such as smiling), but also associated internal feeling states and the cognitively influenced connections among a particular environmental circumstance (such as a greeting from a friend), a feeling state, and a behavioral display. While the socialization of affect is a psychological and cultural process, it occurs only in coordination with a biological substrate that is unique to, and generalized across, our species. In short, there are neurological and hormonal universals in the way humans work; these universals contribute to the mechanisms of emotional socialization and also limit the possible range of variation. Since infants do not enter the world with these or any other biological mechanisms fully mature, observations on the maturationally guided emergence of particular kinds of behavior provide a useful technique for understanding possible universals. Knowing some of the universal elements, the process of tracing environmental influences is much easier.

One of the most dramatic early changes in emotional behavior occurs when a baby is 3 or 4 months old. To the American parent, the baby begins to seem more "like a real person." The third month, it is occasionally said, makes the first two worthwhile. The baby becomes not only less incessantly demanding—often sleeping through the night, for example, and fussing less—but also more reliably rewarding. Many American parents find a qualitative change in the baby's social responsiveness and expressiveness that brings real joy. A similar reaction by Kipsigis mothers in rural Kenya may be reflected in the fact that they begin to refer to their babies as "children" at this time, and no longer as "monkeys."

There is a parallel change at this point in the mothers' behavior in the two cultures: they are more likely to be found holding their babies than they were in the previous month, even though the general trend over the first year is to decrease physical contact (Super, 1980). The kinds of mutual, flowing social play that are salient at this time look very similar in the two groups (see Figures 1-1 and 1-2). Observational recording in the home indicates that Kipsigis mothers and their 4-month-old infants smile and look at each other with about the same frequency as do upper-middle-class mother–infant pairs in Boston, Massachusetts.

Exactly what the behavioral changes in the baby are, and how they become encouraged by the mother's reactions, have yet to be fully documented. Smiling, however, is certainly a central feature of the changes in the baby's behavior. The frequency of smiling in normal infants rises dramatically during the third and fourth months in infants from many different cultures around the world. Figure 1-3 illustrates this for four groups of babies in Israel: those from lower- and middle-class urban families, from a kibbutz settlement with cooperative child care arrangements, and from a group of semi-nomadic Bedouin families in the Negev desert (Landau, 1977). The frequency of smiling by these babies, as observed in the course of a normal day, rises in a similar manner despite substantial differences in the social context of care.

The similarity in the emergence of smiling in the Israeli samples, and in other even more diverse groups, suggests an underlying maturational

**Figure 1–1**    *A Kipsigis mother in Kokwet, Kenya, enjoys a moment of happy play with her 4-month-old baby.*

cause—not a complete and sufficient cause, for maturation can proceed only through interaction with an environment, but still a necessary and driving force. The co-occurrence of this behavior change with a number of other developments at the same age supports the hypothesis of a broad underlying maturational factor. Important transitions at 3 to 4 months have been noted in other areas of emotion as well as cognition, motor skills, and sleep (for example, McGraw, 1946; Piaget, 1952; Spitz, Emde, and Metcalf, 1970). There is evidence for changes in brain structure, most notably rapid myelinization in the cerebral cortex and limbic (emotional) areas of the brain (Yakovlev and Lecours, 1967). Further support is available from studies of blind infants, who show an early growth in smiling that is slightly delayed but otherwise quite similar to development in normal infants (for example, Freedman, 1964; Parmelee, 1955).

Infant distress in response to being left by the mother also appears at a very similar rate in a number of diverse settings. In experiments con-

**Figure 1–2**    *An American mother and infant show the same kind of face-to-face orientation and smiling in their social play.*

ducted in urban America, rural Guatemala, the Kalahari desert of Botswana, and Israeli kibbutzim, infants generally do not cry when the mother leaves until about 7 or 8 months of age, after which point distress becomes more and more frequent until a peak sometime after the first birthday (see Figure 1–4, adapted from Kagan, 1976). The similarity here, it is argued, is not so much in the development of a particular behavior, but rather in a cognitive ability to detect and evaluate (and therefore sometimes fear) unusual and unpredictable events (Kagan, Kearsley, and Zelazo, 1978). Regardless of whether the change is viewed as "primarily" cognitive, emotional, or biological, or as an inseparable blend, the data again point to a remarkably ordered emergence of emotional displays in early life.

## THE SOCIALIZATION OF EMOTIONAL DISPLAYS

As the ability to display particular affective behaviors emerges, and especially as the ability becomes more stable and highly organized, the cultural system engages the infant's responses in particular ways. While

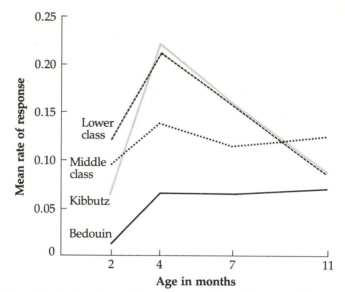

**Figure 1–3**   *Infants from four different groups in Israel increase their rate of sponta-*
*neous smiling in a similar way between 2 and 4 months of age. (Data from R. Landau,*
*"Spontaneous and elicited smiles and vocalizations of infants in four Israeli environ-*
*ments,"* Developmental Psychology, *1977, 13, 389–400).*

the psychological mechanisms that lead to smiling are fundamentally
universal, the opportunities and contexts for smiling in different cultures
diverge. There appear to be two major pathways of cultural divergence
in the emotional training of infants and young children: (1) the direct
expression of parental values or beliefs, and (2) the less intentional structuring of the child's developmental niche by the physical and social
resources for caretaking.

## Parental Values and Beliefs

The most interesting aspect of parental values as they influence early
socialization is that their expression is not usually a direct effort to achieve
some later effect. Their expression is, rather, a more immediate reflection
of adult psychological functioning. That is, values influence behavior
more in the sense of "This is the way I feel like acting with my baby" or
"This is the way I would like to see my baby act," rather than "I want to
train my baby in this skill in order to facilitate social and economic advancement in later life." Socialization values at this age are expressive
goals in their own right, not only means to some later goal. Nevertheless,

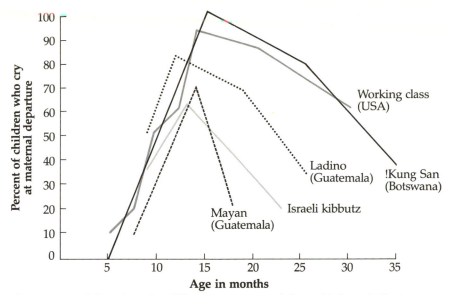

**Figure 1–4**    *Infants from five different groups around the world show similar increases during the first year in the likelihood of crying at maternal departure in an experimental setting, but diverge during later years in the decline of this response. (Adapted from J. Kagan, "Emergent themes in human development,"* American Scientist, *1976, 64, 186–196.)*

the effect of such socialization is usually to provide the infant or young child with practice in culturally appropriate social and emotional behavior.

Examples of concordance between parents' expressive interaction with infants and larger cultural values can be found from all parts of the world. In Uganda, adults and siblings talk and smile to infants more than is true in many other cultures, trying to coax a happy smile in return. It seems the natural way to play with babies. The social skills both expressed and trained in such interaction, however, are talents needed for personal advancement in the relatively mobile Baganda social order. Today, as has traditionally been the case in this group, personal skills are powerful means to gaining status and material resources. Unlike the situation in many traditional African groups, social standing can be individually earned, rather than being ascribed primarily on the basis of sex, age, or lineage (P. Kilbride and J. Kilbride, 1974; J. Kilbride and P. Kilbride, 1975).

Japanese mothers, compared to American mothers, spend large amounts of time soothing and lulling their infants, rather than stimulating them with active "chatting." The kinds of social intercourse that result are consonant with the patterns of interaction at later ages and with the larger patterns of social organization in the two societies. American mothers, partly to fulfill their own expectations of appropriate affective behavior, encourage open, expressive, assertive, self-directed behavior, while the Japanese mothers seek quiet, contented babies (Caudill and Frost, 1973; Caudill and Weinstein, 1969).

In some cases adult beliefs about the nature of infants or about the world in general shape the emotional lives of infants. The Kwoma of New Guinea and Zinacantecans of Mexico, for example, have beliefs about supernatural threats and the vulnerability of infants that lead to keeping their babies close, quiet, and calm (Brazelton, Robey, and Collier, 1969; Whiting, 1971). The cumulative effect on the infants' level of excitement may be substantial, even though the parents' motivations focus primarily on other matters. In contrast, many American parents in the mid-twentieth century were concerned with the possibility of lasting psychological damage that could result from excessive inhibition of "natural" feelings such as jealousy. This belief about the nature of personality development influenced their reaction to some kinds of emotional displays in their young children, for they thought it important to allow emotional conflicts to be expressed and played out where they could be discussed and managed (for example, Spock, 1968, p. 12).

## Structural Features of Care

The expression and regulation of emotional behavior are also mediated by structural features of infant care that are not so obviously related to adult values or beliefs. Many aspects of a young child's environment are influenced by the way families are organized for other purposes. The use of child caretakers to supplement maternal care is an important example. In many societies around the world, the moment-to-moment care of a baby is given to an older sibling or other relative, typically a 7- or 8-year-old sister (Weisner and Gallimore, 1977). While attitudes within any group concerning the desirability of single versus multiple caretakers are probably consistent with the dominant pattern in that group, it would appear that aspects of social organization, such as means of economic production, family size, and mothers' work load, are more effectively related to use of child caretakers than are the values themselves. Certainly in American society over the past decades, it can be argued that maternal employment has been the driving force behind increased group care for young children, while attitudes consistently lagged behind.

In illustrating structural environmental influences on early affective development, and in the remainder of this essay, we describe in some detail the early social life of Kipsigis children in western Kenya. It is difficult, however, to understand the integrating function of a culture's environment for children without some knowledge of the larger cultural system. Before describing structural features of the early environment in Kokwet, therefore, we will briefly present some background ethnographic information.

*The Kipsigis of Kokwet*

The Kipsigis of western Kenya are a Highland Nilotic people (Sutton, 1968) numbering about half a million. Traditionally they lived by herding cattle and raising simple crops; their life was seminomadic as they shifted pasture and field in response to the land and to sporadic fighting with neighboring groups. More permanent residence and land tenure became common in the early part of this century, encouraged by increasing contact with the British settlers and colonial administrators, especially the force of their economics and occasionally their force of arms (Manners, 1967). As in most of East Africa, the period following World War II initiated especially rapid change.

Kokwet, the Kipsigis community where we lived for 3 years in carrying out our investigation, consists of 54 homesteads spread out along 3 miles of a ridge of land formed by 2 streams that drain the Mau forest of the western highlands. To the north and east lie fine, rolling farmland and, a few hours away by dirt road, the tea estates of Kericho. To the south and west, the land dries and slopes down to the savannahs of the Mara, home of zebra and lion and of the Masai people.

The people of Kokwet have adapted successfully as farmers to the national economy. All the families are self-supporting in basic foodstuffs, maize (corn) and milk being major components of the daily diet. Milk, maize, and pyrethrum (a daisy-like flower with insecticidal properties) are grown for cash marketing as well. Each family has about 18 acres of useful land, an unusual situation created by the initial terms of the settlement scheme set up by the Kenyan government at the time of national independence (1963). The land was purchased from a departing white settler and distributed to indigenous citizens. Neighboring lands had never been alienated for European use, and the people of Kokwet moved in from the surrounding areas. The relative abundance of fertile land in Kokwet has permitted, for the present, a continuation of the agricultural adaptation to modern life without disruptive pressures to leave the farm and seek wages in towns or plantations.

While there is no "village center" to Kokwet, households often cluster near the borders of their land to form small groups within the community. The typical round houses, with mud walls and straw roofs, overlook the family's pastures and fields most of the year, sometimes hidden by the tall maize as harvest approaches.

Despite fundamental changes in Kipsigis life, many traditional features persist in Kokwet. Social organization of the community continues to operate at the face-to-face level, with conflicts and disputes confronted and resolved in this context (Harkness, Edwards, and Super, 1981). Communal efforts among households are important for ceremonies, large projects, and some major activites, such as harvesting and weeding groups. Most adults have little or no formal education, and many families consist of one man, his two wives, and their children. While there are major divisions of role by age and sex, all members of a family participate in its maintenance through household chores, agricultural labor, and tending cattle (Figure 1–5). Most children now attend at least a few years of school, but more traditional forms of preparation for adult life continue in the home and in the larger community, for example adolescent initiation and circumcision rites for both boys and girls. Christian missions have been active in the general area for half a century, but most men and women are, in their own words, "not yet" converted.

*The Infant's Niche in Kokwet*

The infant in Kokwet is born into a physical and social setting that is different from the one familiar to Americans. Until the baby is 3 or 4 months old, the mother is almost always with the child. Most of the time, in fact, mother and baby are actually touching; the baby might be sitting propped up in the mother's lap while she prepares food, riding on her back (secured and covered with cloth) as she goes to the river for water, cradled in her arms for nursing, or straddling her hip as she moves around the yard doing chores. By the time the baby is 4 months old, a child caretaker has taken over a large share of the daytime care, holding and carrying the baby and providing entertainment, but often within sight of the mother. A little later the mother may go to the garden, perhaps 10 minutes away, or visit a neighbor while leaving the baby with the child caretaker.

The baby's emotional life is influenced in a number of ways by this organization of care, or niche. Of particular interest here are the embeddedness of infant life in the continuing social and economic functioning of the family, and the adaptations to and by the several caretakers. A

**Figure 1–5**   *Children in Kokwet participate in family chores from an early age. Here, two young boys help their older sister herd cows to the river for watering.*

useful example is the regulation of sleep–wake behavior. Unlike many American families, Kipsigis households do not make major modifications in their living quarters or family routines to facilitate infant sleep. There is no baby's room and no nap schedule. One reason this is possible is that care of an awake infant is more compatible with the mother's daily chores and pleasures. The Kipsigis mother can carry, hold, or entertain the baby reasonably well while sweeping the house, relaxing after the midday meal, fetching firewood, or preparing food (Figure 1–6). This is less true for the American mother who does not have the same customary repertoire of carrying and holding practices, and whose activities include PTA meetings, balancing the checkbook, driving to the supermarket, working in an office, and watching television.

A second circumstance that contributes to the divergence in sleep–wake scheduling is the availability of other caretakers. When the Kipsigis mother needs to be free of the baby for some kinds of garden work or

**Figure 1–6**    *Toddlers can participate in many of the mothers' daily activities, such as shelling maize kernels from the dried cob, to be ground and cooked for the family meal.*

for her peace of mind, there is almost always a sibling caretaker, a co-wife, or another relative to take the child. She does not need to rely on the baby's sleeping for a chance to disengage from continuous care.

As one consequence of these differences in the infant's niche, Kipsigis babies do not sleep quite as much as American infants, and they do not develop long periods of sustained sleep so soon. At 4 months of age, the average Kipsigis baby sleeps just over 12 hours each day, compared to about 15 in America. The longest episode of sleep is about 4.5 hours, compared to 8 (Super and Harkness, forthcoming).

The pattern of adaptation in sleep is related to adaptations in feeding, elimination, and even social interaction. In each domain the Kipsigis infant is likely to have briefer and less regular cycles of activity and rest, while the American baby is likely to have fewer, longer periods of sleeping, feeding, and playful interaction. The circadian flow of behavior has different patterns of tension and resolution in the two niches. The Kipsigis and American babies, in sum, are learning the emotional structure of their cultural niche.

The particular adaptations and embeddedness in each group are only part of the emotional structure of the niche. Of critical importance are the ways the niche can and cannot adapt to the individual characteristics of the infant, for the areas of rigidity and flexibility determine the kinds of behavior that will create upset and difficulty. For the American baby, scheduling activity by the clock may be of considerable importance to the mother because of her value system or because of her own needs. For the baby in Kokwet, adaptation to the different styles of care provided by several caretakers is essential for happy functioning of the family. Within any group, babies vary in their behavioral dispositions (Thomas and Chess, 1977). Regularity and adaptability are dimensions of variation among infants in both cultures, but their significance depends on the typical niche and its points of flexibility. In both groups, a mismatch between the needs and adaptability of the baby and those of the care-taking niche results in a situation that is stressful for all concerned. The early socialization of emotional life includes learning the sensitivities of one's niche.

Long-term adaptations to the niche play another role in emotional life, namely the building of expectations concerning what constitutes normal life and what is bizarre. While infants in Kokwet, as in other communities, are often upset when their mothers leave them for short periods, this response does not not last long. They become accustomed to care by several people, and so maternal absence by itself does not occasion distress. As Figure 1–4 shows, after the universal emergence of distress at separation from mother, at about 1 year of age, there is considerable diversity among cultures in its decline in the second and third years of life. For the American and !Kung San children, for example, who are cared for almost exclusively by the mother, the distress reaction remains frequent for a relatively long time. In the other groups, however, where siblings or other persons play an important role in the day-to-day care of infants and toddlers, there is a more rapid decline in the amount of distress.

Distress at maternal departure ("separation anxiety") is often linked in developmental theory to distress at the approach of a stranger ("fear of strangers"). While the common thread of cognitive competence is important in the emergence of these two responses (Kagan, Kearsley, and Zelazo, 1978), the regulation of the reactions by features of daily life can lead to different patterns in later months. Many American children have a single caretaker but are exposed to a large number of strangers when they visit the doctor's office, the supermarket, and their older sibling's school. In Kokwet, the cast of characters for daily life remains stable and relatively small, despite the fact that two or three individuals are routinely involved in care. Informal observations suggest that fear of strangers is more intense and sustained for Kipsigis children than it is for Americans, even though distress at maternal departure is less so. In each case, the children are making equally successful adaptations to their social niche, minimizing distress in the long run and sensitizing the toddler to unusual situations. The important point for emotional development, however, is that the universal reactions are becoming differentially patterned into the structure of daily life, and that adaptation in the two settings leads to contrasting responses to the identical situation.

## Summary

In summary, parental beliefs and values and the structure of infant care together provide a niche in which the baby develops an emotional life. Various features of the physical and social niche are integrated, in most cases, in a way that both reflects and reinforces larger aspects of the surrounding culture. In the infants' adaptations to the niche can be seen the early, culturally directed organization of emotional behavior and the socialization of emotional displays.

## DEVELOPMENTAL SEQUENCES AND CONSEQUENCES

There is a long history of speculation and inquiry in psychology concerning long-term consequences of early emotional development. Much of this work has focused on possible pathological sequelae of traumatic events or instances of extreme deprivation (Clarke and Clarke, 1976); it does not address several important issues in the continuities of normal development. In the normal case there is not only a continuity of the mind but also some continuity of the environment. It becomes difficult, therefore, to disentangle psychological consequences of early experience from later environmental sequences.

The learning of emotional behaviors does not stop at 3 or 13 or 30, nor does the role of culture in patterning that learning. As the child grows older, he or she encounters a larger variety of social settings. Each setting has a typical cast of characters and scenario, each has a particular meaning and prescription for proper behavior; one way a culture socializes is in the settings it provides (Whiting, 1980). The emotional differentiation of settings in early childhood is part of the culturally regulated sequence of development. Intimately related to the differentiation of settings is the way superficially similar developmental transitions can yield divergent psychological meanings depending on the preceding and surrounding experience. Very few childhood experiences are absolute in their emotional message. The emergent patterning of emotional expression across settings, and the sequence of settings across time, are probably more important for the normal socialization of affect than learning in any one situation. In this patterning and sequencing are intertwined the values, beliefs, customary practices, and ecological forces that are integrated by the culture and that are the cultural context of development (Harkness, 1980).

Cultural divergence in the verbal expression of inner thoughts and feelings illustrates the importance of developmental sequences in socialization. Social interaction during infancy, as indicated earlier, is similar in Kokwet and American settings in the frequency of smiling and mutual regard (face-to-face interaction). The rate of vocalization in Kokwet, however, is only half the American rate; both the mothers and babies in Kokwet "speak" to each other less often than those in an American sample. While the interaction appears equally warm and affectionate in the two settings, it is quieter in Kokwet.

As the children grow through the familiar sequence of crawling, walking, talking, and other milestones of development, there is a variety of skills parents can choose to encourage. Mothers in Kokwet encourage some activities that are relatively neglected by American parents (Super, 1976), but they do not see themselves as having a major role in "teaching" a child to talk. That function, it is believed, is filled by the child's siblings. Mothers' verbal interaction with 2- and 3-year-olds is not as frequent as that found in American homes and has a relatively high frequency of commands. Increasingly as the child moves into early childhood, the mother's verbal communication becomes directing, comforting, and scolding rather than eliciting of verbal reply (Harkness and Super, 1977).

A particular focus of this maternal interaction is the child's initial steps toward becoming a responsible and productive member of the large household. Small tasks start early through a blend of assignment and imitation—watching that the goats or calves do not approach drying produce, carrying small cans of water, helping shell maize cobs. The father, who has had relatively little interaction with his child up to this point, joins in the affectionate responsibility for leading the child toward a maturing role in the family. It is as though the parents' traditional attitude is that children will learn to talk soon enough on their own, but they must be taught to understand requests and instructions and to obey them. The parents' goal for young children is verbal comprehension, not production.

Near the beginning of the transition from toddlerhood to early childhood, generally in the second year of life, the Kipsigis child has been weaned from the mother's breast for feeding, from her back for carrying and comforting, and from her bed for sleeping. Usually a younger sibling has appeared on the scene to take up those places. Interaction with adults actually decreases in the following few years, while siblings, half-siblings, and neighbor children become the main partners in social interaction. Children in the new social group range over several years in age, and while relations are ordered to some extent by the hierarchy of age and sex, a strong camaraderie develops. In this context the children appear as active and vocal as children anywhere, playing games, tussling on the ground, chasing a stray chicken, and swinging from the beams of a maize storehouse. While verbal aggression and precocity may not play the role in such children's groups that they do in some other cultures, there is certainly not the stricture of silence and respect found in the presence of adults.

There are two points to be made from this brief description of the social life of young children in Kokwet. First, the patterning of emotional expression in various settings is as important to affective development as is the character of expression in any one setting. Children are socialized not only into *how* they should behave, but also into how they should behave *where*.

Second, the meaning of how children should behave in different settings depends to some degree on the larger developmental sequences. The transition to early childhood in America shares some characteristics with the Kipsigis case—the pattern of interaction becomes more demanding of obedience, for example. The Kipsigis toddler, however, is already accustomed to having several important social partners to whom can be transferred some kinds of verbally expressive interaction. The meaning of the transition is affected as well by events to follow. Fewer than half of American children witness a similar process in a younger sibling, while in Kokwet more than 80 percent see in their own family that this process is part of everyone's life.

There is a continuing sequence of niches in childhood and maturity, and each culture has its own pattern of continuities and discontinuities. In some cases the thematic parallels are striking. The American baby who is scheduled to bottle and bed is later scheduled to school bell, and still later to time card or deadline. The Kipsigis baby whose state was more personally mediated by several people must as an adult accept community mediation of disputes rather than impersonal and externally imposed judgments (Harkness, Edwards, and Super, 1981). Nevertheless, each life stage has a variety of affective settings, and an individual draws upon the variety of past experiences to know how to feel and how to express the feeling.

## CONCLUSION

The mosaic of emotional behavior expressed by people of different cultures reflects in part their past experience. It is too simple, however, to see that residue of experience only in the shape of personality as traditionally drawn by Western psychology. Any particular expression builds on the motives and the understanding of the world acquired in a long history of culturally constituted experience. The elements of expression are universally human, but they are organized, practiced, and regulated by culture. The values and settings that started the socialization process are at least thematically related to aspects of later functioning, but the patterning and shading of feeling and expression reflect the continuing process of adaptation and growth. So it is with grief, fear, excitement, and pride; so it is with walking in the dark, arguing in a bar, mourning a lost child, chasing in the hunt, and disembarking from the ocean liner in Sydney. We may not need a translator to know how the people are doing it, but we need to know where they have come from to see what they are really doing.

# 2

# Cross-Cultural Assessment of Neonatal Behavior

*Barry M. Lester*
*T. Berry Brazelton*

Little doubt remains that there are differences in newborn behavior among cultural groups around the world. Cross-cultural studies of human infancy enable us to describe the variability of infant behavior and provide a broader understanding of child-rearing practices. The opportunity to see babies before they have been shaped by the postnatal environment and to study the processes by which newborns adapt to the environment in different cultures is a major goal of infancy research and contributes to our understanding of the development of individual differences in our own cultures.

Societies that are minimally influenced by modern technology illustrate variations in child-rearing patterns that may have evolved to facilitate infant survival in different conditions to which the culture has had to adapt. It is also likely that child-rearing practices have developed to maximize the unique behavioral organization of the infants of the particular culture. For example, in hunting and gathering societies, we might assume that child-rearing practices are influenced by the demands of the climate and other environmental conditions, such as the availability of food, but are also affected by the kinds of babies that are produced by the society. And since intrauterine conditions such as nutrition, infections, and motility of the mother, to name but a few, influence the fetus and contribute to the behavioral constellation of the newborn, we can see that at birth the baby is already shaped by the environment. Thus, child-rearing practices may be best understood by accounting for the environmental demands of the culture, the effects of environmental conditions on the mother and fetus, and the nature of the individual infant. Needless to say, accounting for and understanding the interrelationships among these factors is a complex task and requires multidimensional models.

## ON UNDERSTANDING NATURE BY NURTURE

Perhaps the most basic issue in understanding early development is rooted in the nature–nurture controversy. Traditional models assumed that environmental effects in the newborn were, at most, minimal. Thus in the past, cross-cultural differences in newborn behavior were viewed as representing genetic differences. Similarities in behavior were used as evidence that cultural groups were identical at the population level in reflecting genetic predispositions. This model needs to be abandoned for a number of conceptual and methodological reasons discussed below.

There is ample evidence to indicate that the intrauterine environment has a substantial impact on neonatal behavior. Events associated with labor and delivery and perinatal factors also affect newborn performance. To study the impact of obstetrical and postnatal factors on behavior, a number of "at-risk" scoring systems have been developed. The concept of the cumulative at-risk score is based on findings suggesting that, in most cases, single, isolated events have little effect on behavior, but the combined impact of many such events is related to the behavior of the infant. For example, in the at-risk scale developed by Prechtl (1968), 42 factors are grouped into maternal, parturitional (labor and delivery), and fetal nonoptimal obstetric conditions. The at-risk score is simply the sum of the number of nonoptimal conditions that are present. Thus, the more nonoptimal conditions present, the greater the risk status of the baby.

However, scoring each event as present or absent assumes that the relative importance or weight of each variable is the same. A yes/no score also ignores the qualitative aspect of each variable. For example, while it is true that, overall, premature babies are at greater risk than full-term babies, a baby born 10 weeks premature is at a greater risk than a baby born 2 weeks premature. There is also evidence, which we shall discuss in more detail later, to suggest that the impact or weight of at least certain risk variables may vary across different populations. In other words, some populations may be more affected by certain risk factors than other populations. Thus we cannot necessarily generalize the relationships between obstetrical history and infant behavior across cultures.

A popular alternative to studying the effects of these factors on behavior is to attempt to control for their presence by selecting babies on the basis of predefined obstetrical criteria. We often see phrases in the literature such as "All babies were full-term, appropriate for gestational age, normal and healthy, and the products of uncomplicated pregnancies and deliveries." In cross-cultural research the temptation is to assume that by selecting groups on the basis of comparable obstetrical histories we can "eliminate" the environmental effect and view differences between groups as the result of genetic influences.

The logical problem here is, in fact, the same as was raised by Anastasi (1958) with respect to determining the genetic contribution to IQ. We can partition behavioral variability according to the following formula:

*Behavior = genotype + environment + genotype × environment + error.*

Let us pretend we have a perfect universe and eliminate the *error* term. Any further breakdown of this formula assumes that we can separate genetic or environmental influences from the *genotype × environment* interaction. Yet attempting to make such a separation is impossible. We can never measure genotype directly, since our data are anchored in behavior. Behavior (or phenotype) represents the expression of genes manifest in interaction with the environment. The point was made by Anastasi that we should stop asking which affects behavior or how much each affects behavior, and ask instead how they interact. Or, as Hebb (1953) put it, behavior is 100 percent inherited and 100 percent acquired. The interactive question assumes that both genotype and environment affect behavior, but as they can never be isolated, we must assume that we are always studying the interaction. The formulation *behavioral phenotype = genotype × environment* may be an acceptable way of recognizing the interplay of these factors and must be our starting point. Therefore, the only way to interpret mean differences between groups is as a phenotypic expression.

To understand some of the ingredients of the behavioral phenotype of the infant, we need to complement the study of group differences with the study of individual differences. For example, to control for obstetrical risk factors and then compare mean differences between groups ignores the effects of at-risk factors on individual differences. Within an ethnic group we may still find a range of behaviors that is related to values of the at-risk factors, even though the groups were selected on the same obstetrical criteria. To illustrate, let us assume that a birthweight range of 2500 grams to 4000 grams was used to select groups of infants and that the mean birthweight did not differ among groups. It is still possible that the correlation between birthweight and behavior is significant for one group and not for the others. Such a finding would modify how we interpret behavioral differences among the cultural groups. To complicate matters further, we know that risk factors interact synergistically. The notion of synergism, in medicine, refers to the combined effects of two or more agents that are greater than the sum of their individual effects, such as the coordination of the musculature by the nervous system to perform specific movements. The effects of nutrition, for example, are probably best understood from a synergistic model (Lester, 1979; see also Chapter 6 of this book, by Townsend et al). We cannot assume that the selection criteria control for the synergistic effects of obstetrical variables on individual differences, or that these relationships are the same for all infants. In a study in which full-term, full birthweight infants were selected according to optimal obstetric and pediatric criteria, we found that even minimal levels of maternal obstetrical medication had greater neonatal behavioral effects on slightly underweight-for-length infants than on infants with a more nearly average weight-for-length (Lester, Als, and Brazelton, 1982).

This discussion leads to two general conclusions for the cross-cultural assessment of neonatal behavior. First, neonatal behavior represents the phenotypic expression of the interplay of genetic and environmental influences. Second, cross-cultural differences must be studied in terms of group differences *and* individual differences, since behavioral phenotype may be differentially affected by the synergistic relationships among so-called control variables.

# THE BRAZELTON NEONATAL BEHAVIORAL ASSESSMENT SCALE

Our work has focused on the study of the neonate using the Brazelton Neonatal Behavioral Assessment Scale (Brazelton, 1973).* This chapter will mostly summarize our cross-cultural studies with the Brazelton scale. For a more general discussion of cross-cultural studies in infancy, the reader is referred to Super (1980).

Following is a brief description of the Brazelton scale. (For more detailed descriptions, see Als et al., 1979; Als, 1978; and Lester, 1980.) The Brazelton scale was developed to assess the dynamic processes of behavioral organization and development in the neonate. It is a psychological scale for the neonate and, as described by Als et al. (1978), views the infant as part of a reciprocal, interactive feedback system between infant and caregiver. While the exam includes the assessment of reflex responses, it focuses on the infant's capability to respond to the kind of stimuli that caregivers present in an interactive situation.

The scale assesses 16 reflexes and 26 behavioral items. Each reflex is scored as: 0 = absent, 1 = low, 2 = medium, 3 = high, with a 2 considered normal for most of the reflexes. The 26 behavioral items are shown in Table 2–1. Each behavioral item is rated on a nine-point scale. The appropriate state for the administration of each item is shown in parentheses in the table. Six states are defined (Prechtl and Beintema, 1964) as: (1) deep sleep, (2) light sleep, (3) drowsiness, (4) quiet alert, (5) active alert, and (6) crying. Figures 2–1 and 2–2 show a Caucasian infant alerting to a face (items 7 and 9) and following a ball (item 5). Figures 2–3 and 2–4 show a Puerto Rican newborn orienting to a ball and using the hand-to-mouth maneuver to self-quiet (item 26).

As infant behavior is viewed in terms of the infant–caregiver interactive system, the exam focuses on the social interactive capacities of the newborn; that is, we attempt to highlight in the neonate those behaviors that are likely to be typical of future interactions. The examiner plays the role of the caregiver and systematically manipulates the baby from sleep to alert to crying states and back down to quiet states, to bring him through an entire range of situations that captures the baby's coping and adaptive strategies.

---

*Some of the studies reported here are based on an earlier (1968) version of the scale in which some of the items differed from the current (1973) version. Also, different schemes for summarizing the items have been developed as investigators gain more experience with the scale.

**Table 2–1**   *Behavioral Items on the Brazelton Neonatal Behavioral Assessment Scale*

1.  Response decrement to repeated visual stimuli (2,3).*
2.  Response decrement to rattle (2,3).
3.  Response decrement to bell (2,3).
4.  Response decrement to pinprick (1,2,3).
5.  Orienting response to inanimate visual stimuli (4 only).
6.  Orienting response to inanimate auditory stimuli (4,5).
7.  Orienting response to animate visual stimuli—examiner's face (4 only).
8.  Orienting response to animate auditory stimuli—examiner's voice (4 only).
9.  Orienting responses to animate visual and auditory stimuli (4 only).
10. Quality and duration of alert periods (4 only).
11. General muscle tone—in resting and in response to being handled, passive and active (4,5).
12. Motor activity (4,5).
13. Traction responses as he is pulled to sit (3,5).
14. Cuddliness—responses to being cuddled by examiner (4,5).
15. Defensive movements—reactions to a cloth over his face (4).
16. Consolability with intervention by examiner (6 to 5,4,3,2).
17. Peak of excitement and his capacity to control himself (6).
18. Rapidity of buildup to crying state (from 1,2 to 6).
19. Irritability during the examination (3,4,5).
20. General assessment of kind and degree of activity (alert states).
21. Tremulousness (all states).
22. Amount of startling (3,4,5,6).
23. Lability of skin color—measuring autonomic lability (from 1 to 6).
24. Lability of states during entire examination (all states).
25. Self-quieting activity—attempts to console self and control state (6,5 to 4,3,2,1).
26. Hand-to-mouth activity (all states).

*Numbers in parentheses refer to optimal state for assessment.

The examination was designed as a clinical instrument. As such, it depends upon the sensitivity and skill of the examiner to interact with a newborn and to elicit those behaviors that are likely to occur in the future infant–caregiver situations. In this sense, the examiner is as much a part of the examination as the baby, and the impressions and responses of the examiner to the baby's cues become important for clinical evaluation.

Another feature of the Brazelton scale is that the goal is to elicit *best* performance, rather than average performance. We are interested in asking what the infant *can* do, rather than simply what the baby does. Best performance is important for understanding the neonate's potential for

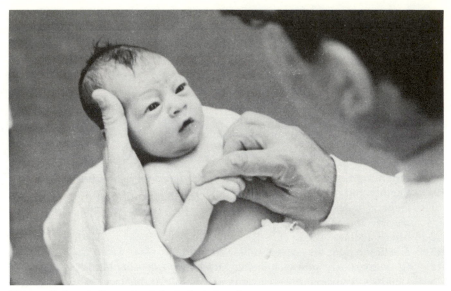

**Figure 2–1**    *A Caucasian infant alerts to a face.*

responding across a range of state changes in a variety of environmental situations and future interactive settings. In a sense, it pushes the limits to maximize the assessment of the baby's coping strategies and to see how the infant uses the examiner and the environment to improve his organization. This places extra demands on the examiner, who must learn the necessary maneuvers to adapt the procedures to the baby.

Important in the scale is the way the baby uses states of consciousness as a base for all behavior. The concept of state is used in two ways. First, because infant behavior is strongly influenced by the infant's state, the exam specifies the appropriate state for the administration of each item. Clearly, this is critical for the notion of best performance. For example, the items relating to social interaction are administered when the baby is maximally available for interaction. The second use of state is as an index of the infant's level of organization. Here we look at dimensions of control and regulation of state. What internal and external mechanisms does the baby use to regulate states? By looking at the pattern by which the infant moves from sleep to alert to crying throughout the exam, we learn the infant's capacity for smooth, modulated state control, the *range* and variability of states, as well as the amplitude of state change.

Flexibility in administration is an important feature of the Brazelton scale and is critical for eliciting an infant's best performance. While the manual does specify the sequence in which some items are administered,

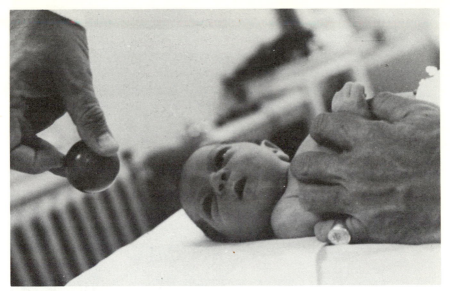

**Figure 2–2**    *A Caucasian infant follows a ball.*

the majority of items are administered when the examiner believes that best performance can be achieved. Successful administration requires that the examiner be sensitive to the signals and cues produced by the baby. The examiner must be able to read the infant—that is, to anticipate the baby's dynamic changes in state organization, his ability to use input from the examiner, and his ability to modulate his behavior in interaction with the examiner. This sensitivity may mean, for example, administering the same items at different points during the exam, as the baby becomes more available for interaction. Hence training to attain reliability in the administration and scoring of the examination is crucial.

## CROSS-CULTURAL STUDIES

To assess neonatal behavioral differences and their natural variations, we have attempted to study them in such various cultural groups as Mayan Indians in Mexico, Ladinos in Guatemala and Puerto Rico, Greeks, Africans in Zambia and Kenya, and Blacks and Caucasians in the United States. In each case we have attempted to establish, in as much detail as possible, the prenatal and perinatal influences on neonatal behavior.

We shall discuss these studies with the following goals in mind: first, to view infant behavior in its appropriate cultural context, both as a

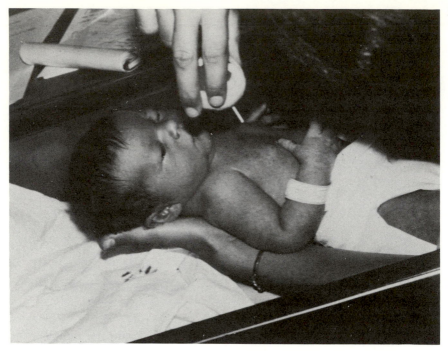

**Figure 2–3**    *A Puerto Rican infant orients to a ball.*

shaper of and as shaped by cultural expectations; and, second, to high-light the complex interaction between genetic and environmental influences on neonatal behavior. Following this discussion, we shall consider some issues surrounding the cross-cultural use of the scale, methodo-logical issues in the cross-cultural study of infant behavior, and a con-ceptual framework for the cross-cultural study of infancy.

## Zambian Infants

We have used the Brazelton scale with African newborns in two studies. In the first study (Brazelton, Koslowski, and Tronick, 1976) we had an opportunity to see the effect of the mothers' expectations that their infants would recover from an initial depleted state. Because of the mothers' undernutrition, the infants were severely depleted of fat and subcutaneous tissue, were dehydrated at birth, and seemed to require very delicate handling. But since the mothers' expectations were based on vigorous neonates from the culture, they *expected* that their infants would respond to vigorous handling. Hence, they ignored the initially limp behavior and handled the infants *as if* they were more responsive.

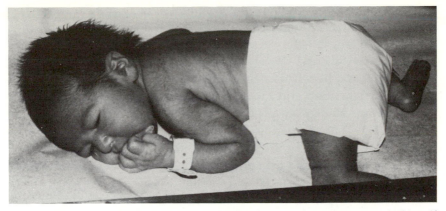

**Figure 2–4**    *A Puerto Rican infant uses the hand-to-mouth maneuver to quiet himself.*

After hydration and initial feedings the babies did become rapidly responsive, as the mothers had anticipated. Since we could see little evidence for neonatal responsiveness when we initially handled the infants, we began to wonder whether the mothers' experience with other babies in the culture led them to expect recovery so that they handled their infants accordingly.

We compared 10 Zambian and 10 Caucasian infants on days 1, 5, and 10. All the mothers were reported to have had normal pregnancies carried to term at 40 weeks, with no bleeding or infection. The American babies were firstborns, from middle-class families, and were delivered without anesthesia to the mother. They were normal and healthy by pediatric and neurological examination with 1-, 5-, and 15-minute Apgar scores of at least 8, 9, and 9. (The Apgar is a scoring system used to evaluate the newborn heart rate, respiratory effort, muscle tone, reflex irritability, and color; each is scored from 0 to 2, for a total possible score of 10.)

The Zambian families were from a semirural, urbanized slum area that surrounds the capital city of Lusaka. The mothers had had several pregnancies in rapid succession, at about 12- to 13-month intervals, and there were at least three children living at home. The babies were delivered in a rather poor hospital in Lusaka, and we were able to meet the families because of our connection with the chief obstetrician. An African nurse introduced us and continued to work with us in our interactions with the families. Her presence was critical to our being allowed to follow them at home.

There was evidence from the history of these mothers of low protein intake, both before and during pregnancy, coupled with a high incidence of gastrointestinal infection during pregnancy. The Zambian babies had a lighter mean birthweight (2,721 versus 3,447 grams) and a slightly shorter birth length (49.5 versus 51.4 centimeters) than the American infants. The weight and size of the Zambian infants suggested that three factors in the mothers had affected the infants: (1) poor protein diet, (2) placental dysfunction and (3) uteri stressed by repeated pregnancies, with placentas inadequate to nurture the fetuses in the period just prior to birth. Signs of intrauterine depletion were evident from the examination of the infants at birth. The infants' skin was dry and scaled, their faces were wrinkled, and the stumps of their umbilical cords were dried and yellow.

Differences in performance on the Brazelton scale between the two groups were seen in the pattern of change from day 1 to day 10, as well as in individual scale items. Table 2–2 shows the mean scores for the items that seemed to be the most sensitive to group differences. The scores of the American infants remained relatively stable over the 10 days, staying within an average range on all three days. In contrast, the Zambian infants showed a recovery curve from initially lower scores to scores within the average range by day 10. For the specific items, on day 1 the Zambian infants showed poorer scores in the items of visually following a ball and the human face, had less overall motor activity, and were less irritable. They cried to very few stimuli. On the reflex items the Zambians had very poor muscle tone, little resistance to passive extension or flexion of the limbs, and poor head control as they were pulled to sit. By day 10, the Zambian infants continued to demonstrate less motor activity than the American infants, but their muscle tone had improved to better than average, and the Zambians scored higher than the Americans in their social interest in the examiner and in overall alertness.

This pattern of recovery in the Zambian infants seemed to be due to improvement from the combination of rehydration and nutrition as the mothers' milk restored the infant's depleted stores after delivery. The breast milk served to overcome the effects of their stressed intrauterine environments. In addition, the child-rearing practices and cultural expectations for early motor and interactive development were very different for them. Zambian babies were taken home at day 1 "to get them to their family." The Zambian mothers actively played with their babies from the first, and everyone in the household handled, jostled, and played with the new baby. The baby was breast-fed frequently, entirely on demand. Weight gain was rapid over the first 10 days, and the infants

**Table 2–2** *Mean Scores for Zambians and Americans on days 1, 5, and 10 for All Measures that Distinguished Between Groups in at Least One Day*

| MEASURES | DAY 1 | | DAY 5 | | DAY 10 | |
|---|---|---|---|---|---|---|
| | ZAMBIANS | AMERICANS | ZAMBIANS | AMERICANS | ZAMBIANS | AMERICANS |
| Motor activity | 3.00 | 4.90* | 5.89 | 5.50 | 4.60 | 5.90* |
| Tempo at height | 3.20 | 5.77* | 5.90 | 5.50 | 4.40 | 6.44* |
| Rapidity of buildup | 3.22 | 4.80* | 5.62 | 4.50* | 3.50 | 5.50* |
| Irritability | 2.50 | 4.40* | 4.40 | 4.70 | 3.80 | 5.00 |
| Consolability | 6.60 | 5.56 | 5.00 | 4.63 | 6.12 | 4.75* |
| Social interest | 1.20 | 4.29 | 6.20 | 5.22 | 6.70 | 4.33* |
| Alertness | 2.40 | 4.20 | 6.30 | 5.11 | 7.40 | 4.80* |
| Follow with eyes | 2.40 | 4.16* | 4.60 | 4.70 | 4.67 | 5.11 |
| Reactivity to stimulation | 3.35 | 4.38 | 5.30 | 4.71 | 6.14 | 4.67* |
| Defensive movements | 3.20 | 4.38 | 5.11 | 5.50 | 4.90 | 6.11* |
| Cuddliness | 3.30 | 4.40* | 5.22 | 5.60 | 6.30 | 5.12 |

*Mean differences are significant at $p < 0.05$.

gained as much as a pound in the first week at home. By contrast, the American babies were in the hospital for 3 days. At home, mothers tended to feed their babies every 3 to 4 hours and played with them at those times. Between feedings the babies were kept in isolated rooms, as mothers were afraid of infections and felt the babies needed "time to themselves in order to recover."

## Kenyan (Gusii) Infants

In the second study we learned that future "motor excitement" of African babies might be seen in the neonates as motor responsiveness. We felt that because they were exciting infants to handle and to play with, mothers responded to them in kind. Maternal responsiveness to their babies' motor behavior reinforced the capacities seen in the neonates. As part of a broad longitudinal study in Kenya's Gusii community, Keefer, Dixon, Tronick, and Brazelton (1978) have reported initial findings from the study of 24 neonates. The maternal obstetrical histories from this sample suggested high risk factors by American standards. In a marginally nourished group of people, we worried about fetal undernutrition. The women in this study were older than an equivalent American sample and of high parity. In addition, the pregnant women either demonstrated weight loss or no weight gain in the third trimester. In spite of these potentially ominous intrauterine influences, none of these factors appeared to have influenced the neonates' outcome at delivery. The infants were clinically healthy by pediatric exam. They were full-term (41 weeks gestation ± 1 week), and their birthweights, lengths, head circumferences, and ponderal indexes (PI) were well within the normal range. (The ponderal index is a weight-for-length ratio: birthweight in kilograms × 100 over birth length in centimeters; it is a direct measure of lean body mass. A low value indicates thinness; a high value, obesity.) Since the PI is an indication of fetal undernutrition, these babies seemed adequately nourished.

The 24 infants were assessed with the Brazelton scale on days 2, 5, and 10 and compared with a group of 54 Caucasian American middle-class infants who had been selected for their low-risk prenatal and delivery variables. We wanted this control group of American babies to reflect optimal neonatal behavior. In spite of the comparison between high-risk African and low-risk Caucasian babies, the African babies compared favorably. On the item of motor maturity, the Gusii infants were significantly better. They were not only more mature in their motor responses, but the excitement they demonstrated as they performed a motor task was striking. For example, as they were pulled to sit by their extended arms, they not only maintained excellent head control in sitting and bringing their heads up parallel to their bodies, but also, with brightened faces, turned their heads to look around the room as they sat. Since the motor behavior we saw did not seem to be captured by the scale's description of motor behavior, the authors expanded the general motor tone scale to reflect how the Gusii infants were able to use their motor capacities. These infants appeared to have remarkable control over their motor reactions; that is, they were able to match their motor responses to the amount of pressure or handling applied by the examiner. For instance, when the examiner turned them on their abdomens, they participated by helping to turn themselves and then lifted their heads off the bed. In contrast to most American infants, the Gusii maintained excellent motor organization as they were handled and as they became excited. In other words, their movements did not become jerky, and the babies did not lose their organization as they became active. Many seemed to enjoy the motor activity and to participate in it as newborns. The result was a rewarding kind of feedback to the adult as he played with the neonate, who matched the adult in each maneuver and provided an exciting interaction.

These findings seemed to be related to the intense motor interaction between the infants and all those around them. At birth the newborns are jostled in outstretched arms. During the day they are played with vigorously, and during the weeks after birth they are picked up by one arm to hoist them on their mother's hip and tossed into the air after a bath to shake off excess water. Vigorous handling practices in this part of Africa resembled that of the Zambian mothers. Since there has been an emphasis on African babies' motor precocity—and, indeed, we did see early motor development—we agree with Super (1976) that there is early and constant stimulation by the environment that reinforces babies' motor behavior. Our feeling was that the cultural child-rearing practices that facilitated early motor development were built on the infants' responsiveness to being handled in the neonatal period.

## Asian-American and Navajo Infants

The argument for biological predispositions of temperament that can be seen in the newborn and that may affect cultural practices was suggested by Freedman in studies of Chinese-American, Japanese-American, and Navajo neonates. Freedman and Freedman (1969) compared 24 Chinese-American and 24 European-American two-day-old babies. The items of the Brazelton scale were divided into five categories: temperament, sensory development, autonomic and central nervous system maturity, motor development, and social interest. Significant differences were found in items that seemed to tap a dimension of excitability/imperturbability. The Chinese-American infants had a less rapid buildup to an excited state of arousal, showed less facial and body reddening, and showed fewer state changes over the exam period. When placed in the prone position, the Chinese-Americans tended to remain inactive, face flat against the bed, in contrast to the European-Americans, who were more likely to lift the head or turn the face to one side. When a cloth was placed on the baby's face in a supine position, the Chinese-Americans were less likely to struggle to remove the cloth than were the European-Americans. Although the groups did not differ in the amount of crying, the Chinese-Americans were easier to console when crying and were better able to stop by themselves, without being consoled. The authors suggested that the dimension of temperamental "imperturbability", seen in decreased reactions to intrusive stimuli, affects what become cultural norms in caretaking practices.

Freedman (1971) then replicated these findings with Japanese-American and Navajo Indian infants. The same pattern of differences seen in the Chinese-Americans described above was again observed. There were a few differences that were unique to the Navajo infants. The Navajos showed a greater tendency to become red when excited and to remain that way for much of the examination than did the Chinese-American or Caucasian infants, although the Chinese showed a greater lability of skin color than the Caucasians. On the reflex items, Navajo infants had less resistance in motor tone when their extremities were straightened. When held vertically, the Navajos were less likely to straighten their legs to support the body, and they did not show walking or stepping movements when leaned forward by the examiner. Freedman suggested that these findings represented temperamental characteristics of passivity and imperturbability and are the basis for the subdued emotionality observed in Navajo children. While others (such as Kluckhohn and Leighton, 1946) have argued that the Navajo temperament is due to the practice of cradle-boarding during infancy, Freedman argues that Navajo babies are particularly suited, both physically and temperamentally, for such practices as cradle-boarding than more active infants would be. In any case, the infants seem to promote their own caretaking and survival by contributing to the development of cultural practices that are adaptive for them. Biological predispositions of the infant may set the stage for the evolution of cultural practices.

## Latin American Infants

Our studies using the Brazelton scale with infants from Latin America are from three populations: the Zinacanteco, Mayan Indians of highland Chiapas in southern Mexico; Ladinos of mixed Latin and Mayan ancestry from Guatemala; and Latin infants from Puerto Rico.

### Zinacanteco Infants

In a study by Brazelton, Robey, and Collier (1969) of the Zinacanteco Indians, we saw how the quiet, alert behavior of the infants, influenced by intrauterine conditions of subclinical malnutrition, infection, and mild hypoxia (low oxygen) due to high altitude, shaped the nurturing environment in the direction of passive caretaking practices that contributed to the infants' ability to adapt to demanding environmental conditions.

In this study, five infants were examined 12 times with the Brazelton scale during the first week of life. Although this may seem like a small sample size from which to draw conclusions, these are the only newborns that have been followed from this very guarded group. The anthropologists, led by Evon Vogt and George Collier, had studied these people for 18 years and were respected by them. Nonetheless, there was a dominant belief that it was dangerous to allow anyone who had not been present and participating in the delivery to see the new baby in the first month. Hence, it was critical that we participate in deliveries. To do this we needed the clearance of the head chief of the village, the grandfather's and father's permission, and the cooperation of the midwives who delivered the babies. In three years, it was finally possible to participate in the five deliveries, and access to the new baby over the neonatal first month was assured. In each case the delivery was easy, and no medication was given to the mother during labor. Toward the end of the second stage of labor (the period of active, strong, and regular contractions), she knelt before her own mother while her husband pulled on a cinch around her waist, putting downward pressure on the full uterus. The midwife instructed her with each labor pain, received the infant on delivery, and tied the umbilical cord. Then the new baby was kept undressed for a 30-minute period in front of the fire, with no protection against the cold other than a blanket at his back, while chants were sung and rituals performed on his behalf. This period provided us a rare opportunity to observe and record the infant's behavior immediately after delivery.

The infants weighed only about 2.3 kilograms, with Apgar scores of 9–9–9 at 1, 5, and 15 minutes. These were small but responsive babies compared to our U.S. infants. In appearance and behavior they were mature, with no apparent difficulties, such as prematurity or intrauterine depletion, to account for their light weights. Although they were the size of premature infants in our country, they had none of the jerky movements or hypertonic rigidity of limbs characteristic of many premature infants. Their limb movements were free and smooth, and they lay quietly on the blanket, looking around the room with alert faces for the entire hour after delivery. In addition to quiet motor activity, they demonstrated a striking sensory alertness. Repeatedly in the first week, all five infants would alert, become quiet, and slowly turn toward a voice. When lighting was adequate in the dark huts, they alerted to the red ball as a visual stimulus and followed it back and forth as it was moved; on one occasion, a baby followed for 60 seconds without interruption. Vertical excursions of 30 degrees from midline were easy to elicit. Frequent head movements were noted to augment such pursuit, and only rarely would startles or jerky motor activity interrupt this attentive state.

To evaluate the distinctive characteristics of these infants, their performance was compared with that of five Caucasian infants to whom the Brazelton scale was administered on each day of their first week of life. These controls had experienced normal, spontaneous delivery from unmedicated and unanesthetized mothers after 40 weeks of normal gestation without any complications of pregnancy. Their Apgar scores were 8–9–9 or over, and pediatrically and neurologically they were normal in the first week after birth.

Our impression was that the Zinacanteco infants' motor activity from birth was freer, more fluid, nontremulous, and only moderate in vigor, without startles or overreaction, which tends to interfere with prolonged or repeated responses to sensory stimuli as compared with U.S. infants. Spontaneous startles of the whole baby were rare indeed; responses to the elicited Moro (a startle response of the whole body when the head is suddenly dropped) were somewhat subdued in the Zinacantecos; the general disorganization of states and lack of coordination we are accustomed to seeing on day 1 and day 2 in U.S. infants was not evident in these neonates. State behavior was also dissimilar to that of U.S. babies, the Zinacantecos maintaining quiet, alert states for long periods, with slow, smooth transitions from one state to another. We recorded none of the deep sleep, intense crying, or intense sucking states observed in the U.S. controls. The apparent control of state and motor behavior in Indian infants seemed to be of a higher order, permitting repeated and prolonged responses to auditory, visual, and kinesthetic stimuli in the first week of life.

The influence of relative hypoxia at this altitude, along with the powerful effects of intrauterine protein malnutrition and infection, and that of constant, regular motor activity of the pregnant female, may be reflected in the neonates by their monitored control of state behavior and their slow, liquid movements. They were not depleted, undernourished, or underhydrated—but they were small. Scrimshaw, Taylor, and Golden (1968) claim that subclinical protein malnutrition produces small babies. Perhaps slow, liquid movements are a behavioral accompaniment. This fluidity, lack of interfering motor activity, and well-regulated state and autonomic control, then, lend a potent background for what appears to be auditory and visual competence in the immediate neonatal period. Whether this apparent competence is based on lack of competition from the motor sphere, coupled with a quiet environment immediately after delivery, awaits other studies. The effect of this behavior for the neonate and for his parent must be a powerful shaper for his nurturing environment.

The immediate perinatal experience—no drugs, no interference with the natural course of labor and delivery, emotional support for the mother, emphasis on subdued, rather passive participation of the mother in the delivery—is then reflected in a similar experience for the newborn. He is left undressed for a period—a stressful period, from an autonomic point of view. He manages the necessary temperature control and is placed in a swaddled, face-covered position beside his mother. She then sets up a model of immediate, contingent responsiveness to his needs, before he can build up to feel the importance of a need, make a demand, and *then* find it gratified. He is rocked, cradled, and breast-fed rather than allowed to cry or become frustrated.

The tendency of these babies to remain quiet and slow in reactivity is reinforced by their subsequent handling in infancy. The infant's role in shaping the environment's response to him was visible in his neonatal behavior and preserved the ground for appropriate reactions from the environment to reinforce his characteristics.

## Guatemalan Infants

The Guatemalan study (Brazelton, Tronick, Lechtig, Lasky and Klein, 1977) was part of a longitudinal project conducted by the Institute of Nutrition of Central American and Panama (INCAP) to investigate the effects of protein and calorie supplementation on mental, motor, and physical development in four subsistence-level farming villages of eastern Guatemala. The INCAP study, described in more detail in Chapter

6 of this book, has been in action for over 10 years. In the process of this extensive study, pregnant women are carefully monitored for their (1) diets, (2) amount of nutritional supplementation, (3) number of infections, and (4) problems around delivery.

The sample consisted of 157 full-term infants examined within the first 30 days. They had a mean birthweight of 2.8 kilograms and a mean length of 48 centimeters. They looked slightly immature at birth, as well as somewhat depleted. Although they were "drier" than usual at birth and their skins were slightly peeling, they were not markedly dehydrated. Hence, they were not severely stressed at birth but seemed to show signs of the chronic undernutrition of their mothers. The infants were divided into four groups, based on their age of testing on the Brazelton scale: 0 to 3 days (N = 43); 4 to 5 days (N = 36); 6 to 8 days (N = 44); and 9 to 28 days (N = 34). The scale items were subsequently divided into four clusters. The items in the first cluster were selected to be the best predictors of good performance, and in the second cluster to be the next best. The third and fourth clusters indicated motor and interactive disorganization in the infant. The infants were then divided into groups on a number of biomedical variables. Performance on the scale was found to improve significantly with increasing gestational age, age of testing, and birthweight. Birthweight was correlated with maternal nutritional intake during pregnancy. Poorer performance was associated with infants whose mothers were shorter in height and who had birth intervals longer than 29 months. On a socioeconomic index, which reflected maternal nutritional history as well as life-style, infants in the higher socioeconomic groups scored significantly better on all items than did infants of lower socioeconomic status.

The behavior of these full-term but low-birthweight and somewhat immature-looking infants was quite striking. They demonstrated poor muscle tone and remained rather limp when handled. Their spontaneous movements were limited, with evidence of both jerkiness and tremulousness. They moved into higher states of arousal slowly and showed little vigor in these states. Their ability to orient to auditory and visual stimuli was poor. There was an improvement in the performance of the higher birthweight infants and in those whose maternal environment and perinatal experiences were less stressed. Even among these less stressed infants, however, the quality of behavior remained poor throughout the next four weeks of the neonatal period.

This pattern of behavior characterizes an underdemanding infant who is a poor elicitor of maternal responses. We can see how the interactive effects of such a passive infant with a nutritionally deprived caregiver in a stressed environment could combine to make chronic malnutrition an almost certain outcome, as well as a causal agent. This leads us to further investigate some of the specific biomedical variables that are related to neonatal behavior.

### Puerto Rican Infants

The purpose of this study (Coll, Sepkoski, and Lester, 1981) was to compare performance on the Brazelton scale between Puerto Rican, Black, and Caucasian neonates. We had two goals in mind. First, we wanted to provide a description of the behavioral features of these groups as a basis for future studies of cultural antecedents of infant–caregiver interaction. The second objective was to study the synergistic effects of biomedical variables on neonatal behavior within each cultural group.

The sample included 72 two-day-old Puerto Rican, Black, and Caucasian newborns (24 from each group). The Puerto Rican infants were examined at the Hospital Municipal de San Juan, Puerto Rico. The Black and Caucasian babies were from a teaching hospital in Florida. All infants were from families of low to lower-middle socioeconomic status and were selected to meet the following criteria: clinically healthy as defined by routine pediatric exam; fullterm (38 to 42 weeks of gestation); birthweight between 2,500 and 4000 grams; born to mothers between the ages of 18 and 34; and delivered by spontaneous vaginal deliveries. The mothers' and infants' medical histories were coded on a list of obstetric risk factors based on Prechtl's list of optimal obstetric conditions (Prechtl, 1968). The infants in this study had a total of not more than four obstetric risk conditions, excluding any chronic maternal disease, premature rupture of membranes, sepsis, or asphyxia. Maternal obstetrical medication was similar across the three groups.

To analyze the data, the individual items on the Brazelton scale were summarized into 7 clusters (Lester, Als, and Brazelton, 1978). This system combines the 26 behavioral items into 6 clusters and uses the 16 reflexes to generate a seventh reflex cluster. Each behavioral cluster is qualitative, with higher scores indicating better performance. These clusters are: *habituation*, the response decrement to the repeated presentation of a light, rattle, bell, and pinprick; *orientation*, the infant's responses to animate and inanimate stimuli and overall alertness; the *motor* cluster, the integrated motor acts and overall muscle tonus; *range of state*, an assessment of the rapidity, peak, and lability of state changes; *regulation of state*, the infant's efforts to modulate his own state control; and *autonomic stability*, signs of physiological stress seen as tremors, startles, and

**Table 2–3**  *Mean Brazelton Scale Scores in Puerto Rican, Black, and Caucasian Neonates and Group Differences*

|  | PUERTO RICAN | BLACK | CAUCASIAN | GROUP |
|---|---|---|---|---|
| Habituation | 3.70 | 5.89 | 6.10 | *** |
| Orientation | 6.80 | 5.89 | 5.72 | ** |
| Motor | 4.61 | 4.92 | 4.43 | * |
| Range of state | 3.57 | 3.22 | 3.55 | |
| Regulation of state | 5.66 | 5.34 | 5.58 | |
| Autonomic stability | 5.17 | 4.69 | 4.71 | |
| Reflexes | 2.67 | 1.95 | 2.04 | |
| Organization for arousal level | 1.60 | 3.10 | 2.90 | *** |

Mean differences are significant at \*\*\**p* < 0.001, \*\**p* < 0.01, \**p* < 0.05.

changes in skin color. The seventh, or *reflex*, cluster is the total number of deviant reflex scores, so that higher scores indicate poorer performance. In addition, an *organization for arousal level* scale was designed as a summary of the baby's overall ability to maintain an adequate level of organization in different states of arousal throughout the exam. We felt the need for providing a systematic, global appraisal of this dimension of newborn behavior, which was not captured by the seven clusters.

Table 2–3 shows the comparisons between the Puerto Rican, Black, and Caucasian infants on the summary scores. Significant differences were found among the three groups for three clusters, and on the organization for arousal level scale, with a fourth cluster approaching significance. On the habituation cluster, the Black and Caucasian infants scored higher than the Puerto Rican infants, indicating that they required fewer trials to inhibit their initial response to the repeated presentation of the stimuli. On the orientation cluster, the Puerto Rican infants showed better performance than the other two groups, reflecting the quality of alertness and the ability to follow animate and inanimate visual and auditory stimuli. The Black infants scored significantly higher than the other groups on the motor cluster. Range of state approached significance, reflecting a trend for Black babies to have more extreme state changes than the Caucasian and Puerto Rican infants. The analysis on the organization for arousal level scale showed that the Puerto Rican babies maintained longer periods of alertness, with a lower level of arousal in spite of increased stimulation. Both Black and Caucasian groups displayed more lability of state, with an average control of arousal

Table 2–4  *Multiple Regression (r) of Gestational Age, Ponderal Index, Apgar Score,* and Number of Obstetric Risk Conditions on Brazelton Scale Summary Scores for Puerto Rican, Black, and Caucasian Neonates

|  | PUERTO RICAN | BLACK | CAUCASIAN |
|---|---|---|---|
| Habituation | 0.60* | 0.44 | 0.20 |
| Orientation | 0.56* | 0.19 | 0.35 |
| Motor | 0.52* | 0.35 | 0.15 |
| Range of state | 0.27 | 0.22 | 0.35 |
| Regulation of state | 0.43* | 0.45 | 0.27 |
| Automatic stability | 0.57* | 0.32 | 0.56* |
| Reflexes | 0.43* | 0.35 | 0.36 |
| Organization for arousal level | 0.21 | 0.31 | 0.12 |

*$p < 0.05$.

ranging from good self-quieting or response to intervention, to poor state control.

A second set of analyses was performed to look at the relationship between the Brazelton scale summary scores and several biomedical parameters within each cultural group. We were curious as to how much of the variation in neonatal behavior the combination of these variables could account for in healthy populations with differing genetic endowments but similar obstetric histories. For this analysis the infant's gestational age, Apgar score, ponderal index, and the total number of obstetric risk conditions were used in a multiple regression on each of the seven Brazelton scale clusters and the organization for arousal level scale for each group. The results of the regressions are shown in Table 2–4. For the Black infants, none of the correlations reached statistical significance. For the Caucasian group there was one significant correlation. By contrast, the Puerto Rican infants' performance on the Brazelton scale was significantly related to the four predictor variables on six of the seven clusters.

The results of this study revealed differences in Brazelton scale performance among Puerto Rican, Black, and Caucasian neonates. The most striking findings were between the Puerto Rican infants and the other two groups. Puerto Rican infants scored lower on the habituation cluster and showed better performance on the orientation cluster and on the organization for arousal level scale. In contrast to the other groups, the Puerto Rican infants came rapidly into a quiet alert state, which was maintained for extended periods. This prolonged alertness was accompanied by a high level of response to animate and inanimate visual and auditory stimuli. These infants took longer to reach higher states of arousal and returned quickly to lower states. Many of the Puerto Rican infants were predominantly in state 4 (quiet alert) and never reached an insulated crying state throughout the entire administration of the scale. On the response decrement items, these infants required more trials to inhibit their responses to visual, auditory, and tactile stimuli than the Black or Caucasian infants. While the responses of the Puerto Rican infants decreased in intensity over the 10 trials, they tended not to meet the criteria for shutdown of the response.

Of the remaining comparisons, the only significant contrast was between the Black infants and the other two groups on the motor cluster. The higher scores of the Black infants may be taken as evidence for the notion of motor precocity in Black infants, although an inspection of the mean motor cluster scores for the three groups (Table 2–3) suggests that this difference is marginal. There was also a tendency for the Black infants to score lower on the range of state cluster, indicating more extreme performance on items that assess the rapidity, peak, and lability of state changes. These differences were also marginal and, as with the differences on the motor cluster should be interpreted with caution.

The regression results illustrate the complex relationship between biomedical variables and neonatal behavior and suggest that these relationships may vary in different cultural settings. That these findings were obtained in groups of infants selected to meet standard criteria for the healthy full-term neonate suggests that within the range of what is considered to be pediatrically healthy, biomedical factors can account for individual differences in neonatal behavior. By supplementing group comparisons with multivariate analyses of individual differences, we may learn more about the antecedents of normal neonatal behavior and the development of infants who may be at risk.

These results also suggest that there may be population differences in the relative effects of biomedical factors on neonatal behavior, as seen in the significant regression analyses among the Puerto Rican infants. The potentiating influences of these factors may vary in different populations, such that some populations are more resistant to the effects of biological factors than others. There may also be threshholds for the synergistic effects of biomedical factors on neonatal behavior. These thresholds may be lower than the thresholds for the effects of single variables and may differ for different populations.

## Greek Infants

In this section we shall discuss a study undertaken in Greece, where the neonatal behavioral results seemed to demonstrate how the cultural taboos surrounding an illegitimate pregnancy had physiological and psychological consequences for the mothers and, ultimately, for the babies. We studied three groups of 30 infants, each assessed on days 1, 5, and 10, with the Brazelton scale (Brazelton, Tryphonopoulou, and Lester, 1979).

The first group was composed of infants whose mothers were cared for in late pregnancy at the Athens orphanage, the Metera, and who had planned to leave their infants at the Metera for adoption. Since an illegitimate pregnancy is still a serious offense in most of Greece, this orphanage has been the only refuge for unmarried young women who become pregnant. The practice, still observed in the mountains and on some of the Greek islands, is that the father and brothers of an unmarried pregnant woman are expected to destroy her before the baby can ruin the family. Hence, it is common for unwed women to attempt to abort themselves, to eat poorly in early pregnancy in order to hide their condition, and to deny their pregnancy. The mothers in this group of our study had followed this tradition. Many reported that they had tried to abort themselves in early pregnancy, and all of them had tried to starve themselves in the first few months in an effort to hide their condition. As a result, although intrauterine conditions changed markedly for the fetus at the seventh month, when the mother accepted her condition and went to the Metera for care, she had deprived the fetus nutritionally in the first few months. No anesthesia and little or no premedication was administered to the mothers at the time of delivery. The babies were seen in the maternity hospital on day 1 and at the orphanage on days 5 and 10.

The second group of Greek neonates consisted of 30 babies from intact, middle-class homes. These mothers had eaten well during pregnancy, and there were no reported attempts to abort any of these infants. Average gravida index was 2.0 (number of babies delivered by the mother). As is the practice in private Greek obstetrics, these mothers had premedication. Spinal or local anesthesia was routinely administered. There were no complications in labor, nor was labor prolonged for any of these mothers. These infants were seen in the maternity hospital on day 1 and at home on days 5 and 10.

The third group of Greek babies consisted of 30 infants of a lower socioeconomic group of laborers' families. They too were of intact families. The mothers were gravida 1.0, except for six who were gravida 2.0. They had all wanted their babies. No medication or anesthesia was administered to this group during delivery. Nutritional histories indicated that malnutrition had not been a problem for these families. Infants were evaluated in the hospital on day 1 and at home on days 5 and 10.

The Brazelton scale items were organized into four clusters that are designed to represent the conceptual dimensions of interactive processes, motor processes, regulation of state, and physiological organization. These items are shown in Table 2–5, which also includes a summary of the statistical findings from this study.

The Metera infants exhibited the poorest overall performance. On nine items (visual orientation to inanimate objects and to the human voice, as well as alertness in general, motor maturity, defensive movements, activity, hand-to-mouth, tempo of movements, and habituation to light), the Metera group had lower scores than the other two groups. The Greek lower-class group, which was to be a control for social class, was in no way comparable to the Metera group, performing significantly better than the Metera infants on all nine items. Also, on two items (inanimate visual orientation and consolability) the Metera infants did not show the significant improvements with age shown by the other two groups.

Using the analysis by dimensions, the interactive dimension showed that the Metera infants performed most poorly in overall social responsiveness. The environment of the infants after hospital discharge differed significantly among these three groups and might well be reflected by the social interactive scores. The Metera infants were isolated in brightly lit white cubicles, similar to the hospital. They were fed on a 4-hour routine, with little extra stimulation provided, whereas the middle- and lower-class groups were fed frequently and on demand, and were offered the personal interaction of parents and others at home. Since this interactive dimension reflects the infants' important ability to elicit responses from and to give feedback to their environment, this difference becomes an important predictor of both the infants' capacity to elicit necessary nurturing and the parents' perception of the infants.

The Metera and the middle-class Greek babies performed significantly more poorly than the lower-class group on the items in the dimensions of motor processes and state regulation. In the Metera babies, it is easy to postulate that their performance was affected by intrauterine conditions. Since the middle-class babies were not nutritionally stressed in utero, their depressed performance on these dimensions seemed to reflect the effects of medication given mothers at delivery.

**Table 2–5**  *Summary of Significant Effects for Three Groups of Greek Neonates [Derived from Analyses of Variance (Anova)]*

| BRAZELTON SCALE ITEMS | ANOVA EFFECTS | | |
| --- | --- | --- | --- |
| | GROUP | AGE | GROUP × AGE |
| **I. INTERACTIVE PROCESSES** | | | |
| Orientation inanimate visual | *** | *** | *** |
| Orientation inanimate auditory | | ** | |
| Orientation animate auditory | ** | *** | |
| Alertness | *** | *** | |
| **II. MOTOR PROCESSES** | | | |
| Motor maturity | * | *** | ** |
| General tonus | | ** | |
| Defensive movements | ** | *** | |
| Pull-to-sit | | *** | |
| Hand-to-mouth | * | *** | |
| Activity | | | ** |
| Vigor of movements | | *** | |
| Tempo of movements | * | *** | |
| **III. REGULATION OF STATE** | | | |
| Habituation to light | ** | *** | |
| Rapidity of buildup | *** | | |
| Lability of states | * | * | |
| Irritability | | ** | |
| Consolability | | *** | ** |
| Self-quieting | | | |
| **IV. PHYSIOLOGICAL ORGANIZATION** | | | |
| Tremulousness | *** | *** | *** |
| Amount of startles | ** | *** | |
| Lability of skin color | * | *** | |

$*p < 0.05$, $**p < 0.01$, $***p < 0.001$.

# ISSUES IN THE CROSS-CULTURAL USE OF THE BRAZELTON SCALE

The widespread use of the Brazelton scale in a variety of research and clinical settings has generated a number of important issues regarding the understanding of the scale, training in the administration and scoring of the scale, populations for which the scale is appropriate, and the data reduction and analysis of the scale items. These issues and reviews of studies using the scale have been discussed elsewhere (Als, 1978; Als et al., 1979; Lester, 1980). In this section we would like to highlight issues that are particularly relevant for the cross-cultural use of the Brazelton scale.

The dynamic model of the organization of neonatal behavior on which the scale is based assumes considerable change in scale performance during the neonatal period. To measure the adaptation and coping strategies of the neonate, a series of examinations is necessary. The scale was not intended to provide a "one-shot" assessment of the neonate—which is not to say that there is no validity to scale performance on a given day. The scale *can* provide an accurate description of the behavioral functioning of an individual at a given point in time; however, that assessment is not necessarily predictive of organization at some later date. A single assessment takes a time slice of a dynamic process and, as such, cannot capture the process itself. We expect the predictive validity of the scale to come from the pattern of recovery reflected in repeated assessments over the first few weeks of life, rather than in a single assessment. By plotting each neonate's performance over time, we can study individual differences in recovery curves, which may then been used to understand the coping capacities of the neonate and to predict later developmental outcomes.

Related to this is the relative stability of performance over a series of repeated assessments. As the scale is based on a process model, an individual's pattern of performance over time should show relative change. In a study of 54 full-term healthy infants examined seven times during the first 10 days of life, Lester (1980) reported an average cumulative test–retest correlation of 0.49 for the 26 behavior items. The correlations ranged from 0.23 to 0.90, with the lower correlations reflecting the more dynamic processes, such as social interaction. Most of the correlations are statistically significant but low to moderate in magnitude, suggesting that the relative rank order of individuals changes over time. In terms of the study of individual differences, this makes sense, since the scale is a way of assessing the process of organization of the baby as he responds to stress and recovers.

In cross-cultural work, the patterns of performance over time give us additional insights into the interaction between the behavioral organization of the infant and ethnocentric cultural practices and expectations. We may expect to find recovery curves that typify one culture more than another. These curves may reflect the demands of the culture on the fetus in utero. Within a culture, individual differences in patterns of recovery over time may further indicate the adaptation which that infant had made in an infant–caregiver relationship and then become a reflection of the cultural matrix. The Zinacanteco study showed us depressed patterns of recovery due to prenatal and perinatal stress conditions of undernutrition, as well as an undemanding, quiet pattern of maternal interaction. In contrast, the more rapid recovery curve seen in the Zambian infants appears to reflect maternal expectations for early motor and social development as the infants overcame their initially depleted physical condition.

Clearly, the context in which the exam is performed will influence the administration and results of the exam. This was the thrust of the argument made by DeVries and Super (1978) as they tested infants from four groups in Kenya in a variety of environments ranging from modern hospitals to traditional mud and wattle homes. They felt that home testing, for example, was complicated by low light levels, lack of furniture, varying noise and temperature levels, demand feeding, swaddling, and the presence of other family members and even domestic animals. As the authors pointed out, the sensitivity of the examiners to the context in which the exam is administered may provide a better understanding of the infant's adaptation to his postnatal environment. We would take this argument a step further and suggest that contextual variables, rather than being seen as disruptive, should be incorporated into the relationship the examiner establishes with the infant. The administration of the exam should be flexible, and the examiner must accommodate to the baby as part of an infant–caregiver interactive system, and use the physical and social context to bring out the adaptive capacities of the infant in *his* setting. Then we can estimate the practices that are likely to be used for an individual infant in his familial and cultural context. As was pointed out by Keefer et al., (1978), using the scale as a rigid set of stimulus–response contingencies is too restrictive an approach if one wants to learn about individual differences in behavioral organization, especially in a different culture.

We have also found that the context in which the scale is used can influence the reliability of the examination. When we have rechecked examiners for reliability after a stint of cross-cultural research, we have noted that an examiner's reliability may sometimes slip for particular scale items. Often these items are clues to understanding the essential differences in the population of interest. Since they are witnessed so often, the examiner brings these very items to a mean level that is appropriate for the culture studied but which may be different from U.S. norms. These items can then become the most sensitive ones to differences in the particular culture. In the Gusii study, the examiners' familiarity with the normative U.S. behavior on which the scales were developed and standardized enabled them to capture the unique motor behavior of the infants. They noted how they used the scale to organize their observations in a descriptive and exploratory way and focused more on the scale descriptors than on the quantitative scale scores. Moreover, too heavy a reliance on the individual scale points may force the infant to conform to the exam and may be too restrictive for cross-cultural research, if the goal is to highlight the behavioral features that are unique to a culture.

## METHODOLOGICAL ISSUES IN INFANCY RESEARCH

There are special problems that any observer of infants and small children must face. Cultures that have safeguards or taboos designed to protect the integrity of their group have established especially strong taboos around their small infants. Since the infant is seen as the most vulnerable member of the society, he is usually protected by such beliefs as his vulnerability to the "evil eye" (Africa) or the "heat" of the stranger (Yucatan). Unless the observers can become identified with the midwives or curers who participate in labor and delivery, they are not likely to be admitted to the newborn baby's household for a ritual period of protection (usually 30 days). This means that the observers will miss an observation in the critical period of early infancy, when a baby might be evaluated for behaviors that are influenced by his prenatal experiences, and when his responses are less influenced by extrauterine experience.

The ritual beliefs and practices that surround pregnancy, labor, and delivery are often just as closely guarded. And, until the observers have established credibility with a group, their chances of getting reliable data by questioning informants is likely to be minimal. Since these practices are guarded in order to exclude influence by outsiders, the more threatened the culture is by change, the less likely people within that culture are to impart to outsiders their crucial ingredients.

Another methodological problem is that, as we have seen from the studies discussed earlier, infant behavior is influenced not only by cultural practices but also by other factors that vary within a cultural setting, such as the maternal obstetric history. In other words, culture is only one of many variables that need to be examined to understand the behavioral organization of the infant. We view culture as a matrix within which to study variations in behavior as related to within-culture variables that may be operative. By collecting data on factors that can serve as alternative explanations, their contribution to behavior can be assessed statistically, both alone and in interaction with other factors. Rather than setting up an "either" culture or "other" argument, it may make more sense to assume interactions and study influences on behavior in the cultural context. Then we can ask what is unique about the culture that fosters certain constellations of behavioral processes. Culture then becomes a summary descriptor of the underlying processes within the demands of a given setting, and we can study the coping strategies of infants to that setting.

Thus, we may study variations in behavior within a local population to learn what are the determinants of behavior in that setting. The inclusion of other independent variables can be used to provide additional explanations, to help sort out interactions, and to widen the window on behavioral processes. They become expounding, rather than confounding, variables. Comparisons across local populations and between cultures enable us to look for patterns of differences and commonalities. Patterns of differences between populations may suggest how common processes are expressed and shaped by a culture. For example, we saw from the Zambians and Gusii how motor and social interactive processes are integrated into the unique handling practices of each culture. This approach also strengthens our theoretical explanations because, as Cole, Gay, Glick, and Sharp (1971) pointed out, it is more difficult to provide alternative explanations for patterns of differences than for single differences.

One corollary of these sentiments is to shy away from group designs where the thrust of the study is a series of mean comparisons. Rather, the focus would be to investigate interrelations or correlations among variables within a local population and then to compare differences in patterns of relations among variables. The arguments against mean differences, aside from the inevitable confounding with other independent variables, is that mean differences reflect group, rather than individual, differences. Differences or similarities in behavior between groups is entirely separate from (and statistically independent of) patterns of individual differences for that behavior. For example, we might find that two ethnic groups do not show significant mean differences on the social interactive items of the Brazelton scale. The two distributions of social interactive behavior overlap to have similar means, but there is still a range of social interactive behavior, and we need to ask what accounts for this variability in the two groups. By studying individual differences, we may learn why some infants perform higher than others within each group. The Puerto Rican study showed us that even in pediatrically normal and healthy samples, individual differences in the behavior of the Puerto Rican infants were related to obstetrical factors, both for clusters that differed between groups and for clusters that showed no group differences. Thus, individuals may have differential susceptibility to obstetrical effects, and obstetrical effects may interact with other variables that affect behavior.

The final difficulty we wish to discuss with cross-cultural research as a methodology is that: Because it is often used as a methodology, much cross-cultural work suffers from a lack of theoretical focus. The investigation of patterns of differences and their replication among populations rests on the articulation of at least a set of a priori hypotheses. A theoretical model serves as a guide toward deciding which variables to measure, how they should be measured, which are plausible confounding variables, and which differences and patterns of relationships to investigate. An atheoretical approach may result in simply cataloging behaviors that differ between two cultures, calculating mean differences between the cultural groups, and then generating post hoc explanations for those differences. This can be especially dangerous when the lack of a theoretical model results in the projection of one's own cultural biases and prejudices onto the beliefs and mores of another culture.

## CONCEPTUAL MODEL

The application of a psychobiological model to the cross-cultural study of the organization of neonatal behavior is illustrated in Figure 2–5. We view the infant as a biological–psychological system that proceeds developmentally from less complex to increasingly higher and more differentiated levels of organization. Organization refers to the biological tendency to coordinate and integrate processes into systems or structures that are both biological and behavioral—or "biobehavioral." These biobehavioral systems are dynamic and are accessible for investigation through the study of the process by which they develop; that is, we focus on the *how*, rather than the *what* or *why*, of development. Thus, infant behavior becomes a way of documenting biological processes of organization and development.

Because of the dynamic quality of biobehavioral processes, infant behavior must be studied serially. These processes become visible through observing the coping and adaptive strategies of the neonate to the new environment. By plotting the pattern of neonatal performance over time,

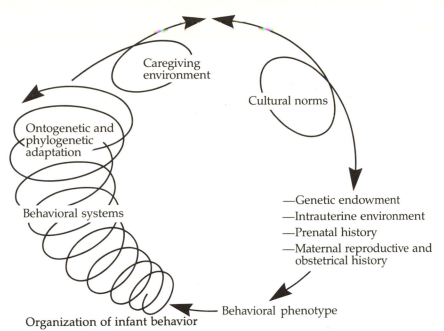

Caregiving environment

Cultural norms

Ontogenetic and phylogenetic adaptation

—Genetic endowment
—Intrauterine environment
—Prenatal history
—Maternal reproductive and obstetrical history

Behavioral systems

Behavioral phenotype

Organization of infant behavior

**Figure 2–5**    *A psychobiological model for the cross-cultural study of the organization of infant behavior.*

we can study individual differences in developmental patterns that reflect the processes of organization of behavioral systems. Cross-culturally, we can study how organization in different cultures proceeds.

This approach is also holistic, or organismic, and assumes that behavior is best understood in the context of the total functioning of the organism in the caretaking environment. While we are creating a taxonomy or catalog that documents the selective responses of infants to environmental stimuli, these isolated bits of behavior need to be resynthesized into a meaningful whole that preserves the dynamic quality of the organization of infant behavior. For the organismic model (cf. Werner, 1957, 1980), organization and development form a novel synthesis, rather than a simple summation, of previous systems and structures. Development is viewed as a process of increasing differentiation and integration that proceeds hierarchically, such that the present level or status of the system cannot be explained by the component elements or parts of the system. The problem is somewhat like stopping a bicycle and taking it apart to learn how it works: By having the parts strewn on the ground we may learn what the individual components of the system look like; but how they become integrated into a dynamic, functional whole can only be learned by observing the system in motion.

Implicit in this model is also the assumption that much, if not all, behavior is adaptive, and that the neonate emerges with a preprogrammed response repertoire that is designed to maximize the survival of the individual and of the species. The form of adaptation as evidenced in neonatal behavior reflects both the evolutionary, or phylogenetic, history of the species and the particular, or ontogenetic, history of the individual's development. The neonate is viewed as a competent organism that is skilled, selective, and socially influential, who actively interacts with and makes demands on the caretaking environment. As shown in the figure, the organization of neonatal behavior is represented by the increasing integration and differentiation of biobehavioral systems. At birth, this organization is the product of the synergistic relationship among several classes of variables. These include the obstetrical and reproductive history of the mother, the genetic endowment of the child, and the prenatal environment (which includes the conditions and complications associated with pregnancy and delivery—directly, such as nutrition, and indirectly, such as the effects of maternal attitude).

Subject characteristics—for instance, the infant's age (from conception, as well as from birth), size, weight, and sex—also need to be considered. These forces act to produce a behavioral phenotype, the expression of genetic endowment in a particular environment. This behavioral phenotype is predisposed to act on and respond to the caregiving environment in ways that represent the phylogenetic adaptation of the species to a given cultural setting. While basic organizational processes may remain constant from culture to culture—for example, infants universally become more alert and develop increasing interactive skills in the first few weeks of postnatal life—the range and form of adaptation for a particular culture will depend upon the demands of that culture. The behavioral repertoire of the individual newborn represents a homeostatic adaptation, with the limits set by adaptation of the species to a particular culture and the ontogenetic history of that individual. Thus, in the neonate we see already a blend of cultural practice and biological predisposition. And by considering the variability in neonatal behavior as adaptive, we can afford to expand our concepts of normality as we witness modes of organization that are unique and functional in one setting or another. Once we understand the significance of a culturally unique pattern of organization, we can ask how this pattern becomes integrated into processes of development and what are the antecedents of the pattern.

Returning to the figure, we see that the infant, now a product of his phylogenetic and ontogenetic history, elicits from the caregiving environment what he needs for his own organization and for the preservation of the species through the culture. This sets up the parent—infant dyad as a microcosm of the culture at large. The infant, by the range and form of adaptation, sets the limits and puts focus on the dyadic interaction. He shapes the practices and expectations of the culture. At the same time, the infant is shaped by postnatal environmental forces. These forces include methods of care and handling, the familial constellation and ecological milieu, the physical setting, and the larger goals, expectations, and needs of the culture. In this dynamic feedback system, a neonate becomes a respository of cultural expectations and in the process shapes the culture. The development of infant–caregiver interaction will proceed as infant and parent cycle through phases of homeostatic equilibrium as they strive to facilitate their own development and the mores of a culture.

Culture, then, becomes a way of broadening our perspective on underlying processes of development and provides a context within which we can learn about and understand the capacities and strategies of infants. It presents an opportunity to enlarge our perspective of the range and variability of forms of adaptive behavior and enables us to expand our basic principles and understanding of the processes of organization and development. Culture and biology are as inseparable as heredity and environment: Each is the expression of the other, and together they extend the range and potential of human experience.

# 3

# Culture and the Language of Socialization: Parental Speech

*Ben G. Blount*

Human infants are born with a potential for social and cognitive development that allows them to become members of their society. The potential is realized through socialization, the process through which children acquire the culture of their society. An infant's parents or caretakers play a critical role in socialization from the early stages of infancy. Parents assist in structuring the learning environment of their children. As members of society themselves, parents have a stock of knowledge about the world, about the social relationships that exist in it, and about the kinds of behavior that are expected of members of the society. Using that knowledge, parents channel children's activities to facilitate the children's learning about the environment and the social beings in it.

Socialization begins early in an infant's life. From birth, infants can respond to their surroundings and interact with their environment, including their caretakers. Communication between caretakers and infants is limited at first. An infant's capacity for communication at birth is undeveloped, but as an infant matures and the complexity of the interaction between infant and caretaker advances, communicative skills expand. Eventually, through social interaction, an infant begins to acquire language, the association of sound and meaning. The acquisition of meaning is the beginning of the acquisition of culture. As children gain more knowledge, their ability to function as members of society increases.

The transition from early, limited communication to the beginnings of cultural acquisition is a fundamental part of the socialization process. This chapter is devoted to a discussion of that transition. En route, it will be necessary to describe the nature of parent–infant interaction, paying particular attention to the activities of parents and infants. We want to know what parents do to encourage infants to interact and how they direct and influence interactions once these are established. The ways that parents speak to infants are central mechanisms in fostering and sustaining interaction, and if we can begin to understand how that process works, we will advance our knowledge of socialization. Toward those ends, parental speech is the major subject of discussion here.

To provide a proper context for a discussion of parental speech and its role in the socialization of children, it will be necessary for us to consider two related topics. The first is a review of the concept of culture, which is defined in numerous ways. For the sake of clarity, a brief historical account will be given. In particular we want to emphasize that culture is knowledge and that members of society organize knowledge into categories that are useful and meaningful to them. Categories of interest here are features of parental speech—in effect, knowledge that parents have of how to speak to infants. The second topic is the concept of communication and its general relationship to culture. A review of the meaning of communication will be useful to us in our consideration of infant–parent communication and the relationship of culture to that communication.

Once the concepts of culture and communication have been outlined and reviewed, we will again turn our attention to the nature of parent–infant interaction. A first consideration will be the capacity of infants for communication and their increasing ability to interact. We will be especially concerned with vocal interaction. As infants become more proficient in interaction, their parents are able to use the proficiency to assist the infants in their acquisition of meaning. Parental speech is instrumental in the interactions, and we will identify and describe the characteristic features of parental speech as used in English and Spanish. Usage frequencies of the features will be established, and differences will be highlighted according to language, culture, male–female speech, and the roles of the features in socialization.

## CULTURE AND COMMUNICATION

Adults in every human society possess a large body of information about the world around them. Under normal circumstances, a person has extensive knowledge about a wide variety of physical objects in the environment, and he or she has regular contact with several categories of social beings. People possess knowledge about how to act or behave in relation to the characteristics of physical and social entities. Their knowledge allows them to orient themselves to one another, to behave and communicate in ways that are more or less predictable and that convey meaning.

Although one can easily appreciate that members of society have an abundance of information about their society and how to behave in it, a description of the information is difficult. The sheer volume of the information defies easy description, but it is not difficult to conceptualize the entire array of knowledge. The sum total of knowledge that people in a society possess has been summarized conceptually as culture. A historically early definition of culture, for example, was "Culture or civilization . . . is that complex whole which includes knowledge, belief, arts, morals, law, custom, and any other capabilities and habits acquired by man as a member of society" (Tylor, 1871, p.1).

Tylor's definition of culture, as we can see, encompassed the totality of knowledge of a society. If one views culture in that perspective, the definition can be applied holistically to any given society. In other words, we can speak of the culture of the Navajo Indians or the Mayan Indians or the Yoruba people of Nigeria. To think of culture in a holistic way is useful in some respects. Differences in behavior, dress, language—lifestyle in general—are usually easy to discern, at least in broad outline. Every society is different from every other society, and culture is a convenient concept to summarize the differences. The Blackfoot Indians are different from the Cherokee Indians; they each have different cultures.

If we began, however, to look in more historical detail at Blackfoot culture and Cherokee culture, we could see that the two cultures differed in many dimensions. The kinship systems were not organized in the same way, marriage systems were different, and the subsistence patterns were not the same. To generalize, different aspects of culture will be involved, depending on which aspect of a society one wants to investigate and describe, and slightly different definitions of culture will be needed. Studies, for example, that emphasize continuity in the transmission of knowledge across generations will focus on cultural knowledge that is relatively unchanging and traditional. If the focus is on societal knowledge that facilitates adaptation to the environment, then a stock of cultural knowledge about climate and natural resources will be emphasized. An emphasis on one or another aspect of culture is consistent with the necessity for selectivity about the kinds of knowledge and behavior that one wishes to study. A selective approach to the study of culture can be called an institutional perspective.

A holistic approach to culture was the first to be used historically, and it is useful for comparing societies on a general level. The institutional perspective was developed later and is useful when a particular aspect of culture, such as kinship or marriage, is to be described.

Still more recent is an internal perspective of culture. To explain what internal perspective means, we need to return for a moment to Tylor's definition of culture given above. His definition is, in effect, descriptive. It lists the categories of knowledge according to preestablished ideas about art, religion, and so on. The approach to a society's culture from his perspective is external, on the one hand relying on preestablished categories to help organize information about the society, and on the other hand attempting to fit descriptions of behavior—individual instances of behavior—into those categories. An internal perspective also uses categories, but the ways in which they are identified and established are quite different. First, the categories must be identified rather than created. The task confronting a researcher is to identify the categories that members of a society themselves use.

An assumption in an internal perspective of culture is that people do indeed rely on categories in the organization of their behavior. In some instances, reliance on categories is clear. A kinship system is a case in point. All societies have kinsmen, people recognized as related to one another in defined ways. Moreover, in all societies, there are prescribed ways of behaving with respect to kinsmen. Individuals have behavioral obligations toward kinsmen as opposed to nonkinsmen, and the obligations vary according to the category of kin, such as grandfather, brother, or cousin. Kinship categories are real entities that people use in making decisions about their behavior.

In other instances, categories of culture are present but not as easy to discern, as for example in speech behavior. Although it is clear that a member of society does not speak in the same way to everyone that he or she addresses, the categories of speech often can be identified only by careful study. All societies do, however, possess categories of speech. Some categories are appropriate to the person to whom one is speaking. One speaks differently to a friend than to a stranger. Other categories depend on other factors. One does not always speak to a friend in the same way. A discussion of a sports event does not involve the same ways of speaking as a heart-to-heart talk or an apology. An individual who spoke the same way in all contexts and with different individuals would be viewed as anomalous and probably pathological in all societies. To speak appropriately, individuals rely on categories of speech.

To recapitulate, an internal perspective of culture involves searching for the categories of knowledge that members of a society have and use in organizing their behavior. A formal definition of culture in this perspective states that, "a society's culture consists of whatever it is that one has to know or believe in order to operate in a manner acceptable to its members, and do so in any role that they accept for any one of themselves" (Goodenough, 1957, p. 167). We can think of culture as information that members of society have and use in organized ways to: (1) regulate their own behavior and make it meaningful to other individuals with whom they have social contact, and (2) interpret the behavior of other individuals in the society who in turn are making efforts to make their own behavior meaningful.

The culture of a society is realized, that is, made apparent, in the behavior of its members. One can "see" culture operating when members of a society interact with one another. Only some aspects of culture will be revealed in any given social encounter or interaction between members, but the important point is that culture becomes evident when people interact with one another. People make available to each other information that can be shared, understood, interpreted, or in some fashion made meaningful.

We now turn our attention to the concept of communication. Communication is a complex process of signal interchange usually involving several channels of information, conveyed simultaneously. By channel, we mean the medium by which information is transmitted. A channel can be vocal, gestural, facial, and so on. To take an example of the use of multiple channels, if a man meets an acquaintance on the street, and he wishes to acknowledge that person's presence, he may express the intent in multiple ways. The man might say "hello," and he might also send several facial signals. He might, for instance, use an eyebrow flash, quickly raising and lowering his eyebrows. He might smile, or depending on his intent, frown or scowl. He might also nod his head, raise his head momentarily, slow his pace, quicken his pace, wave, and so on.

Whatever an individual chooses to do in social situations where greeting behavior is expected, his choice will be communicative. Even a failure to give any greeting at all communicates, often strongly. What one chooses to say, how one actually says the greeting, and what nonverbal actions accompany the greeting all contribute to how the social interaction is to be interpreted.

Several important points can be made about greeting routines, communication and culture. First, members of a society know—that is, they can recognize—when a greeting is socially expected. To participate as a member of society, an individual has to be able to function in greeting routines, and each member of society acquires the cultural knowledge needed to make appropriate decisions regarding greetings. Second, an individual has a set of greeting formulae that he or she can use as needed. A person has knowledge of what will serve or count as a greeting. The knowledge is cultural in origin. One has to learn what words, phrases, and the like are acceptable and interpretable as greetings. It is also necessary that a person become enculturated (that is, acquire cultural knowledge) about how the meanings of verbal formulae can change depending on how one says them. Giving a greeting extra loudly or softly, or with exaggerated intonation, or with excessive breathiness can all convey meaning.

Several additional points are necessary concerning speech, communication and culture. Greetings are only one kind of speech act that members of a society must know. Many other speech acts, such as promising, arguing, denying, and confirming, must be acquired as a person becomes enculturated. Regardless of the speech act, however, an individual must learn what is acceptable behavior. In a greeting, a person could say "hello" in an unusual speech register such as falsetto, or he could say "hello" when "goodbye" is appropriate. In either instance it is likely that the behavior would communicate, but it would probably not be acceptable. A general point then is that communication can occur in the absence of culture, but by definition the behavior that communicates in that way is outside the realm of acceptability and is difficult to interpret. Culture, again, is a specific kind of knowledge that members of society use to make behavior meaningful, that is, acceptable and interpretable.

## PARENT–INFANT INTERACTION

A distinction between communication and culture is useful in our consideration of parent–infant interaction. Parents communicate with their infants in a variety of ways and through several sense modalities. Parents attract the attention of their infants, and they seek to establish and maintain concerted activity with them. Several motives may promote their communication with infants. In an immediate sense, they may merely derive pleasure from the social interaction. Over a period of several months, however, parents make an effort to introduce symbolic meaning to the interaction. They begin to rely more and more in the interaction on the use of words, in effect, vocal sounds that stand for—that is, symbolize—objects in the environment. If we trace the activities of parents in their interactions with infants through time, it is reasonably accurate to say that through communication, parents begin to introduce culture to infants.

During their first few months of life, infants are not able to use cultural knowledge in the way we have defined it here. They do, however, have the ability to communicate and to interact in limited ways. Infants use several sense modalities, both to initiate and to respond in interaction with adults. The major modalities are touch, vision, and sound. Our central concern in this chapter is with sound, but some general features of communication through touch and vision should be noted.

Tactile communication has an important role in the development of infants. Infants in all societies are held, cuddled, and in general stimulated through body contact and touching. It has been known for many years that infants who are grossly deprived of tactile communication will become listless and may develop behavioral disorders (see Spitz, 1945, 1946). Tactile communication is necessary for normal development, but relatively little research has investigated the ways that parents and infants use touch to communicate. The amount and duration of tactile communication between parent and infants appear to vary considerably across societies. The amount of touching is in part a function of the number of people who have access to the infant. In some societies in East Africa, for example, mothers and infants are kept in virtual seclusion for several days after a child's birth, and after the period of seclusion ends, only close relatives have access to the child. In other societies, such as the Eskimo, many more individuals will participate in infant care and have contact with infants. General societal attitudes toward children and child rearing are also responsible for the amount of tactile communication an infant receives.

Vision is another important channel of communication between parents and their infants. Infants are able to use vision to a limited extent soon after they are born (Mendelson and Haith, 1976). Vision is a major means by which infants can attend to their surroundings. Within a few weeks after birth, an infant can recognize its mother's face and voice (Culp and Boyd, 1975). Eye contact, though limited in frequency and duration, nevertheless is established and sustained for brief periods. Infants only a few weeks old will vocalize in response to a caretaker's vocalizations, especially if eye contact has first been established (Stern, 1974). It has been suggested that eye contact plays an important role in establishing mother–infant and father–infant bonds (Klaus and Kennell, 1976). Eye contact appears to be a powerful stimulus to interaction and development, and its absence, in cases where infants are blind, can lead to abnormal interaction patterns between mothers and infants (Fraiberg, 1974).

As infants mature and gain greater control of their sense organs, vision undoubtedly becomes more important in their communication systems. Infants learn to distinguish individuals with whom they are in contact, usually their mothers at first and then other categories of individuals, including strangers. Vision is increasingly integrated with other aspects of communication such as smiling and laughing, and the role of vision becomes more specialized as the communication system is further differentiated. Eye contact between a mother and her infant in early development may at first establish only a momentary affective tie, but in later development eye contact may be a means of attracting and sustaining an infant's attention so that other interaction may follow (Stern, 1977).

Infants have the ability to vocalize from birth onward. They can, of course, cry from birth, but within a few weeks they begin to make vowel-like sounds. They also exhibit within a few weeks a responsiveness to parental vocalizations, and parents and infants engage in relatively brief exchanges of vocalizations. The sounds that infants make during their early vocal interactions with their parents are devoid of any linguistic meaning. They certainly aren't words—the sounds have no referential meaning—but they do serve as a medium of social interchange between an infant and caretaker (Blount, 1972). Limited at first to only one or two turns of vocalizations by each "speaker," the vocal exchanges increase in frequency and duration as infants become older and more proficient in interaction.

Through time, not only do the parent–infant exchanges become longer, with each participant taking more turns vocalizing, but the characteristics of the vocalizations change, especially in the speech of the parent. In the beginning stages, parents often imitate, roughly, what an infant vocalizes, and those parental vocalizations are thus also devoid of any linguistic meaning. Episodes of parental speech early in the development of the child may consist solely of vocalizations, that is, sounds unrelated to linguistic meaning. Some of the parental speech, however, may consist of words and phrases ordinarily used in their language, although the way those items are articulated may be nonordinary. In time, parental speech begins to contain more and more words, and the speech could accurately be characterized as verbalizations. For the sake of convenience, however, parental speech to infants will be referred to here in general as vocalizations, although in actuality the speech that parents address to infants may contain some verbalizations.

Parental speech is not random or haphazard overall. Parents interact with their infants in regular and systematic ways. One of the systematic ways in which caretakers use their vocalizations is in joint referential activity (Bruner, 1975). An infant's attention is focused on an object (or an action) through joint infant–caretaker action, and the caretaker names the object (or action) involved in the transaction. Repeated instances of that behavior serve as the basis for a child's learning the association between the object and the sounds that "accompany" it. An example is a mother who hands her infant a cup, says "cup," gives the cup to the child, takes the cup back from the child, says "cup," and repeats the exchange over and over. Joint referential activity is an early basis for acquisition of vocabulary (Ninio and Bruner, 1978). There are also other ways in which caretakers pattern their vocalizations when they are talking to infants at earlier developmental stages. These are discussed below.

Parents are faced with a special communication problem when they interact vocally with infants who are in the prelinguistic stage of development. Infants at that stage cannot understand what is said to them, at least not in the usual sense in which speech has meaning. Yet parents in all societies do interact vocally with their prelinguistic infants. The parental vocalizations may be regular expressions that could be used with practically anyone, but more often they are tailored to addressing children who have limited or even no linguistic skills. The parental vocalizations may, as noted, be made up exclusively of nonsense sounds, and they may be imitations of sounds that the infants themselves make. The absence of semantic content in parental speech, however, does not really matter in the early phases of interaction. The speech can still be communicative. Infants respond to it with surprising regularity and consistency, and after several months of practice interacting with their parents they can participate in prelinguistic vocal interactions or "conversations." Parents and infants interact in a conversational form, with each member taking turns in a round, and rounds following each other in succession. In other words, a parent may say "mama," the infant takes a turn by repeating "mama," the parent begins a new round with another turn, "mama," and so on.

It is recognized more and more that prelinguistic vocal interactions play an important role in the socialization of children. They constitute a fundamental pattern of behavior that infants learn early in development and continue to employ throughout their acquisition of language. The pattern is instrumental in the acquisition of language, which in turn is a major vehicle of learning about the environment and about oneself. In a recent study of prelinguistic conversations, Freedle and Lewis (1977) presented evidence for the importance of interactional behavior in children's development. They found that mother–infant interactions constitute a social system. The system is situationally bound, with particular behaviors occurring only in specific environments. Waving goodbye, for example, occurs only when someone is leaving. A pattern of behavior is established, and the prelinguistic behavior is the framework through which language is later acquired. After learning to wave goodbye in a particular situation, a child then has a basis for learning to say "bye-bye."

Children less than a year of age can participate in prelinguistic interaction, but their interactional skills are limited. Most of the work to foster the interactions must be done by the parents. What do parents do to establish interaction patterns? Several basic interactional requirements have to be met. First, a parent must attract a child's attention and alert a child to the possibility of interaction that can be accomplished through different modalities—touch, vision, vocalization—or combinations of modalities. Once attention is obtained, it is necessary to focus the attention on an activity, usually through the exchange of vocalizations, or an object, or both. Still a third function of parental speech is the introduction of linguistic meaning into the interaction. Parents begin to name the actions and activities in the interactions and to treat the interactions as if they were semantic.

Parents can accomplish the above objectives by employing a number of special linguistic devices in their speech (Blount and Padgug, 1977). Almost all the utterances that parents make to prelinguistic infants contain features of speech such as falsetto, high pitch, and exaggerated intonation. The presence of those features gives the speech a special character. Sometimes referred to as "baby talk," parental speech is a form of speech (a register) that is acknowledged by members of a society to be especially appropriate for talking to infants (Ferguson, 1965).

Each society has its own register of baby talk, its own socially approved ways of speaking to infants who cannot respond with language. Linguists have studied and described baby talk form in languages as diverse as Berber (North Africa), Marathi (India), Gilyak (Siberia), Cocopa (American Indian), and Luo (East Africa) (see Ferguson, 1977, for a summary description). Parental speech registers in each language, however, will have their own sets of sounds and words. Each register will be unique in its total configuration, although considerable similarities exist in registers across societies and languages. The similarity is due in part to the fact that parents in all societies face the same problems in communicating with infants. Some common features of parental speech, for example, are reduction of consonant clusters in words, reduction of the number of syllables in words, and the use of short, simply constructed sentences.

Parents in all societies also use special articulatory features in their speech to infants. One category of those features is prosody, which consists of the volume, pitch, and tone of speech, duration (the period in which sounds are sustained), and juncture (the period of silence between syllables and words). Another category is paralinguistic sounds, which accompany sounds that are necessary for meaning but are not themselves directly involved in the meaning. For example, the word *you* can be pronounced with excessive lip-rounding, that is, with the lips protruding and rounded, but the meaning of *you* is not thereby changed. Other paralinguistic features that are commonly used in parental speech are nasalization, palatalization (placing the tip of the tongue on the palate during articulation), and labialization (extra use of the lips in articulation).

Most of the characteristics of parental speech seems to be designed to facilitate children's perception of speech and, after they have begun to acquire language, their comprehension of it. To demonstrate those functions it is necessary to study parental speech and its effects longitudinally. One has to consider parental speech in actual interaction with infants across a developmental age span. That approach was employed in a project on English and Spanish parental speech. To illustrate some of the scope, complexity, and functions of parental speech in socialization, the study will be reported in detail here.

## PARENTAL SPEECH IN ENGLISH AND SPANISH

Interpersonal communication between parents and children in English- and Spanish-speaking families in Austin, Texas, has been the subject of a recent study. The long-range goals of the project are the description of parental speech in each language, a comparison for the purpose of illustrating cultural differences, and an assessment of the roles of parental speech in fostering the acquisition of communicative skills in children.

To date, the descriptions and analysis have centered on the parental speech patterns. Features of speech modification by the parents have been identified, and profiles of feature usage have been established for each of the families and parents in the study (Blount and Padgug, 1977).

The differential use of features by mothers and fathers has also been described, and English and Spanish comparisons have been made to identify cultural differences in feature usage across languages as well as sex of speaker (Blount and Padgug, 1976). Changes in feature selection, longitudinally, have been noted in relation to language development of the children (Blount and Kempton, 1976). These findings are reviewed below, but first some comments about methods and procedures are in order.

Tape recordings were made of parental speech to young children in four English-speaking and four Spanish-speaking families in Austin, Texas. The families were chosen on the bases of ages of the children and of the children having no other siblings. The age range of the children was 9;0 to 18;0 months (9 months, 0 weeks, to 18 months, 0 weeks) for the English speakers and 8;1 to 13;1 and 18;1 to 22;2 for Spanish speakers. All were children of university students, and all the English-speaking families were native speakers of American English. Three of the Spanish-speaking families were from Latin America—one family from Mexico, one from Chile, and one in which the father was from Peru and the mother from Argentina. The fourth family was native to Texas.

Efforts were made to record under as natural conditions as possible. At the beginning of the project, we repeatedly emphasized in discussions with the parents the necessity of obtaining samples of natural interactions. The parents were encouraged to record conversations with their children that were typical of everyday interactions, and they were requested to avoid staged productions that would be unrepresentative of children's interactional routines. All the families reported that there were special times of the day when they were most likely to interact with the children, and they attempted to record during those times.

A tape recorder was left with each family for 24-hour periods, ideally every week (although on some occasions recordings were made only every 2 or 3 weeks). During a 24-hour period, parents would tape about 30 to 45 minutes of interaction. A minimum of 9 recording sessions was made for each child, and the maximum was 14 sessions.

Observers were not present during the recording sessions. Valuable behavioral information was thereby sacrificed, but pretesting had shown that the presence of an observer–outsider in the home severely constrained the behavior of the children. Even after several visits and long periods of habituation, the children were still reluctant to vocalize. That, in turn, interfered with parental speech behavior and naturalness of interaction. The parents all reported, however, that they had no difficulty in making the recordings when only they and the child were present, and none of them believed that the presence of the tape recorder hindered their behavior or the child's. They all stated that naturalness of setting and interaction was not a problem, and none felt that they had attempted to teach or instruct the children any more than they would have under other circumstances.

After taping had been completed, it was necessary to identify the units of speech that would be scrutinized for parental speech features. The basic units in the transcriptions of the interactions were utterances. An utterance was defined as parental speech offset by children's vocalizations or by pauses—that is, interactional turntaking was the structural criterion. Whatever occurred verbally in a turn was one utterance, whether it was a monosyllabic nonsense form or two or more sentences.

The number of parental utterances addressed to each infant varied across sections, families, and sex of speaker. No effort was made to record in comparable settings or activities, as for example, during feedingtime or bathtime. As discussed above, we wanted the interactions to be part of each family's normal routine, and consequently no attempt was made to control for variation. We merely note here that the average number of parental utterances per session was 161 for the English-speaking sample and 80 for the Spanish-speaking sample.

Native speakers of English and of Spanish first listened to each utterance to decide if the speech could be considered parental. Although we knew that parents often speak to infants in special ways, we did not know how much of their speech to infants would contain parental features. The judgmental criterion was appropriateness of the speech to children and general inappropriateness to adults. In effect, the decisions were made on cultural grounds, on the basis of knowledge that members of the speech community have about what forms, or registers, of speech are appropriate for talking to which kinds of individuals—in this case, infants. Somewhat to our surprise, virtually all the utterances were parental. More than 97 percent of the speech addressed to the infants was in parental speech register.

After each utterance had been scored as parental or nonparental, native speakers next listened to each utterance to identify features that led to the classification of utterances as parental. Initially only the more obvious features were noted—exaggerated intonation, high pitch, falsetto, special lexical items—but the investigation soon led to the discov-

**Table 3–1**   *Parental speech: Prosodic, Paralinguistic, and Interactional Features*

| | FEATURES | |
| --- | --- | --- |
| PROSODIC | PARALINGUISTIC | INTERACTIONAL |
| Breathiness | Phonetic alteration | Special lexical items |
| Breath held | Creaky voice | Nonsense form |
| Whisper | Tenseness | Personal pronoun |
| Lowered volume | Nasality | substitution |
| Raised volume | Rounding | Grammatical deviation |
| Falsetto | Phonetic substitution | Tag question |
| High pitch | Lengthened vowel | Instructional |
| Low pitch | Shortened vowel | Hmm? |
| Exaggerated intonation | Lengthened consonant | Attentionals |
| Singing | Shortened consonant | Turn substitution |
| Slow tempo | | Repetition |
| Fast tempo | | Imitation |
| | | Interpretation |

ery of the identification of 34 prosodic, paralinguistic, and interactional features that characterized the speech as parental. A list of the 34 features by category is given in Table 3–1.

The list of features in Table 3–1 shows the wealth of special speech features available to parents in English and in Spanish. Although the list was compiled from the records of all the parents, the majority of the features appeared in the speech of each parent at one point or another in the study. One major finding of the study was that all the parents used a large number of different features in their speech to infants. None of the parents relied on only a few features, and that indicates, as will be discussed below, the existence of cultural patterns for parental speech and the efficacy of speech in stimulating and facilitating parent–infant interaction.

Several other points should be made about the information in Table 3–1. The meaning of the terms *prosodic* and *paralinguistic* have already been discussed, but an explanation should be given about the general category *interactional*. In one sense all of the 34 features are interactional. They all are indicators of a speech style that is considered appropriate for use with young children, and they all have a pragmatic function of fostering and promoting joint action of parent and child. Some of the features, however, are defined as components or units of the interaction itself. To take only one example, *repetition* is the repeat of an utterance by a parent that had been made to a child. Often a child failed to respond to a parental utterance, prompting the parent to repeat the utterance. *Repetition* is part of the structure of the interaction.

Many of the parental speech features in Table 3–1 are well known or self-explanatory. *Whisper* and *falsetto,* for example, are features of speech that are well known, and *breathiness* and *breath held* mean merely that greater and lesser amounts of air, respectively, are released in utterances than would normally be expected. Some features, however, are probably not obvious in their meaning. A list of those features with definitions is given in the appendix at the end of this chapter. The appendix contains only the lesser-known features that are relevant to this paper. Several features are of low frequency and need not concern us here (see Blount and Padgug, 1977, for a complete description).

## FEATURE PROFILES: ENGLISH AND SPANISH

Once the features were identified and described, the parental utterances were coded for each of the 34 features, again by native speakers. If a feature occurred at least once in an utterance it was scored as present, otherwise as absent. Multiple occurrences of a feature in an utterance were not individually scored. The present/absent rate provided a rate measure, not an absolute frequency of occurrence for the features. To date, the rate-measure profiles have been established for the composite records of parental speech to each of the nine children, that is, not for the individual weekly sessions but for all the sessions for each child.

Five individuals were responsible for coding the features, three native speakers of English and two native speakers of Spanish. All were graduate students at the University of Texas. For English, coder reliability was high across the 34 features. Comparisons of selected samples during the coding of the speech revealed no significant differences among the coders. The coders were consistent in their identification of the features in the English parental utterances.

The two coders for Spanish were also consistent in their identification of the features, but considerable variation appeared on four features, *high pitch, fast tempo, slow tempo,* and *attentionals.* Coder 1 showed rates that were significantly above or below what appeared in the whole sample, English and Spanish combined. Her scores on those four features were not used in the calculations. This limitation on methodology should be noted. In general, the Spanish results, as compared to the English ones, are more problematic, due to the coder variation on the features above, two as opposed to three coders, and more diverse background of the families. Despite the limitations, coder reliability was high on 30 of the 34 features, and the results are in the range of acceptability.

In the first phase of the analysis of parental speech, profiles of the feature rate measures were established for each child and for each recording session. In other words, each weekly session for each child contained a list of the rate scores at which each feature appeared in the speech of the mother and father. By viewing the sessions in sequence for each child and for each language group of children, longitudinal records of parental speech were available, and the speech could be viewed in terms of longitudinal changes. The possibility existed, then, of investigating developmental functions of parental speech. At the present, the analysis includes only the longitudinal profiles for speech to each language group and not to each individual child.

The speech profiles reveal several interesting points. The most striking is a remarkable uniformity, overall, of rate measures across the children for each feature. The uniformity of parental speech is most striking when we consider the features with the highest rate scores. In the English samples, *exaggerated intonation* was by far the most frequently occurring features, appearing in more than 60 percent of the utterances in the speech of each parent. *High pitch* also showed great uniformity across speakers. Spanish also showed a high degree of similarity on the top-ranked features, *repetition, exaggerated intonation, instructional,* and *attentionals.*

For purposes of comparison and summary, the composite rate measures of each feature and for each language have been ranked. This, again, is the totaled rates of occurrence summed across parents. Rankings of the ten most frequently occurring features are given in Table 3–2.

An inspection of Table 3–2 shows that 6 of the 10 most frequent features in each language are common to both: *exaggerated intonation, high pitch, lengthened vowel, repetition, lowered volume,* and *instructional.* Each language has four specific features. In English they are *breathiness, creaky voice, tenseness,* and *falsetto.* In Spanish, they are *attentionals, fast tempo, raised volume,* and *personal pronoun substitution.*

Speakers of each of the languages are similar in a high utilization of pitch, intonation, vowel duration, and lower volume on the one hand, and the use of repetition and instruction on the other. The English-speaking parents relied more heavily on control of air volume and prosodic and paralinguistic features, whereas their Spanish-speaking counterparts showed greater utilization of speech tempo and interactional features. Exactly what these differences mean in developmental terms is not yet clear, but if we keep in mind that in all the families, the initiation

**Table 3–2**  *Ranking 10 Most Common Features in English and Spanish*

| ENGLISH | SPANISH |
|---|---|
| 1. Exaggerated intonation | 1. Exaggerated intonation |
| 2. Breathiness | 2. Repetition |
| 3. High pitch | 3. High pitch |
| 4. Repetition | 4. Instructional |
| 5. Lowered volume | 5. Attentionals |
| 6. Lengthened vowel | 6. Lowered volume |
| 7. Creaky voice | 7. Raised volume |
| 8. Instructional | 8. Lengthened vowel |
| 9. Tenseness | 9. Fast tempo |
| 10. Falsetto | 10. Personal pronoun substitution |

and maintenance of interaction with the children was the focus of care-taker-child activity, we can see that there are two distinct cultural styles to achieve those ends. In English, parents modulate the prosodic and paralinguistic properties of their speech, and in Spanish, social interactional properties are more readily invoked.

Another expression of cultural differences is in the overall rate of feature usage. Parents in the Spanish sample, as a group, showed a rate of 436.8 features per 100 utterances. English-speakers showed a rate of 318.8 per 100 utterances. Thus, Spanish speakers used 37 percent more features than English speakers.

## MOTHER AND FATHER SPEECH

Men and women in all societies have different ways of speaking. In extreme cases they may have completely different languages; more likely, they share the same language but use its features differently across situations. An area where one would expect to find differences in male and female speech is in the speech addressed to infants. To consider differences in mother and father speech the 12 most frequently occurring features in their speech were compared. The mothers' and fathers' records in each language group were combined, allowing us to compare sex differences in feature usage across languages.

Looking first at the English speakers, mothers and fathers share 9 of the 12 most frequently occurring features listed by sex of speaker. The most notable aspect of the speech, then, is that mothers and fathers are much more alike than they are different. Mothers and fathers tend to talk to their infants in much the same way. If their speech is contrasted, however, the features that best characterize mother speech, based on the comparisons and differences in rank order, are *lengthened vowel, falsetto,* and *high pitch.* Those that best characterize father speech are *lowered volume, creaky voice,* and, secondarily, *low pitch* and *breath held.* In effect, mothers rely more on duration and higher pitch registers, and fathers rely more on lower pitch registers and breath control.

Turning now to the Spanish record, mothers and fathers share 11 of the 12 ranked features. As in English, we find that in Spanish parental speech, mother and father are more alike than different. If we focus on the differences, mother speech is best characterized by *lengthened vowel, personal pronoun substitution,* and *exaggerated intonation.* Father speech is best accounted for by the features *raised volume* and *fast tempo.*

A consideration of the features that best characterize the speech of mother and father in English and Spanish leads to the conclusion that there are culturally differentiated sex-specific preferences for feature usage. In both languages, the mothers tend to use the same features at the same rates to a greater extent than do the fathers. This consistency would be expected, given the mother's traditional role in child socialization. Mother speech also shows preferences for features that tend to be associated with nurturant relationships, whereas father speech has comparatively more speech that marks interaction as meaningful in terms of language content. The fathers' speech appears to be more related to the problems of understanding content and intention in interaction. English-speaking fathers make their speech lower and more tense, and Spanish speaking fathers make their speech louder and faster.

It should also be noted that the speech profiles for mother and father speech exhibit differences that are consistent with other accounts of male and female speech. Several studies show that female speech tends to have higher pitch levels and greater intonational movement and is less forceful than masculine-role speech, which tends to be low in pitch and volume (Addington 1968; Berko-Gleason 1975; Kramer 1974).

Differences in the speech of mothers and fathers are likely to be important in the speech socialization of children. They appear to place different communicative demands on children, mother speech emphasizing affective ties and relationships and father speech emphasizing understanding in interaction. Since their expectations are different, children are likely to learn to respond differently, and consequently their communicative skills will be enhanced while at the same time they will be learning cultural patterns and preferences for speaking. Those seem, at least, to be probable consequences, although our lack of knowledge here does not allow us to make those claims with certainty.

## DEVELOPMENTAL FUNCTIONS
## OF PARENTAL SPEECH

Rather than emphasizing differences, we can turn to the similarities in the speech of the parents and make further observations about these features. The similarities that are found across languages and across sex lines are likely to be due to practical requirements that parents face in trying to interact with children who have limited communicative skills. It has been noted that the following features have high occurrence rates in the speech of the majority of the parents: *exaggerated intonation, repetition, high pitch, lowered volume, lengthened vowel,* and *instructional.* These features are definitive of parental speech primarily because of the demands placed on parent–infant interaction. Before interaction can be established, parents must first attract an infant's attention, and since infants can distinguish pitch, tone, and volume differences long before they can make semantic distinctions, parents use exaggerated prosodic features abundantly. A second interactional requirement is that attention, once obtained, be focused, and the high usage of *repetition* and *instructional* are consistent with that task.

The developmental patterns that occur in parental speech are also interesting. At the beginning of the project we had assumed, again somewhat incorrectly, that speech would change significantly over the age range of the children, a range of approximately 9 to 22 months. Only a few features, however, showed changes in rate measures consistent with age increases. *Repetition* had a higher rate in speech to the two youngest children than to the older ones in the English sample. *Interpretation* showed the opposite pattern; it was 3 to 10 times higher in speech to the two oldest children. Spanish showed a similar pattern for *interpretation* and *slow tempo.* Again, it should be recalled that the composite records, not the weekly sessions, of parent–child interaction are under consideration. Analyses of each parent's record longitudinally might reveal more clear-cut developmental patterns.

In an effort to look for changes in combinations of features that might express developmental patterns, the functions of various speech features were examined. Not all features appeared to function in the same way to promote and sustain interaction. Some prosodic and paralinguistic features—those involving dimensions of tone, duration, pitch, phonetic quality, and volume—seemed primarily to convey affect, and they were used by parents to attract children's attention. Other features were more directly interactional in character, relating to the sequences of vocalizations by interacting parents and children. Repetition of an utterance and an adult's imitation of a child's vocalizations are examples. The features appear to function to direct children's attention to speech as an activity. Still other features were used to relate speech to the environment in meaningful, referential ways.

The functions of attracting attention, focusing attention, and introducing meaning were assumed to represent parental strategies in interactions with their children. Three interactional strategies were thus posited: (1) affective-interactional, reflected in speech by prosodic and paralinguistic features, and functioning to attract attention; (2) didactic-interactional, reflected in speech by interactional features, and functioning to focus attention once it has been obtained; and (3) semantic-interactional, reflected in speech by features that attribute meaning to the interaction, and functioning to relate the interaction to the environment referentially (see Blount and Kempton, 1976). A distributional analysis was carried out on the features *exaggerated intonation, instructional, imitation,* and *repetition* in relation to each other and to the other features in the study. In other words, we wanted to know if these features tended to occur together or separately. The goal was to find either inclusion (co-occurrence) or mutual exclusion patterns that would allow us to see distinct patterns and changes in patterns during the 12- to 13-week developmental period. The distributional analyses showed that diachronic changes did occur for some children. First, there were changes in the usage patterns between *exaggerated intonation* and *instructional*. Initially issued in the context of exaggerated intonation, *instructional* speech came to be issued principally in the context of normal intonation. Distributional relationships between *instructional* and *imitation* showed a similar pattern of development. They tended to be separated in speech to children in the later weeks of the study, and to co-occur in the early sessions.

These patterned aspects of parental speech relate to a telescoped version of developmental social interaction. Parents are confronted with the task of communicating with individuals who do not know what the fundamentals of interaction are. Young children must learn that speech is to be attended to, that their own vocalizations and those of their caretakers warrant attention, that the attention can be sustained, and that within that framework, speech can be exchanged and ultimately serve as a vehicle of meaning. Parental speech appears to be organized in precisely those ways. Parental activities establish the groundwork for language socialization by providing children with fundamental behavior patterns for discovering their language and its appropriate use.

## SUMMARY AND CONCLUSIONS

Human societies are composed of individuals who share to greater and lesser degrees knowledge about their social world. The knowledge that enables them to act in meaningful ways to interpret the behavior of their fellow members is called culture. Infants are born into society in an "acultural" state. To become members of their society, they have to undergo a process of socialization. Through socialization, they begin to acquire the culture of their society.

Although infants are born without culture, they do have the capacity to communicate. They can respond to their environment through several sense modalities, and within a short time after birth they can engage in brief but concerted action with their parents or caretakers. The interactions are important vehicles of socialization. Parents play a directive role in the interactions, on the one hand channeling infants' attention to what they consider to be important, and on the other hand assisting infants in their acquisition of language.

An important part of the socialization of infants is the transition from communication to regular, concerted or joint interaction. The transition develops over a period of months, beginning during the final quarter of the first year of life. Since the interactional skills of infants are limited at that age, parents play a critical role in initiating, fostering, and sustaining interaction. Parents use a number of devices in fulfilling those ends—in particular, special ways of talking to infants.

In all societies, parents speak to infants and young children using special features in their speech. In a comparative study of English and Spanish, 34 special "baby-talk" features were identified in parental speech. The list is probably not exhaustive; other features may occur in these and other languages. Prosodic, paralinguistic, and interactional features all are presented in parental speech, and they seem well designed to facilitate social interaction. Some features serve to establish affect between infants and caretakers, providing a convenient means for attracting an infant's attention. Other features serve to focus an infant's attention on ongoing activities. Still other features encourage the use of language. These three functions of parental speech meet the requirements basic to social interaction and to the acquisition of language.

Parental speech also represents an expression of a society's culture. Parents, as members of a society, possess knowledge about categories of speech and the appropriate use of the categories. Parents use that knowledge in their interactions with prelinguistic and language-learning infants. Speakers of English and of Spanish use all 34 features, but they do not use them at the same rate. There are cultural preferences. English speakers relied more on prosodic and paralinguistic features, whereas Spanish speakers relied more on rate of speaking and interactional features. Spanish speakers also used more kinds of features in their speech.

Another expression of culture is found in the differences between mother and father speech. In each language, males and females have specific preferences in their use of features. The gender-specific patterns of parental speech represent knowledge that speakers have about speech and its appropriateness.

Although we can discern the functions of parental speech in socialization and can identify and describe cultural variation and differences acorss language and sex, we do not know the effects of parental speech on children's styles of speaking. We do not know what gender-specific instructional value the differences between male and female speech have for infants acquiring language. At some stage in their socialization, infants begin to acquire gender-specific speech, and the differences between mother and father speech seems to be a likely source. This is a fertile area for further study. We would also like to know if parental speech to male infants is significantly different from speech to female infants. We expect that there will be differences. To answer those and other important questions, we need more studies in different societies on parental speech, its role in socialization, and its cultural definitions.

## APPENDIX: DEFINITIONS OF SELECTED SPEECH FEATURES

**Attentionals**  Words that are used specifically to attract children's attention so that interaction can proceed. The most commonly used items were the children's names and the interjections *Hey!* and *Look!* and their Spanish equivalents *Oye!* and *Mira!*

**Creaky voice**  Articulations that result from making sounds deep in the throat (laryngealization) while holding the cheek and throat muscles tense and holding one's breath.

**Exaggerated intonation**  Speech that contains exaggerated contours of pitch. The pitch of the voice may be unusually high or low, and changes in pitch level that are excessive compared to normal speech may be involved.

**Imitation**  Parental mimicry of a child's preceding utterance. Imitation appears to function as confirmation that a round was initiated (thereby calling for a response) and that the content of a child's utterance was read (as in: child, "That'sa bear"; parent, "That'sa bear").

**Instructional**  A feature of speech that emphasizes the active, or pragmatic, function of the utterance. Instructional includes several features that are often viewed as separate features in adult speech to other adults. The central feature is heavy stress, and accompanying features are flat intonation contour and increased volume. An example of *instructional* is a parental response of "no, that's a ball," said in response to a child's incorrect naming of the object. "Ball" would receive heavy stress, and the contour of the utterance would be flat and sustained.

**Interpretation**  The attribution by a parent of lexical meaning to a child's utterance even if it was not clear that the child had uttered a word or had intended a particular meaning. For example, a child might say "ta-ta," and his mother would respond with "Yes, that's right, thank you." In effect, the parent interprets the child's utterance as semantic and proceeds as if it had meaning.

**Lengthened vowel**  Vowel sounds that are sustained, that is, continued to be articulated, for a duration longer than normal. The vowels in the word "mama," for example, can be lengthened, which is sometimes indicated in writing as *maamaa . . .*

**Personal pronoun substitution**  The substitution of a personal pronoun (I, you and so on) for one that normally occurs. A child's mother will, for example, sometimes refer to herself as *she* and to the child as *I* or *me*.

**Special lexical items**  Words used especially for speech addressed to children. An example is *choo-choo* for train.

**Tenseness**  Sounds made while holding the cheek and throat muscles extra tense.

# 4

# The Development of Picture Perception in Children from Different Cultures

*Gustav Jahoda*
*Harry McGurk*

## LEARNING TO PERCEIVE IN THE PICTORIAL MODE: PERCEPTION OF PICTORIAL OBJECTS

> Take a picture in black and white and the natives cannot see it. You may tell the natives, "This is a picture of an ox and a dog," and the people will look at it and look at you and that look says that they consider you a liar. Perhaps you say again, "Yes, this is a picture of an ox and a dog." Well, perhaps they will tell you what they think this time. If there are a few boys about, you say, "This is really a picture of an ox and a dog. Look at the horn of the ox, and there is his tail!" And the boys will say, "Oh yes! There is a dog's nose and ears!" Then the old people will look again and clap their hands and say, "Oh yes! It is a dog." When a man has seen a picture for the first time, his book education has begun. (Laws, 1901)

This is an early example of numerous reports by missionaries, anthropologists, and latterly psychologists suggesting that many non-Western people have difficulties in understanding pictures. Thus Kidd (1904) at the turn of the century described how he tried to show pictures to Kaffirs and how many were unable to understand them, wondering what the smudge on the paper was supposed to be. Herskovits (1950) relates how he showed an African woman a photograph of her son, whom she failed to recognize.

Apart from such natural situations, psychologists concerned with testing came across similar problems. Thus Biesheuvel (1952) wrote: "When constructing tests for the classification of African mine workers, for example, we used the Kohs Blocks Test to make candidates reproduce pictures of familiar objects such as a native hut and an earthenware cooking pot, decorated with a conventional tribal pattern. Very few could identify the hut and a large number also failed to recognize the pot. The candidates apparently perceived them only as pieces of coloured cardboard."

These particular examples suggest that the acquisition of the ability to identify the objects represented two-dimensionally in pictures is not something that is normally part of the development of perceptual processes, but rather that it requires specific learning. Thus it has been argued by Segall, Campbell, and Herskovits (1966) that a photograph can be regarded as an arbitrary convention, representing something large and three-dimensional on a small scale on a flat surface. They point out that photographs have stimulus characteristics, such as the white band around the edge, which might well interfere with content perception; hence we should not be unduly surprised if an understanding of such conventions is not universally shared.

A much more elaborate theoretical formulation of this kind has been put forward by Goodman (1968), who places great stress on the contrast between pictures and the real world they represent. According to him, a picture is more like a language consisting of arbitrarily assigned pictorial labels. To understand the meaning of a picture, one has to learn what the labels stand for. Since the labeling system may vary across cultures, and presumably some cultures may lack such a system, differences in the ability to "read" pictures are to be expected. The position taken by Goodman is a rather extreme one. A more usual view is that of Miller (1973). After reviewing the cross-cultural evidence he concluded that "the ability to perceive anything in a pictorial representation requires some experience with pictures in order to acquire the set that pictures can represent more than a flat surface."

There is, however, one famous study that creates considerable problems for the Goodman–Miller standpoint. Hochberg and Brooks (1962) prevented a child from coming into contact with pictures until he was 19 months old. The child was then shown a series of pictures of objects, a line drawing always preceding a photograph of the same object, and was asked to name it. The result, checked by independent judges, was 17 clearly correct responses out of 21, another one being doubtful. The authors claim that the lack of any specific learning opportunities implies that there must be "*some* irreducible minimum of native ability for picture recognition. If it is true also that there are cultures in which this ability is absent, such deficiency will require special explanation; we cannot assert that it is simply a matter of having not yet learned the 'language of pictures'."

Miller (1973) was inclined to discount this study, partly because the sample was so small (N = 1) and partly because the child may not have been completely deprived of pictorial experience by seeing, for instance, simple illustrations of objects. He contends that even very limited experience may be sufficient to trigger the "insight" necessary to overcome the flatness cues, to which Miller attached great weight. However, the findings of Hochberg and Brooks (1962) fit in well with the theoretical position of Gibson (1966, 1971). In direct opposition to Goodman, Gibson holds that there is an important "natural" and nonarbitrary resemblance between a three-dimensional object and its pictorial representation. He argues that the information contained in the restricted optical array emanating from the picture is in several important respects the same kind of information as that carried from the object in the ordinary environment.

Thus there would seem to be a sharp conflict between two opposing theoretical stances: either the ordinary nonpictorial environment is sufficient for learning to understand pictures, in which case the difficulties reported from some cultures would appear inexplicable, or the results of the Hochberg–Brooks study become very puzzling. Actually the conflict is perhaps more apparent than real, and it must be admitted at this stage that it has been highlighted to draw attention to the basic problem. The reason the issue appears so intractable is that the evidence cited at the outset is either somewhat anecdotal, or a by-product of studies not primarily concerned with pictorial perception as such. The remainder of this section will therefore be devoted to a review of studies directly focused on pictorial perception, followed by a brief discussion of their theoretical implications.

First, studies employing photographs will be considered, since with these the correspondence between pictorial and environmental optical information is closer than with line drawings. One of the earlier, somewhat impressionistic studies was that of Doob (1961), who presented subjects in northern Nigeria with an array of photographs. He reported that they were generally able to identify specific objects but often found it hard to make sense of the picture as a whole. Winter (1963) examined the responses of adult Bantu workers to safety posters that, while not actually photographs, were closer in style to photographs than to line drawings. There were numerous misperceptions, especially among subjects from a rural background. However, since the posters also had captions and employed what were clearly symbolic conventions of a culture-specific nature, few firm conclusions can be drawn from such work. A more systematic approach was adopted by Deregowski (1968), who studied adults and children in a rural area of Zambia where there was no tradition of graphic arts apart from rudimentary geometric wall decorations. On the other hand, there was a primary school in the area where illustrated textbooks were used. For the experiment Deregowski employed a set of models of animals, some familiar and others unfamiliar to the subjects. The procedure consisted of presenting a photograph of a model and requiring the subject to pick out the appropriate animal from an array of models in front of him. Both adults and children did significantly better than chance in identifying the animals in the photographs, but adults did better with the familiar animals, and children with the unfamiliar animals.

The studies considered above were all undertaken in Africa by psychologists. The next study was carried out by an anthropologist working in New Guinea. Since it presents some particularly interesting features, it will be described in detail. Forge (1970) studied the Abelam of New Guinea, who have highly developed arts of both carving and painting, but whose productions are stylized and only partly representational. Forge states that in spite of more than 30 years of contact with the West, the Abelam have an almost total inability to understand photographs. However, from his own detailed description below, it is obvious that the matter is more complicated.

Photography has been known to the Abelam since the first contacts with Europeans in 1937. Nowadays, when all young men go away for at least a two-year stint of labour on the coast, they bring back photographs of themselves in all their modern finery, usually taken by Chinese photographers. The subjects stand rigidly at attention facing the camera, either singly or in groups, against a background of either a white sheet or a wall. No Abelam had any difficulty "seeing" such a photograph and in recognising and naming the individual concerned if they knew him. But when shown photographs of themselves in action, or of any pose other than face or full figure looking directly at the camera, they cease to be able to "see" the photograph at all. Even people from other villages who came specially because they knew I had taken a photograph of a relative who had subsequently died, and were often pathetically keen to see his features, were initially unable to see him at all, turning the photograph in all directions. Even when the figure dominated (to my eyes) the photograph I sometimes had to draw a thick line round it before it could be identified, and in some cases I had the impression that they willed themselves to see it rather than saw it in the way we do. Photographs of ceremonial houses and objects were easier, although in black and white people could identify a house as a ceremonial house rather than say which house it was.

. . .

Since I needed identifications from photographs of yam exchanges, brawls, ceremonies and debates, I trained a few boys to see photographs; they learnt to do this after a few hours of concentrated looking and discussion on both sides. (Forge, 1970, p. 287–288)

It is clear that there are certain kinds of photographs that the Abelam could recognize with ease. These were the photos of persons facing the camera and featured against a homogeneous background. On the other hand, if the people were depicted in a natural setting they were no longer able, in Forge's words, to "see" the photograph. It is not entirely clear whether they could not make out anything in the picture or, as seems more likely, were able to recognize some objects but not to identify particular individuals. It would seem that, as reported by Doob (1961) from Nigeria, they found it hard to make sense of the photograph as a coherent whole. The Abelam had somewhat less trouble when the pictures were seen through a viewer and in color. Since these factors were not separately examined, it is not possible to judge how far color as such enhanced comprehension. The viewer certainly eliminates many of the flatness cues of an ordinary photograph and reduces the saliency of the picture edges. Similarly, absence of head movements reduces flatness information and enhances the effectiveness of depth cues within the picture.

As in many previous reports, it would appear that older people had much more trouble with the photographs then younger ones. Most important of all, Forge reports that a few hours of training were sufficient to make young boys capable of correctly identifying individuals in action in natural settings. Such rapid learning, which agrees with the early observation of Laws (1901), fails to bear out Goodman's theory (1968).

One problem with most photographs is that they contain a multitude of complex visual cues. Hence the task of understanding them usually goes well beyond mere pictorial recognition of objects and requires a comprehension of the spatial relationships between persons and objects depicted. One can of course use simple photographs, as Deregowski (1968) did, or prepare suitable line drawings. There have been a number of studies using such material, the earlier ones being designed for other purposes such as test construction, as done by Brimble (1963) in Barotseland, or the value of visual symbols in health education in Kenya (Holmes, 1963). Both of these obtained high rates of correct responses for simple line drawings. More recently Kennedy and Ross (1975) carried out a more theoretically oriented investigation among the Songe of Papua, who are culturally similar to the Abelam studied by Forge. They were concerned with three main questions: (1) Can the Songe understand line patterns representing objects or parts of objects?; (2) Can they interpret color or texture discontinuities represented in outline?; and (3) Can they correctly interpret the mobility of objects represented by static displays? The findings show that with regard to the first question, the success rate was of the order of 80 to 90 percent, showing that the subjects generally experienced little difficulty. With regard to the more specialized aspects, the performance was at a much lower level, but the representation of motion, as for instance of a river or fire, involves a large element of conventionalization, so the Songe's difficulty with these is hardly surprising. It should also be mentioned that there was a sharp age contrast, older subjects again doing relatively poorly. Kennedy and Ross (1975) argue that this may be an age effect per se rather than lesser "Westernization"; in particular, it is proposed that the lesser cognitive flexibility of older people may be a handicap. The salient finding, however, is that the Songe had little trouble understanding outline pictures of familiar objects.

The burden of evidence thus shows that people in non-Western cultures are generally able to recognize objects in line drawings. This is also supported by recent work in secondary schools that concluded that line drawings in textbooks were equally effective learning aids in several African countries, India and Scotland (Jahoda et al., 1976). Unfortunately all the work discussed so far suffers from the weakness that none of the cultural settings can really be regarded as a totally nonpictorial environment. All have been influenced to a greater or lesser extent by Western influences, especially schools that normally have illustrated textbooks.

There are two main ways of dealing with this problem. The first, which is becoming increasingly difficult, is to find a culture that has so far remained almost completely isolated from the outside world. The second is to study very young children who have not been exposed to pictorial material. There are two studies that have employed the first and second approach respectively, thereby avoiding the problems of contamination that plagued most others.

Deregowski, Muldrow and Muldrow (1972) investigated a remote Ethiopian tribe, the Me'en, whose cultural milieu contains no pictorial art. The pastoral lowland branch of the tribe has also had minimum contact with the outside world, and few of them would ever have seen a picture. On a preliminiary visit, subjects who were shown pictures of animals would take the paper and crinkle it and listen to the sound, or even smell it, but ignore the picture. This reaction may have been due to the unfamiliar material arousing greater interest than the surface patterns, and for this reason the material subsequently used in the main study was a coarse whitish cloth familiar to the Me'en. Three pictures were printed in black ink on the cloth: the first two showed single animals, a standing buck and a running leopard, and the third was a more complex hunting scene. Pictures were presented in that order to subjects who were asked "What do you see?" with follow-up questions when necessary. The highland subjects experienced little difficulty in recognizing the animals, and even among the lowland ones there were few who failed to do so. On the other hand recognition was not always immediate with the latter, and they had to put some effort into the task. Here is an example of a protocol from a male lowlander in his mid-30s:

*Experimenter* (points to picture):   What do you see?
*Subject:*   I'm looking closely. That is a tail. This is a foot. This is a leg
     joint. Those are horns.
*Experimenter:*   What is the whole thing?
*Subject:*   Wait. Slowly, I'm still looking. Let me look and I will tell you. In
     my country this is a water buck.


Evidently the subject was gradually building up the picture from its components before the whole was adequately recognized. There were indications that the task was a stressful one for some of the subjects. A woman and a young girl tried to run away when the third picture was shown, and several others displayed signs of some disturbance. However, these reactions must be viewed in the light of the fact that no subject failed altogether to make sense of any of the pictures. It would seem, therefore, that when simple objects are clearly represented on familiar material, even people from virtually pictureless environments are able to understand them, even if this comprehenshion requires some initial effort.

This conclusion is confirmed by the last study to be cited, which dealt with children aged about 3 in areas of Ghana and Zimbabwe where pictures of any kind were very rare and unlikely to have been seen by any of the children (Jahoda et al., 1977). When shown color photographs of simple objects, the children had an overall correct recognition rate of 86 percent. A second part of the study used another sample of children in an urban area, some of whom were attending a model nursery school lavishly provided with pictures, while the remainder lived in homes where there were hardly any pictures and did not go to any nursery school. The correct recognition rates for these two groups of children were almost exactly the same, thereby confirming the findings of Hochberg and Brooks (1962).

The evidence concerning pictorial recognition throws fresh light on some controversial issues. First, there is the theoretical debate about the nature of pictorial representation, which has been lucidly discussed by Hagen and Jones (1978): as far as the representation of simple objects is concerned, the evidence strongly supports the Gibsonian view, which stresses the common elements in the information derived from an optic array for both natural three-dimensional objects and their two-dimensional representations. This evidence applies both to photographs of objects displayed against a uniform background and to line drawings that clearly show the outlines of objects or that employ shading and texture. Given such conditions, no extended "learning to read pictures" appears to be necesssary. Deregowski (1968) has pointed to another factor neglected in the past, namely the potentially distracting effect of the material on which the picture is presented. This factor probably accounts for findings such as Biesheuvel's (1952), where subjects became so interested in the colored pieces of cardboard that they failed to concentrate on what was on them.

When line drawings are made of nonsolids such as fire, steam, or flowing water, the absence of sharp outlines makes it necessary to resort to conventions. Goodman's theory (1968) applies in such cases, and where there is a pictorial tradition the conventions may be culture-specific and therefore have to be learned; otherwise, misinterpretations occur. Thus in the work of Holmes (1963) a supposedly steaming pot was sometimes understood as a pot with plants in it.

What has been said so far of course applies only to the recognition of simple pictorial objects. Most pictures are not limited to a single object but show different ones against a nonhomogeneous background. Hence the task becomes more complex, since it is necessary to understand the relationships between the various parts of the picture.

# THE PERCEPTION OF PICTORIAL RELATIONS

In the normal environment, light arriving at the eyes carries three categories of information about the spatial arrangement of objects in the environment and their distance from the viewer. First, binocular disparity, arising from the differences in view between the two eyes, is a cue to depth and, in the absence of other information, can be responded to as such. Second, as the observer moves through the three-dimensional world, motion parallax is generated, again providing information about the differential distances of objects from the observer and from each other. Third, there are the so-called static cues to depth, cues that would be available to a one-eyed stationary observer. These include linear and aerial perspective, superposition (overlap or occlusion), texture gradient, elevation (position on the retinal plane), familiar size (visual angle), and shadow. The cues in the third category are sometimes referred to as pictorial cues to depth, for the information they contain can be presented on a single, two-dimensional surface to create a two-dimensional representation of a three-dimensional scene. Such cues have served as the primary basis for conveying depth information in Western representational art since the Renaissance, and they provide the depth information available in photographs. Thus when an adult observer looks at a picture—for example, one of Canaletto's paintings of the Grand Canal in Venice—he is able not only to recognize the different objects depicted therein but also to see that some of these objects (houses, boats, people) are nearer to him than others. If asked to describe the scene after having viewed the picture, the observer would probably use spatial terminology.

It is important to stress that pictorial cues to depth are not merely an arbitrary set of conventional symbols. On the pictorial plane they carry information of a similar quality to that carried by them in the three-dimensional reality. As Gibson (1971) has argued, in the real world the visual angle projected by an object decreases in a lawful gradient as distance between object and observer increases. To transcribe the three-dimensional world onto a two-dimensional surface the artist must, of necessity, employ the laws of perspective geometry. If these laws are correctly applied then the resultant picture, under specified viewing conditions, will provide precisely the same depth information as contained in the pictured scene and may be indistinguishable from it. The viewing conditions in question are as follows: (1) both the picture and the real scene should be viewed monocularly; (2) there should be an aperture in front of the eye to conceal the boundaries of the picture; (3) the picture should be upright and at right angles to the line of vision; and (4) the picture should project the same visual solid angle as is projected by the real scene.

The effect of the viewing conditions specified by Gibson is to remove information for flatness of the pictorial scene by eliminating such cues as binocular disparity and motion parallax, while enhancing information for depth by adopting the correct viewing station and eliminating picture boundaries. Thus the conditions for the perception of pictorially represented depth are maximized. However, as Hagen (1974) and Pirenne (1970) have pointed out, these are decidedly not the conditions under which pictures are normally viewed. Usually pictures are viewed with both eyes open, from the *wrong* viewing station, with picture boundaries in full view and with information for the flatness of the pictorial surface available both from the texture of the surface itself (canvas, paper, photographic print) and from motion parallax. Yet, under these conditions of conflict, with information for the flatness of the pictorial surface and for three-dimensionality of the pictorial scene simultaneously available, adult viewers are highly adept at perceiving the spatial relationships between objects depicted in the scene and at perceiving pictorially represented depth. It is to consideration of the development of this capacity that we now turn.

## THE DEVELOPMENT OF SENSITIVITY
## TO PICTORIAL DEPTH: WESTERN STUDIES

It is only within the last decade or so that developmental researchers have begun to investigate the ontogeny of pictorial depth perception, and there have been few programmatic inquiries in the area. The evidence is therefore fragmentary and derives from a number of disparate studies employing a wide range of methodologies and measurement procedures. However, results from investigations involving Western subjects suggest that the capacity to respond to pictorial information for depth is entirely absent at birth but develops over the first few months of life and is detectable, at least in embryonic form and under monocular viewing conditions, by around 6 months of age (Bower, 1965, 1966; Yonas, Cleaves and Pettersen, 1977).

Evidence for developmental progress beyond the infancy period is dependent to a considerable extent on the procedures and measurement techniques employed. Two-year-old children are able to point reliably to the nearer or farther of two pictorially depicted objects, provided that cues to depth are unambiguous; where this is the case, their judgments appear uninfluenced by the amount of depth information available. This finding obtains across a wide variety of viewing conditions, and there appear to be few age-related differences in this ability between 2 and 6 years (Olson, 1975; Olson and Boswell, 1975, 1976). On the other hand, when preschool children are asked to make judgments about the relative sizes of pictorially depicted objects, their accuracy is influenced by viewing conditions (Yonas and Hagen, 1973) and by the amount of depth information available (Jahoda and McGurk, 1974a). Moreover, age-related changes in performance are evident from 3 to 10 years (Yonas and Hagen, 1973; Jahoda and McGurk, 1974a), although even preschool children perform at well above chance levels with relatively impoverished stimulus materials (McGurk and Jahoda, 1974).

The results summarized above have been obtained under conditions where subjects have to reach or point to the nearer or farther of pictorially depicted objects or have to make judgments about the relative sizes of objects in a pictorial scene. A somewhat different set of findings has been obtained in studies where, using solid objects, children are required to reconstruct a three-dimensional scene from its pictorial representation. From a developmental perspective this is a relatively insensitive procedure for assessing ability to discriminate pictorial depth if scoring is based on spatial arrangement alone. Accurate performance is not reliably present until around 6 or 8 years of age, although thereafter it develops rapidly to near-perfect levels by 10 years (Brown, 1969; Jahoda and McGurk, 1974a; McGurk and Jahoda, 1974). However, perception of depth relations in a picture is one thing; the re-creation of these relationships in three dimensions is quite another, and there is no necessary relationship between the two abilities. Performance on a reconstruction task is likely to be more influenced by subjects' understanding of spatial relationships in general than by their ability to discriminate pictorially represented depth.

## THE DEVELOPMENT OF SENSITIVITY TO PICTORIAL DEPTH: CROSS-CULTURAL STUDIES

### The Hudson Studies

Although there have been one or two independent assessments of cultural differences in children's ability to perceive depth in pictures (for example, Vernon, 1965), the vast majority of such investigations derive from the series of studies conducted in South Africa by Hudson (1960,

1962a, 1962b, 1967). Hudson's primary materials comprised a series of six black-and-white outline drawings depicting a hunting scene, each of which featured an elephant, an antelope, and a man holding a spear in the throwing position. There was also a black-and-white photograph depicting a modeled reconstruction of the scene represented in the drawings. Hunter, elephant, and antelope were the same size, relative to each other, in each of the pictures and always occupied similar locations on the pictorial plane (see Figure 4–1). Cues to pictorial depth used by Hudson included elevation on the pictorial plane, interposition, linear perspective, and familiar size, but these cues varied in unsystematic fashion among the different pictures, as is evident from the figure. Hudson's subjects were required to identify the figures in each picture and to respond to questions about whether the hunter was aiming at the antelope or the elephant, and whether the elephant or antelope was nearer the hunter. Subjects were classified as 2D or 3D perceivers according to their replies to these questions. It was assumed that a 3D perceiver would judge that the spear was being aimed at the antelope and that the elephant was farther from the hunter than the antelope.

Hudson tested large samples of black and white South African children and adults. His major finding was that black adult mineworkers were less efficient at perceiving pictorial depth than white adults or black or white school children. However, even black children attending school were poor perceivers of pictorial depth, although it is noteworthy that, despite the apparent simplicity of the test, no group of subjects, black or white, young or old, achieved a score approximating perfect performance across all pictures.

A number of other investigators have employed the Hudson materials to assess pictorial depth discrimination among African children. Thus Mundy-Castle (1966), using four pictures from the Hudson series, tested a group of Ghanaian children between 5 and 10 years of age and reported a very low rate of 3D response. Only one subject in his sample gave consistent 3D responses to all four pictures. Kilbride, Robbins and Freeman (1968) used two of Hudson's pictures to assess depth discrimination among Baganda subjects between 4 and 20 years of age. They found little evidence for sensitivity to pictorial depth in children younger than 11 or 12 years of age, with improvement thereafter. In a study of Zambian schoolboys and adult male domestic servants, Deregowski (1968) employed the entire set of Hudson materials. He found that the schoolboys were more sensitive to information for pictorial depth than were the domestic servants, although neither group produced as many 3D responses as the comparable samples of black South Africans originally

**Figure 4–1** *Examples of items from the Hudson test. (From W. Hudson, "Pictorial depth perception in subcultural groups in Africa,"* Journal of Social Psychology, 1960, 52, pp. 183–208.)

tested by Hudson. Interestingly, however, a significant proportion of subjects who were classified as 2D perceivers on the Hudson test built 3D models on the basis of exposure to pictorial representations of geometric forms that contained various cues to depth. Deregowski concluded, therefore, that although his findings confirmed previous reports of deficiency in perceiving pictorial depth on the part of black African subjects, inability to perceive depth in the Hudson pictures should not be taken to mean that the subject is incapable of perceiving depth in any kind of 2D representation.

## Criticisms of Hudson

Results from studies employing the Hudson materials have generally been interpreted as replicating his original study and as producing comparable findings, pointing toward the twin conclusions that the majority of black African school children fail to respond to depth cues in pictures and that black African children lag behind white children in their acquisition of pictorial depth discrimination. Elsewhere we have presented an extensive critique of studies based on the Hudson test, arguing that the grounds for comparability of the findings reported by different investigators are rather shaky (Jahoda and McGurk, 1974c). Firstly, as is evident from the brief review above, different investigators have employed different numbers and combinations of pictures from the set developed by Hudson. These pictures differ from each other in the ways in which depth is depicted (see Figure 4–1) and it is known that they are not equally effective in eliciting 3D responses (Hudson, 1960). Thus, except where corresponding materials are employed, there is no proper basis for comparison of findings. Of the studies discussed above, only those by Hudson (1960) and Deregowski (1968) are directly comparable in this respect. Further, there is evident variation in the scoring criteria employed by different investigators when classifying subjects as 2D or 3D responders. Some researchers have required appropriate responses to two critical questions ("What is the hunter doing?" and "Which is nearer the hunter?") before classifying the subject as 3D; others have relied on answers to only one question. Clearly, with two equiprobable responses to each question, chance expectation of being classified as 2D or 3D differs according to the scoring system employed. Such differences are sufficient to invalidate direct comparison between studies employing different procedures.

Apart from these procedural differences between studies ostensibly employing the same methodology, a number of other deficiencies in the Hudson test are worthy of mention. First, availability of some of the depth cues in the pictures is dependent on correct identification of the objects depicted therein. Hudson (1960) found that failure to identify items was related to 2D responding. This finding should hardly be the occasion for surprise when it is noted that the road, for example, was frequently identified as an elephant trap! Thus through poor picture construction the intended cue of linear perspective was entirely eliminated for some subjects. Similarly, Mundy-Castle (1966) found that many of his Ghanaian subjects misidentified the elephant as a pig or rabbit or other small animal. This being the case, the (familiar) size-distance relationships in the pictures are altered and responses rendered uninterpretable. In this connection it is interesting to note that Omari and MacGinitie (1974), working with Tanzanian children, found that when the animals in the Hudson pictures were replaced with animals more familiar to the children, depth-perception scores increased significantly.

A further ambiguity in the Hudson pictures is the handedness of the hunter. It is not apparent whether the back or front of the hunter's body is depicted. If the former, he is right-handed; if the latter, he is left-handed. The effect of this ambiguity is unknown, but any tendency to perceive the hunter as having his back toward the viewer and his spear in his right hand would result in the impression that the spear is being aimed at the elephant—which would be classified as a 2D response!

Finally, a number of commentators have remarked on the ambiguity of the critical question, "Which is nearer the hunter, the antelope or the elephant?" Ambiguity arises because it is not apparent whether the question refers to spatial relations on the pictorial surface (in which case the elephant is nearer) or in the scene depicted by the picture (in which case the antelope is nearer). That the question may have posed something of a dilemma for Hudson's African subjects can be inferred from the fact that some of them took as long as one hour to respond!

These criticisms of the Hudson materials and of the scoring and other procedural differences evident among various investigations employing his test combine to cast considerable doubt not only on the validity of direct comparison of findings from different studies but also on the validity of the Hudson test as a measure of pictorial depth perception. The inevitable conclusion must be that our knowledge of cultural differences in children's perception of pictorial depth is much less well established than is commonly believed.

It was in this context that we undertook an extended cross-cultural investigation of the development of pictorial depth discrimination. Previously we had developed a new test of pictorial depth perception (Jahoda and McGurk, 1974a; McGurk and Jahoda, 1974). The new test made only modest demands on verbal comprehension and entirely avoided the use of relative terms of quantification (bigger–smaller, nearer–farther), which are known to pose difficulties for young children (Donaldson and Balfour, 1968; Omari and Cook, 1972) and they also present problems of precise translation into different languages (Leach, 1977). The test was therefore eminently suitable for administration to children across a wide age span and from different linguistic–cultural communities. Previously the test had been successfully used to plot the development of pictorial depth discrimination among Scottish children between 4 and 10 years of age. Now it was intended to use the new test to assess the development of pictorial depth discrimination among children from a diversity of cultural backgrounds. A second objective was to make specific comparisons between performance on the new test and on the Hudson test, again involving children from widely differing cultural backgrounds.

Essentially, the new test presents the child with a construction task. Test items comprise a series of chromatic pictures depicting a landscape scene in which two female figures appear, one on the right side of the picture and the other on the left. The figures are identical, apart from size, and are intended to represent either two children or two adults or a child and an adult. The figures are of tan complexion and have medium-length black hair. Facial detail is indistinct, and the figures are intended to appear neutral with respect to race.

In each scene one figure is in the foreground, the other in the background. They are therefore at different relative distances from the viewpoint of a 3D perceiver. Background figures are two-thirds the size of foreground figures, and children are two-thirds the size of adults. Hence in a child-foreground–adult-background picture, both figures subtend equivalent angles, but for a 3D perceiver the height of the background figure would appear to be greater. Different cues to depth appear in different test series. In one series the elevation of the figures on the plain represented in the picture is the primary depth cue (elevation cue). In the second a road extends somewhat diagonally across the plain, and the figures are located on the road (linear perspective cue). The third series depicts the same plain and road but also has a fence extending along the far side of the road (element size and interspace cue). Examples of test pictures appear in Figure 4–2.

Using large and small model dolls, the subject is required to reconstruct the pictorial scene in three dimensions on a green rectangular response board intended to represent the pictorial ground. Following a familiarization procedure, test trials are presented, eight trials under each cue condition. Responses are scored independently for size accuracy (indexed by the relative sizes of the dolls chosen to represent the pictorial figures and by the right–left location of these dolls on the response board) and for spatial accuracy (indexed by the spatial alignment of the dolls on the response board; as is apparent from Figure 4–2, the correct alignment is diagonal). The child is told that each picture portrays two "ladies," two "girls," or a "lady and a girl," thus avoiding possible semantic confusion associated with using explicit terms denoting relative size. The child has to decide which is which and construct the response accordingly, ensuring that the 3D figures are placed in a location that corresponds to their location in the picture.

The goal of assessing the development of pictorial depth perception among children from different cultures was facilitated by contrasting performance on the new test by samples of children from Scotland, Hong Kong, and Zimbabwe (Jahoda and McGurk, 1974b). The Scottish sample

**Figure 4–2**  *Examples of items from the new 3D test. (From G. Jahoda and H. McGurk, "Pictorial depth perception: A developmental study,"* British Journal of Psychology, *1974, 65, pp. 141–149.)*

comprised children at 4, 6, 8, and 10 years of age from central Glasgow. These children were from families of skilled and semiskilled manual workers. There were two Hong Kong samples. One comprised a group of girls drawn from an urban school catering largely to children of lower-middle-class parents. It had been planned to include a comparable sample of boys, but a catastrophic flooding, leading to closure of all schools, made this impossible. Girls in the urban sample ranged from 5 to 9 years of age.

The second Hong Kong sample was composed of "boat children," so called because they spend most of their lives on trading junks. It is only relatively recently that the parents of these children have been persuaded to send them to school. They do not start school until the age of 7, and some start even later. This sample, comprising boys and girls, ranged from 7 to 10 years of age. Testing of both Hong Kong samples was carried out in Cantonese by local researchers.

The Zimbabwian children were all African and came from rural villages and a small township near Salisbury. All were from families of low socioeconomic status. Testing was carried out in the local dialect of the Shona language, although a few of the oldest subjects were tested in English. Inadequacy of records made it difficult to establish the precise ages of some of these children, so the number of years of schooling was used instead in data analysis. Age and years of schooling, of course, are highly correlated, and the age range covered in the African sample—from about 4 to about 10 years—is comparable to that in other samples.

Working with these samples served to establish the cross-cultural validity of the new test. Using back-translation methods it was found that test procedures translated readily and accurately between languages. Also, task requirements were readily understood by children of all ages in all the samples tested. Data for all four samples are presented in Tables 4–1 and 4–2. The maximum score possible under each cue condition is 8 both for size and for spatial responses.

With respect to size responses, examination of Table 4–1 reveals that in all four samples accuracy tends to increase with increasing age (years of schooling). The absolute magnitude of the effect, however, differs between samples and is statistically significant only in the Scottish and African samples. The influence of pictorial information for depth was evident in the responses of subjects from all four samples, and in each case the effect was statistically significant, indicating that among children from each culture, size-response accuracy increases with increase in amount of depth information available. However, even among African children with no formal education, size-response accuracy, although

**Table 4–1**   *Mean Number Correct Size Responses by Age (or Years of Schooling) Under Three Conditions of Pictorial Cues to Depth*

| SAMPLE AND AGE OR SCHOOLING (YEARS) | N | ELEVATION | LINEAR PERSPECTIVE | ELEMENT– INTERSPACE SIZE AND FREQUENCY | ALL CONDITIONS |
|---|---|---|---|---|---|
| Glasgow | | | | | |
| *Age* | | | | | |
| 4 | 15 | 5.1 | 5.4 | 5.8 | 5.4 |
| 6 | 15 | 5.6 | 5.2 | 5.9 | 5.6 |
| 8 | 15 | 6.1 | 6.7 | 6.7 | 6.5 |
| 10 | 15 | 6.0 | 6.7 | 7.0 | 6.6 |
| All samples | 60 | 5.7 | 6.0 | 6.4 | 6.0 |
| Hong Kong (Urban) | | | | | |
| *Age* | | | | | |
| 5 | 12 | 5.0 | 5.3 | 4.9 | 5.1 |
| 6 | 12 | 4.8 | 5.2 | 5.4 | 5.1 |
| 7 | 12 | 5.3 | 5.9 | 6.3 | 5.8 |
| 8 | 12 | 5.3 | 5.7 | 5.9 | 5.6 |
| 9 | 12 | 5.3 | 6.0 | 6.2 | 5.8 |
| All samples | 60 | 5.1 | 5.6 | 5.8 | 5.5 |
| Hong Kong (Boat children) | | | | | |
| *Age* | | | | | |
| 7 | 12 | 4.2 | 4.3 | 4.6 | 4.4 |
| 8 | 12 | 4.3 | 4.8 | 4.9 | 4.7 |
| 9 | 12 | 4.7 | 5.2 | 5.4 | 5.1 |
| 10 | 12 | 4.7 | 4.9 | 5.1 | 4.9 |
| All samples | 48 | 4.4 | 4.8 | 5.0 | 4.7 |
| Zimbabwe | | | | | |
| *Schooling* | | | | | |
| 0 | 23 | 3.4 | 3.1 | 3.9 | 3.5 |
| 2 | 18 | 4.1 | 5.3 | 5.5 | 5.0 |
| 4 | 18 | 6.0 | 6.2 | 6.1 | 6.1 |
| All samples | 59 | 4.5 | 4.9 | 5.2 | 4.8 |

**Table 4–2** *Mean Number Correct Spatial Responses by Age (or Years of Schooling) Under Three Conditions of Pictorial Cues to Depth*

| SAMPLE AND AGE OR SCHOOLING (YEARS) | N | PICTORIAL CUES | | | |
|---|---|---|---|---|---|
| | | ELEVATION | LINEAR PERSPECTIVE | ELEMENT–INTERSPACE SIZE AND FREQUENCY | ALL CONDITIONS |
| Glasgow | | | | | |
| *Age* | | | | | |
| 4 | 15 | 0.7 | 1.0 | 0.7 | 0.8 |
| 6 | 15 | 2.6 | 1.9 | 1.3 | 1.9 |
| 8 | 15 | 5.1 | 4.5 | 3.5 | 4.3 |
| 10 | 15 | 7.2 | 7.0 | 6.5 | 6.9 |
| All samples | 60 | 3.9 | 3.6 | 2.9 | 3.5 |
| Hong Kong (Urban) | | | | | |
| *Age* | | | | | |
| 5 | 12 | 2.5 | 2.6 | 1.8 | 2.3 |
| 6 | 12 | 4.6 | 4.8 | 4.8 | 4.7 |
| 7 | 12 | 5.7 | 4.7 | 4.6 | 5.0 |
| 8 | 12 | 6.7 | 6.3 | 5.8 | 6.3 |
| 9 | 12 | 7.1 | 6.5 | 6.5 | 6.7 |
| All samples | 60 | 5.3 | 5.0 | 4.7 | 5.0 |
| Hong Kong (Boat children) | | | | | |
| *Age* | | | | | |
| 7 | 12 | 5.8 | 5.8 | 4.3 | 5.3 |
| 8 | 12 | 4.4 | 4.8 | 4.8 | 4.7 |
| 9 | 12 | 6.4 | 5.3 | 5.2 | 5.6 |
| 10 | 12 | 6.5 | 6.3 | 6.6 | 6.5 |
| All samples | 48 | 5.8 | 5.6 | 5.2 | 5.5 |
| Zimbabwe | | | | | |
| *Schooling* | | | | | |
| 0 | 23 | 0.6 | 0.7 | 0.5 | 0.6 |
| 2 | 18 | 3.4 | 3.0 | 2.7 | 3.0 |
| 4 | 18 | 6.5 | 5.7 | 4.8 | 5.7 |
| All samples | 59 | 3.5 | 3.1 | 2.7 | 3.1 |

From G. Jahoda and H. McGurk, "The development of pictorial depth perception: Cross-cultural replication," *Child Development*, 1974, *45*, 1042–1047. © 1974 The Society for Research in Child Development, Inc.

poorest of all, was significantly above chance level under the minimal (elevation) cue condition. The difference between Hong Kong urban and boat children of comparable age cannot be precisely interpreted but possibly reflects, among other things, the cultural and educational deprivation of the latter.

Examination of Table 4–2 indicates that for spatial responses as well there was a tendency for accuracy to increase with increasing age (years of schooling). The effect was statistically significant for all groups except the Hong Kong boat children. The most common spatial error among children from all samples was for the dolls in the subjects' 3D constructions of the pictures to be aligned horizontally rather than diagonally. Interestingly, in all four samples there was a general tendency for such errors to increase with the increase in the number of cues to depth. Once more the effect was statistically significant for all groups except the Hong Kong boat children.

Considered against the great diversity of cultural experience represented by the children in these samples, the impressive feature of the findings from this study is the correspondence in the pattern of the data from different cultural groups. Thus, children in all samples and at all ages revealed some sensitivity to information for pictorial depth, as evidenced by the accuracy of their size responses and by the way in which such accuracy was enhanced by the increase in the amount of depth information available. Of course, there were fluctuations in the levels of size-response accuracy achieved by children from different cultural groups, but with the exception of the somewhat depressed scores achieved by the 10-year-old Hong Kong boat children, the oldest subjects in all samples scored at relatively high, if less than perfect, levels. In particular the African children, who started off well below all the others, exhibited a sharp increase in performance with increasing age and schooling, and the top group caught up with older children from the other samples.

With regard to spatial responses, the data again reveal a considerable degree of correspondence. There was a pronounced and highly significant age trend in all samples except the Hong Kong boat children. The youngest subjects among the latter were 7 years old, and at this age they were already scoring relatively highly, with little further improvement among older subjects. On the other hand, younger children in the remaining samples had little success. This was particularly evident among the youngest Scottish children and among the African children with no schooling. Both groups were almost totally unable to cope adequately with this aspect of the task. However, increasing age and years of schooling had a significant impact upon performance and, once more, the top African group achieved performance levels not far removed from those displayed by their peers from other cultures. Thus neither on the basis of size responses nor on the basis of spatial responses is there evidence from this study for the proposition that black African children display gross backwardness in discrimination of pictorially represented depth. As indicated earlier, the degree of correspondence in the performance displayed on this test among children from a diversity of cultural backgrounds is more impressive than fluctuations in performance between cultures.

It is interesting to note that the finding that an increase in linear perspective information (linear perspective cue and element size and interspace cue) led to a *decrease* in the number of correct spatial responses was replicated in every one of the samples in the present study and was statistically significant in all cases with the exception of the Hong Kong boat children. Elsewhere we have argued that spatial responses on this task are influenced by the extent to which the child is able to ignore competing frames of references save those provided by the internal organization of the picture (Jahoda and McGurk, 1974a). The most common spatial error at all ages and in all cultures is for response figures to be aligned horizontally rather than diagonally. Such errors, which decrease with increasing age, can be accounted for if it is assumed that younger subjects employ the rectangular contour of the pictorial array as the major form of reference and thus align response figures with the lower horizontal boundary of the picture. With increasing age subjects appear to attend more to frames of reference within the pictorial array itself and thus are more likely to produce diagonal adjustments. However, the presence of straight lines and edges when linear perspective cues are employed can disrupt this process, leading to an increase in errors under such conditions. This argument is analogous to Piaget's account of the child's construction of the projective line (Piaget and Inhelder, 1956; Laurendeau and Pinard, 1970). Predictions following from this interpretation were tested and confirmed in a series of experiments by McGurk and Jahoda (1974). These experiments and the present data indicate that the spatial part of the task involves skills and abilities beyond those involved in pictorial depth perception per se. In children from all cultures in which the new test has been employed, evidence for sensitivity to information for pictorial depth, as indexed by size responses, has been found to appear developmentally prior to its being manifested in the spatial organization of responses.

## The Hudson Test and the New Test Compared

To facilitate direct comparison between performance on the new test and on the original Hudson test upon which so much of the previous cross-cultural research has been based, we undertook a further cross-cultural investigation, this time involving samples of primary school children from Scotland and Ghana (Jahoda and McGurk, 1974c; McGurk and Jahoda, 1975). For the new test, procedures were identical to those described earlier, although there were some modifications of materials. Primarily these modifications involved substituting black-and-white drawings for color photographs, but in addition a cue to depth—texture gradient, not previously used in our studies—was incorporated into some of the drawings. Otherwise, the test involved presenting subjects with the same task as before, that of making a 3D construction of the size and spatial relationships between the two figures represented in each picture. Altogether there were four sets of stimulus pictures in which depth cues were systematically manipulated with eight pictures in each set. One set contained elevation cues alone; another contained elevation plus texture gradient; a third contained elevation plus linear perspective, and the fourth contained elevation, texture gradient, and linear perspective cues.

The published version of the Hudson test, comprising six line drawings and a photograph of the hunting scene previously described, was also administered to subjects. For each item the subject was asked to report what the man was doing and to state whether the antelope or the elephant was nearer the hunter. Responses to any particular picture were given a score of 1 only if replies indicative of 3D perception were made to each question. All other responses were scored 0, so that the maximum possible score was 7.

The two tests were administered to samples of primary school children from a working-class district of central Glasgow and from the Staff Village Primary School attached to the University of Ghana at Legon; the parents of these children include clerks, porters, stewards, and laborers employed at the university. The structure of the sample is depicted in Table 4-3. It can be seen from the table that Ghanaian children were substantially older and that, as is usually the case in Africa, each class represented a greater age range than in the Scottish sample. The primary independent variable is therefore the number of years of schooling.

Testing with Hudson's measure and with the new material was carried out individually. Scottish children were tested in English. In Ghana the tester used the child's own vernacular (mainly Ga or Twi) or English (the

**Table 4–3**  *Ages of Children: Means and Standard Deviations (N = 20 for each class)*

|  | SCOTLAND | | GHANA | |
| --- | --- | --- | --- | --- |
|  | MEAN | STANDARD DEVIATION | MEAN | STANDARD DEVIATION |
| Primary 2 | 6.5 | 0.3 | 7.2 | 0.5 |
| Primary 4 | 8.5 | 0.3 | 9.8 | 1.1 |
| Primary 6 | 10.5 | 0.3 | 11.9 | 1.1 |

language of the school) or some mixture congenial to the child. Half the subjects within each class started with the Hudson test followed by the new test, and the remainder were exposed to the reverse sequence.

Size and spatial responding on the new test have been contrasted in considerable detail elsewhere (McGurk and Jahoda, 1975) and will be discussed here only very briefly. For Scottish and Ghanaian children, size-response accuracy increased significantly with increase in pictorial depth information, and spatial accuracy increased with age. Sensitivity to pictorial information for depth was found in the size data prior to its appearance in the subjects' spatial responses.

Of more concern here is the contrast between perception of pictorial depth as indexed by subjects' responses to the Hudson materials on the one hand and by their size responses to the new test on the other. For this purpose, responses on the new test were averaged across all stimulus conditions to yield an operative maximum score of 8 with a chance score of 2. The corresponding scores on the Hudson test are 7 and 1.75 respectively. Data from the performance of Scottish and Ghanaian children on the two tests are presented graphically in Figure 4–3.

As is evident from the figure, the level of performance of all three Ghanaian groups was significantly below chance levels on the Hudson test (P2, $p < 0.001$; P4, $p < 0.001$; P6, $p < 0.02$). The scores of the two younger groups of Scottish subjects did not differ significantly from chance, while P6 subjects scored significantly above chance ($p < 0.01$). When data from Scottish and Ghanaian samples were entered into an analysis of variance, there was a significant trend for grade level ($p < 0.05$) and a highly significant cultural difference ($p < 0.001$).

With respect to performance on the new test, the mean scores for every sub-sample, Ghanaian as well as Scottish, were well above chance expectation ($p < 0.001$ in each instance). Analysis of variance again yielded a highly significant cultural difference ($p < 0.001$), but there was no significant effect for age.

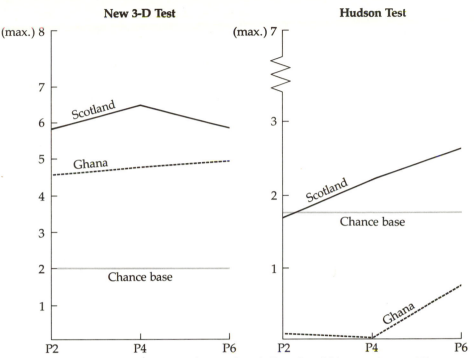

**Figure 4–3**   *Mean performance of Scottish and Ghanaian children on the new 3D test and on the Hudson test. (From G. Jahoda and H. McGurk, "Pictorial depth perception in Scottish and Ghanaian children: A critique of some findings with the Hudson Test," International Journal of Psychology, 1974, 9, pp. 255–267.)*

These findings confirm that the Hudson materials yield a depressed estimate of children's ability to discriminate pictorial depth. This is particularly marked in the case of Ghanaian subjects, though as indicated above, only the oldest of the Scottish children achieved a score significantly above chance level. On the new test the Ghanaian children still lag behind their Scottish counterparts, though now the difference between the two groups is relatively small compared not only with the origin but also with the chance base. Indeed, only one Ghanaian child obtained a score of less than three times the standard error above chance on the new test. Thus under appropriate conditions even the youngest Ghanaian subjects were capable of responding to depth information in pictures.

A further factor requires consideration when evaluating the performance of Ghanaian children on the new test. In the test pictures the stimulus figures were dressed identically and could only be discriminated as girls or women in terms of represented size. However, the short skirt worn by the figures suggests either schoolgirls or "modern" women. The bulk of "traditional" women, who constitute the majority in the environment of the Ghanaian children, wear a wraparound cloth reaching to the ankles. This possible source of confusion, which probably also obtained for the sample of African children tested in the earlier study reported above, had become apparent in the course of pilot work, and every effort was made to deal with it by explaining, in the vernacular as appropriate, that the adults in the pictures were educated ladies. An analysis of error patterns was undertaken as a check upon the effectiveness of this precaution. Had no such source of confusion existed, the girls should have been mistakenly identified as women as frequently as the reverse—and this is precisely what happened with the Scottish children. However, five times as many Ghanaian subjects responded more frequently by selecting a "girl" doll when it should have been a "lady" than the other way around. On a two-tailed binomial test this outcome has a probability of less than 2 percent and is unlikely, therefore, to be due to chance. This means that even with the new test the estimate of ability of Ghanaian children to discriminate pictorial depth is probably on the conservative side. Once again, therefore, we find little evidence for the proposition that African primary school children are seriously deficient in their ability to respond to depth cues in pictures.

## SUMMARY AND CONCLUSIONS

In this chapter we have sought to demonstrate that earlier generalizations concerning gross cross-cultural differences in the ability to recognize pictorial representations of objects and in the ability to perceive depth relations in pictures are misleading. We have also presented evidence for the conclusion that the development of pictorial depth perception follows a similar pattern among children from a wide diversity of cultural backgrounds, and we have argued that our own test procedures are more sensitive in assessing children's abilities in this respect than are those devised by Hudson. It has to be acknowledged, however, that the data base on which to make cross-cultural comparisons of the development of picture perception in general and of pictorial depth perception in particular is relatively sparse. For example, with the exception of our own study in Zimbabwe (Jahoda and McGurk, 1974b) and a study that involved 3-year-old Chinese children (Dawson, Young and Choi, 1974), there have been few other cross-cultural investigations of pictorial depth perception that have reported data on preschool children. Similarly, we know of no cross-cultural comparisons in this area that have involved infants. Thus, although some data are now becoming available from Western studies of infants, we are relatively ignorant of the origins of pictorial depth perception among children younger than school age in other cultures. Accordingly, there exists no basis at present to determine whether such differences as do appear in middle and later childhood arise because of differences in cultural and educational experiences or because of differences in the point of origin for the development of the perceptual processes involved. It would perhaps be surprising if the latter turned out to be the case, but at present the evidence is unavailable to determine the point.

In our investigations we have found that in all cultures studied, even the youngest children tested have been sensitive to the amount of information available for pictorial depth. In all the samples we have worked with, accuracy of size judgments has increased significantly with increase in the number of depth cues contained in pictures. Also, we have found that the minimal depth information provided by elevation of figures on the pictorial plane is sufficient to induce perception of pictorial depth in young children from a variety of cultures. Beyond this, however, there is little systematic evidence on the influence of different cues on judgments of pictorial depth among children from different cultures. This might be a fruitful area for further researh, for the evidence that could be derived from systematic evaluation of different cues to depth would be of considerable value in designing illustrations for books and other educational materials intended for use in particular cultural settings.

As noted earlier, E. J. Gibson (1969) has suggested that in unsophisticated viewers, the perception of depth in pictures may be suppressed by the co-occurrence of information for flatness provided, for example, by binocular and motion parallax. Yonas, Cleaves and Pettersen (1977) and Yonas and Hagen (1973) found that elimination of information for flatness enhanced pictorial depth discrimination in infants and young children respectively. Although some comparative data are available for adult subjects (Leibowitz and Pick, 1972), this is an issue that, as far as we are aware, has never been investigated cross-culturally from a developmental perspective. Such study would have considerable theoretical relevance, for evidence on the role of information for the flatness of the pictorial surface is crucial to the resolution of the still lively issue (see, for example, Hagen and Glick, 1977) as to whether J. J. Gibson's (1971) hypothesis of equivalence of information between pictures and real scenes is valid, or whether pictorial perception is a matter of learning to respond to a relatively arbitrary set of conventions, as argued by Good-man (1968). If elimination of information for flatness were found consis-tently to enhance pictorial depth discrimination among children from diverse cultural backgrounds, this would represent strong evidence in support of the Gibsonian argument. It is from research of this nature, within a coherent theoretical framework, that our understanding of the development of pictorial perception will be advanced. As outlined in this chapter, there is now abundant empirical evidence to demonstrate that the relevant question is no longer *whether* young children, of whatever culture, perceive pictorial objects and pictorially depicted spatial rela-tions, but rather under what conditions such perception is manifested and by what processes it is mediated.

# 5

# Ontogeny in the Study of Culture and Cognition

*Daniel A. Wagner*

## THE SOCIALIZATION OF COGNITION

The term *socialization* has two psychological connotations when referring to the domain of culture and cognition. First, there is the sense of "social" or "societal," and the implication concerning the impact of sociocultural influences on thinking. Given this perspective, we find that cross-cultural research bases interpretation on independent variables such as societal institutions, child-rearing patterns, language, and customs. Second, socialization connotes ontogenetic (age-related) or developmental effects on the individual or group of individuals. In developmental laboratory and school-based research, the chronological age of the child is used as a measure of previous learning and biological maturation. (For a broader interpretation of comparative approaches see Wagner and Paris, 1981).

There would seem to be a necessary link between cross-cultural and ontogenetic perspectives. Cross-cultural researchers generally assume that cultural factors are the basis for observed psychological and behavioral differences, which presumably are a function of growing up in (that is, experiencing) a given social and physical environment. Thus, as we shall see a little later, a difference in physical environment is the imputed factor in observed differences in perceptual ability between two different cultural groups. The physical ecology does not act synchronically (that is, at the particular moment of testing) upon adult perception. Rather, the cross-cultural analysis almost always assumes a diachronic or historical interpretation in which the physical ecology (or any other independent variable) acts on the individual over time. In other words, even though research may be conducted on adults only, interpretation usually necessitates a historical, diachronic, or ontogenetic assumption. Interestingly, much cross-cultural research on cognition makes such an assumption *without* collecting either longitudinal or cross-sectional data that would allow a direct link to antecedent origins of adult behavior.

In the following sections we shall explore this problem in two research domains that have been of considerable long-term interest in culture and cognition: perception, with studies of susceptibility to visual illusion; and memory, with studies of recall and recognition.

## PERCEPTION: SUSCEPTIBILITY TO VISUAL ILLUSIONS

In the middle of the nineteenth century, when psychology was established as an experimental science, visual perception emerged as a central focus of interest. A number of prominent investigators became interested in the fact that human beings may misinterpret or misjudge visually observed events; that is, visual perception may be nonveridical. The experimental paradigms employed often tested the individual's tendency to adopt or to resist a holistic or contextualized (and nonveridical) interpretation of a given visual stimulus. Prominent among these experimental paradigms were tests for susceptibility to visual illusions. Such tests were particularly useful in that they made it possible to calibrate very accurately the degree of individual susceptibility to a wide variety of illusion-inducing stimuli.

It is not surprising therefore that W. H. R. Rivers took along stimuli for illusions on his famous anthropological expedition to the Torres

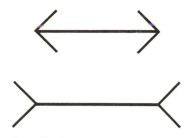

**Figure 5–1**    *The Muller-Lyer illusion.*

Straits (Rivers, 1905). Rivers was motivated in part by the need to supplement basic anthropometric data with some measure of mental ability.
Rivers used the Muller-Lyer illusion (see Figure 5–1) and other perceptual
tests on a very isolated ("primitive," in the jargon of that era) group of
native inhabitants. The results of his testing were mixed, but one interesting finding was that the local population showed less susceptibility to
illusion than educated subjects of the same ages in Great Britain. Explanation of this finding was, and remains, difficult, because it is not clear
whether to attribute low susceptibility to high or low perceptual ability.
To attribute low susceptibility to high perceptual skill would imply that
native perceptual skills were superior to English upper-class norms. To
imply the converse (that is, English superiority) would run counter to the
finding that on the Muller-Lyer illusion skilled adults show less susceptibility than children.

Despite problems of interpretation, Rivers' work stood for several decades as an example of cross-cultural inquiry into cognitive processes. His
work was given new life in the 1960s by Segall, Campbell, and Herskovits
(1966), who undertook the first large-scale cross-cultural study of cognitive processes. Following the work of Rivers, Segall and his colleagues
decided to use susceptibility to visual illusions to test hypotheses about
the cultural origins of perceptual ability as a major step toward the systematic study of culture and cognition. They hypothesized that an individual's physical environment might well affect the individual's habits
for making perceptual judgments. For example, it was suggested that
cultural differences in susceptibility to the Muller-Lyer illusion were a
function of the individual's tendency to view the illusion stimulus as a
three-dimensional representation. This tendency might be especially
likely, they surmised , for individuals growing up in urban "carpentered"
(that is, right-angled) physical environments. In principle, this "carpentered world" hypothesis could be at least partially tested by measuring

susceptibility among peoples who lived in urban versus rural environments. Results obtained from the testing of adults in more than two dozen societies seemed to confirm the "carpentered world" interpretation. Urban dwellers seemed to be more susceptible than rural dwellers in many different cultures.

There were, however, two problems with this conclusion. First, as in all comparative studies, there is the question of confounded or overlapping variables. In this study we might wonder if any other variable or variables besides "carpenteredness" vary more or less systematically with rural and urban environments. Indeed, the rural environments were virtually all selected from populations in Third World (primarily African) nations where factors such as schooling, literacy, and contact with pictures were much less a part of the life of the rural samples than of the urban samples, which were usually composed of white university students or educated adults. A second problem lies in the ontogenetic development of susceptibility to illusions. If "carpenteredness" experience leads, over the life course, to higher susceptibility, then children should be less susceptible to the Muller-Lyer illusion than adults. Yet, Segall and his colleagues found exactly the opposite result. In their study and in others, children are generally more susceptible than adults. However, the researchers did not make systematic and age-graded comparisons of children with adults, and again there was little control of factors such as education. Segall and his colleagues were not unaware of this conflicting result, and several of their students spent considerable effort in reconciling the "carpentered world" hypothesis with other results. (For a review of this material, see Segall, 1980.)

As argued earlier, the cross-cultural (adult) and ontogenetic comparative problems in interpretation are inevitably linked by the underlying assumption that individuals are subject to cultural and environmental influences diachronically as they develop in the context of societal experiences. In a well-known paper, Campbell (1961) pointed out that the interpretation of cross-cultural comparisons of any two groups of individuals is virtually impossible due to the large number of rival explanations that might explain these differences. The present argument would add a further dimension to his admonition. That is, without some measure of the ontogenesis of the behavior in question, theories based on the cross-cultural comparison of adult groups fail to satisfy the necessity of diachronic confirmation of development. Let us look again at the study by Segall and his colleagues. If ontogenetic data were not collected, the "carpentered world" hypothesis might have been generally accepted in spite of other problems. The ontogenetic data called into question the very basis of possible interpretation by showing a contradictory trend in the socialization of susceptibility to the illusion

Another advantage of the ontogenetic approach should be noted: such comparison may allow for analysis of trends within a culture rather than simple comparisons between means. Since most cross-cultural hypotheses imply the influence of some variable on individual or group socialization, an ontogenetic analysis of trends within a given population may be just as important as cross-cultural comparisons between two cultures. (For a further discussion of this point, see Schweder, 1973.)

To gain a better idea of the mutual and separate influences of ontogeny and culture on cognition, a two-year research project was undertaken in Morocco, in the northwest corner of Africa. A variety of cognitive tasks were adapted to the local cultural setting , and these data form the basis of much of the research presented in this chapter. Before turning to the results of the visual illusion experiments, it is necessary to provide a brief description of the Moroccan cultural context in which these data were collected.

## THE SETTING IN MOROCCO

Morocco has been a crossroads of diverse cultural influences from Africa, the Middle East, and Europe for at least a millennium. Originally populated by indigenous groups of Berbers, Morocco has seen the influx of peoples and religions from all its neighbors. The most important impact came from the great Islamic invasions of the eighth and ninth centuries, which provided a Muslim overlay on local social institutions and which, over the centuries, have had a profound effect on the daily lives and social fabric of the peoples of Morocco.

A second foreign influence came from the comparatively recent colonialization by the French and Spanish in the late nineteenth and early twentieth centuries. The colonial period brought a number of important institutions that continue to affect the lives of children, such as the modern school, which has become a prominent part of Moroccan society (see Figure 5–2). Interestingly, unlike many other colonized African nations, Morocco already had a functioning formal school system. In Morocco, as in most Middle Eastern Muslim nations, traditional Islamic (or Quranic) schools trained young children (mostly boys) from the ages of 5 to 15 and continued to train exceptional students through the university

**Figure 5–2**    *A classroom in a Moroccan modern public school.*

level. In today's Quranic schools (see Figure 5–3), children still learn the basics of reading and writing through intensive memorization of the holy Quran (Koran). Most children attend Quaranic school for about two years and then go on to modern public school or to no school at all (Wagner and Lotfi, 1980).

As in many Third World nations, urbanization and contact with Western cultural and economic values—both through personal experience and mass media—also influence the socialization of Moroccan children. Some urban areas, such as Casablanca and Marrakesh, provide stimulation very much akin to what American children might experience in an urban environment. On the other hand, in rural mountainous areas children (and adults) remain relatively isolated from modern trends, values, mass media, and so on. Also, both Quranic and modern schools are found much less frequently in such rural areas.

Morocco is linguistically diverse. About half the population consists of native Arabic speakers, while the other half are native speakers of one of four Berber dialects. Many Berber speakers are also fluent in Arabic. Due to the country's colonial past, many Moroccans speak French and Spanish, with fluency depending on geographic location and degree of

**Figure 5-3**   *A traditional Quranic school in Morocco.*

education. Literacy skills (in Arabic and French) are a function of experience in Quranic or modern public schools, or both, though adult literacy is estimated at less than 40 perrcent. Skilled reading seems to be mainly a consequence of modern public schooling, but elementary literacy skills may be acquired after only a few years in the Quranic school.

This very brief description of the cognitive "ecology" of Moroccan children provides a beginning basis for the study of societal influences on cognition. Schooling, urbanization, mass media, and literacy have all been surmised to be factors in the production of cognitive skills and cognitive styles. In the following sections we will look at how these variables interact with cognitive development in Morocco.

The population studied included 384 Moroccan children and young adults who were selected so as to complete a three-way factorial design: four age groups (7, 10, 14, and 19 years of age), two environmental settings (urban and rural); and two schooling contexts (those who had gone to school and those who had not). Urban subjects lived in the city of Marrakesh, which includes a *medina* (or "casbah") and a modern quarter—both of which would be considered to be highly carpentered. Rural subjects lived in small villages where most of the houses are made of packed earth. While the houses are often rectangular, there is little else in this region that could be characterized as carpentered in the sense of Segall et al. (1966).

## STUDIES OF SUSCEPTIBILITY TO ILLUSIONS

In the first experiment, children were tested on the Muller-Lyer illusion provided in the booklet of illusions developed by Segall and Campbell (1969). Each child was also interviewed for background variables to assess contact with urban life and mass-media as well as socioeconomic status. The degree of susceptibility to the Muller-Lyer illusion was calculated for each of 16 groups; detailed statistical analyses are provided in Wagner and Heald (1979). It was found that both urbanization and schooling produced significantly increased susceptibility, while an age-related decrease in susceptibility across all groups was almost significant ($p < 0.10$). However, a separate analysis of variance for the nonschooled groups indicated a significant ontogenetic decrease in susceptibility. Further, a significant schooling by environment interaction indicated that schooling had more impact in the urban setting.

This complex pattern of susceptibility to the Muller-Lyer illusion reveals the importance of including systematic ontogenetic data. Groups that had not been to school showed a decrease in susceptibility of about 50 percent between ages 7 and 19, while groups in school seemed to maintain levels of susceptibility into adulthood. The "carpentered world" hypothesis gains some support from the finding that all urban groups tended to be more susceptible than their rural counterparts of the same age. Attendance at school also had a major impact on increased susceptibility. Furthermore, it is interesting to note that the susceptibility shown by the Moroccan groups is generally of the same magnitude as that found in the study by Segall and his colleagues. That is, urban schooled and rural nonschooled Moroccans showed about the same level of susceptibility as schooled Americans and nonliterate Africans respectively.

The value of considering ontogenetic trends may be seen in this study. Here we find a way to disentangle the seemingly conflicting findings of earlier reserach. We have some indication that susceptibility is augmented by carpenteredness and decreased in ontogenesis. The ontogenetic curves provide information about general trends that allow us to ignore minor variations across the age groups and focus on general tendencies.

We will now briefly consider a second study of susceptibility to illusions. This time we turn to the Ponzo illusion, the effects of which have been the subject of considerable debate. Several configurations of the Ponzo illusion (sometimes called the "railroad tracks" illusion) used in the study are depicted in Figure 5–4. These four configurations—of which the "abstract," context-free stimulus is best known—were devel-

**Figure 5–4**    *Ponzo illusion configurations used in Wagner (1977). The configurations are listed in the text as: Track (top left); Field (top right); Abstract (bottom left); and Control (bottom right). (From Daniel Wagner in* International Journal of Psychology, *vol. 12, p. 165. Courtesy of North-Holland Publishing Company, Amsterdam.)*

oped by Leibowitz, Brislin, Perlmutter, and Hennessey (1969) to measure the importance of contextual information on susceptibility.

According to Gregory (1966) and others, contextual information and inferences derived from such information provide a major basis for inducing susceptibility to visual illusions. The "carpentered world" hypothesis is derived from the same inference system. In the present study, the illusion stimuli are embedded in increasingly rich pictorial displays— from the Abstract version to the Field and Track contextual configurations. If susceptibility were a function of the subject's inferences about the relative distance (or depth in the third dimension) of the two stimulus lines, then differences in interpreting depth cues in pictures should produce systematic differences in susceptibility. Unlike the studies of Segall and his colleagues, the present study not only invokes global ecological factors but also suggests another set of mediating factors that produce susceptibility. Schooling and contact with pictures and cinema, as well as contact with carpentered environments, might all lead to perceptual skills used in interpreting context in pictures such as those in Figure 5–4. By examining how perceptual skills that affect susceptibility relate to cultural and ecological factors, our understanding of these phenomena is greatly enhanced.

The populations studied were the same as those in the Muller-Lyer illusion study. Eight trials of each of the four stimulus configurations were used to determine individual susceptibility for each configuration. In addition, the Children's Embedded Figures Test (CEFT, from Witkin, Oltman, Raskin, and Karp, 1971) was used as an independent measure of perceptual development. Finally, each child was given a relatively simple test of depth perception based on ability to interpret three-dimensional representation in the Track and Field stimulus configurations. (Further details are available in Wagner, 1977, 1978b.)

The results of group susceptibility to the Ponzo illusion configurations may be seen in Figure 5–5. The most striking feature of these results is the contrasting ontogenetic pattern of susceptibility to each configuration. Older children showed increased susceptibility to the Track and Field conditions (summed over children), decreased susceptibility to the Abstract condition, and no trend for the Control condition. As in the Muller-Lyer study, schooling and urban environment led to greater susceptibility, but only for the Track and Field configurations and not for the Abstract configuration. The depth perception measure provided a means of classifying individuals as "high" and "low" depth perceivers (that is, those skilled and those less skilled in seeing depth in a two-dimensional pictorial display). Analyses indicated that high depth perceivers were significantly more susceptible than low depth perceivers to the Track and Field conditions, but not to the other two conditions.

Correlational analyses were conducted between illusion susceptibility, chronological age, depth perception, CEFT scores and contact with urbanization and mass media. Susceptibility to the context-free Abstract configuration was relatively unaffected by the socialization and background of the subjects but was negatively correlated with chronological age. In contrast, susceptibility to context-rich configurations was affected substantially by the subject's perceptual development (as measured by the CEFT), depth perception skills, and contact with urbanization and mass media.

These results point to the necessity for careful understanding of the ontogeny of susceptibility to different illusions and illusion configurations. This is apparently so, because the configurations themselves engage different perceptual skills in the growing individual. Such a conclusion follows directly from the analyses of the effects of socialization experiences that act through depth perception skills and perceptual development—using both individual differences and groups varying in

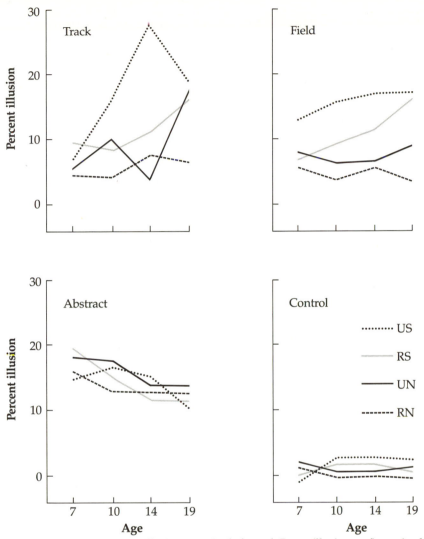

**Figure 5–5**    *Mean percent illusion magnitude for each Ponzo illusion configuration by age and by group. (Groups: US = Urban/Schooled; RS = Rural/Schooled; UN = Urban/ Non-Schooled; RN = Rural/Non-Schooled.) (From Daniel Wagner in* International Journal of Psychology, *vol. 12, p. 167. Courtesy of North-Holland Publishing Company, Amsterdam.)*

age, urbanization, and schooling experience to pinpoint the factors underlying illusion susceptibility. The foregoing study not only tells us something about cultural influences on perception of visual illusions, but also points to the need for complex models to deal with multifactor psychological issues that go beyond the domain of illusion susceptibility.

## MEMORY STUDIES IN MEXICO AND MOROCCO

The study of cultural variation in memory ability is usually said to have begun with the monograph of Sir Frederick Bartlett, *Remembering*, published in 1932. In that volume, Bartlett set forth a major research theme that would guide subsequent investigators. Briefly, he suggested that cultural variation in memory ability originates in variation in information or knowledge available to members of the culture. Bartlett was primarily concerned with memory for oral and written discourse, and found that cultural knowledge about the material to be remembered had an important effect on both accuracy and amount that an individual could recall.

Recent cross-cultural research on memory has dealt primarily with the influence of culture on the acquisition of memory skills, or "mnemonics," as aids in remembering. In Liberia, for example, Cole, Gay, Glick, and Sharp (1971) sought to determine the degree to which clustering strategies in a free recall task were employed by groups that varied in modernization and education.

The memory research to be presented here began in 1971 in the Yucatan peninsula of southern Mexico. At the time the study was carried out, a consensus was beginning to develop concerning the importance of memory strategies in the ontogeny of memory and in individual differences in adult memory. It was not clear, however, how children acquired such strategies for remembering, even though children at different ages demonstrated relatively distinct patterns of strategy use. Children's day-to-day experiences with cognitive tasks and in meeting cognitive requirements seemed a possible source of their acquisition of strategies.

This hypothesis was tested by studying children who had been socialized in different cognitive environments. The school itself seemed to be a cognitive environment very important for children's cognitive growth and an environment in which memory requirements were presumed to be high. Since virtually all American and European children attend some type of formal school, it has been generally impossible to study the influence of the covarying but separate factors of increasing years of age and schooling. We decided therefore to study the socialization of children in a society where some of the children attended school and others did not.

One model of memory, proposed originally by Atkinson and Shiffrin (1968), distinguishes between structural features (akin to "hardware" in computer terminology) and control processes (strategies, or "software") in memory. Ontogenetic models (Brown, 1975; Hagen, Jongeward, and Kail, 1975) proposed that memory *structure* develops in early life, while *control processes* develop more slowly through childhood. The hypothesis in the present studies is that control processes may be more sensitive to environmental experience (such as schooling) than structural features. In turn, structural features should appear in stable fashion from an early age in children from widely varying socialization contexts.

In the series of memory studies begun in Mexico (Wagner, 1974, 1975), children from the highly contrasting environments of urban and rural Yucatan tended to have similar scores and component skills (for example, "primacy" and "recency" effects in short-term recall) when they were in comparable grades in school. Older children from rural Yucatan had little or no access to schooling beyond the third grade. After that age, significant differences in performance began to appear between urban schooled and rural nonschooled children. While this finding was a clear demonstration that the ontogeny of memory was affected by experience, the experimental design did not allow a separation of the independent effects of urbanization and schooling.

The research undertaken in Morocco was designed to discover to what degree these and other experiential factors influence specific memory processes. The subjects were the same 16 groups of Moroccan boys described earlier in the experiments on illusions. Additional groups of subjects were also tested in order to consider possible culture-specific influences on memory skills. For example, Quranic scholars from a traditional Islamic school were included in the sample for the recall task, since they were alleged to have extraordinary memory abilities. A short-term recall task and a recognition memory task were chosen for study in these experiments because they both tapped aspects of structure and control processes as described above.

The first experiment explored the development of short-term recall. A serial memory task of the type used in the Mexico study required the subject to locate an animal drawing in a series of seven briefly presented drawings, where the drawing to be remembered varied in position from trial to trial over 14 trials. The subject was first shown each of the seven cards briefly after which they were placed face down. Following the presentation of the seven cards, the subject was shown a single "probe" card with an animal drawing on it, and had to find the same animal in the linear array of face-down cards.

This memory task has been particularly useful because it provides a serial position curve, where the primacy effect (that is, recall of the early items in the list) has been shown to be a function of verbal rehearsal strategies (Hagen et al., 1975). Also, the recency effect (recall of the most recent items) provides a measure of short-term memory, considered to be a structural feature of memory. A middle-positions score was calculated as the average of the outcomes on the central three positions in the seven-item series, so as to provide a measure with less of the presumed recency and primacy effects. Finally, the task provides an overall recall measure by calculating the percentage of responses correct over 14 trials.

Statistical analyses showed that recency recall was stable and relatively invariant across all population groups studied, regardless of age, schooling, and environment. The middle-positions measure was low and relatively stable across age, though there was a small but consistent effect for schooling. Primacy recall developed with age only for schooled subjects, and in a somewhat diminished form for nonschooled children who lived in an urban setting. More importantly, primacy recall appeared to be the most important factor in improved overall performance in the older schooled groups. The Quranic scholars' performance was similar to that of rural nonschooled subjects, who showed little primacy effect and no increase in recall with age. The influence of urbanization did not interact with age, but resulted in moderately increased recall for urban subjects of all ages. In the similar experiment undertaken in Mexico, urbanization also had an effect on overall recall. However, in both Morocco and Mexico, number of years in school appeared to be the most important factor in producing the primacy effect and increased overall recall.

In general, the short-term recall experiment provided evidence that formal schooling and urbanization may contribute independently and positively to the development of control processes, or mnemonics. The use of mnemonic strategies, such as verbal rehearsal, seemed to be linked to certain cultural experiences such as schooling, while short-term memory—a structural feature measured by the recency effect—seemed to be present in all individuals, regardless of age or special cultural experiences. It should be emphasized that the *ontogenetic* trends were crucial for understanding what promotes recall memory. By analyzing the components of memory processing as they develop in children growing up in differing social contexts, we gain a better understanding of the basis for cultural differences between adults.

Let us now turn to a second experiment that involves another kind of remembering—recognition memory—that will provide further evidence on the distinction between structure and control processes. Developmental studies of recognition memory—in contrast to recall—have often been characterized by a lack of age-related trends in performance (Brown, 1975). Such invariance with age is often considered to be evidence of the degree to which recognition memory does *not* require mnemonic strategies (Brown, 1975). Some recent recognition memory studies have demonstrated developmental increases, usually by using complex tasks where verbal or perceptual strategies may be used (for example, Dirks and Neisser, 1977). On the other hand, other studies have shown that forgetting rates (the continuous decay of information from memory as a function of time or intervening information to be remembered) are invariant from childhood through adulthood (for example, Wickelgren, 1975). The second experiment was designed to look at overall pictorial recognition performance, as well as to provide a component score that measures the rate at which material is forgotten as a function of intervening time and information (that is, the "forgetting rate").

The children for the second experiment were the same as those in the recall experiment, except for the addition of two more groups: adult Moroccan rug sellers and University of Michigan students. The stimuli consisted of black-and-white photographs of Oriental rugs, chosen to provide culturally familiar task items. Rugs and weaving are very important in the lives of Moroccans, and these stimuli generate considerable interest and enthusiasm. The experimental task was made up of different rug patterns and exact duplicates, which were arranged in a sequential array so that duplicates formed "lags" of 1, 5, 10, and 25 intervening items. Both practice and experimental stimuli were arranged in large notebooks, so that when the next pattern was exposed, it covered the previous pattern. The subject was instructed to look at each rug carefully, and say whether the present pattern was appearing for the first or second time.

Results of the second experiment were analyzed on the basis of total correct responses and component scores for measuring forgetting rates over the four lags (see Wagner, 1978a). The general findings were: (1) chronological age produced little or no reliable effects; (2) schooling produced a significant effect, but primarily at longer lags; (3) the effect of environment was highly significant but, contrary to the recall task, rural Moroccans were superior on total correct recognition; and (4) Michigan students and rug sellers performed as well or better than all other groups, while the Quranic students scored near the bottom.

In general, the data on recognition memory support previous research that indicates little age-related change in forgetting rates. Furthermore, forgetting rates were invariant with respect to schooling and environment. While it was unclear why rural subjects performed so much better than urban subjects on the total number correct, one hypothesis is that rural subjects were more familiar with rugs than urban subjects. Finally, the rug sellers (with little formal education) scored as well as or better than all other Moroccan groups. While familiarity might again be invoked as an explanation, it is also possible that rug sellers were able to pick out distinctive features in rugs as a function of occupational experience. Furthermore, other evidence suggested that some rug sellers used categorization strategies as part of daily commerce to aid in recall of rugs.

Quranic students were originally thought to have special memory abilities, either due to their selection for study at the Quranic school or as a function of daily memorization of the Quran. On both tasks, however, Quranic students showed poor memory performance and little use of memory strategies or mnemonics. This poor performance may be due to the fact that the usual requirements of Quranic study involve recall of meaningful verbal material embedded primarily in religious literature. Thus, the recall and recognition tasks, which used pictorial stimuli, may not make use of the subjects' knowledge, semantic network, or schemas (Bartlett, 1932). Although young Moroccan children may learn the Quran by rote and therefore not comprehend the words they are repeating, older Quranic students may use mnemonic skills on oral or written narrative discourse. Quranic students appear to have well-developed schemas for embedding new information about the Quran, while such schemas are relatively nonfunctional for the processing of spatially presented pictures used in the recall task. In contrast, public school children often memorize a large array of more or less meaningful items for limited periods of time (a semester or a year), while Quranic students build on learning over much longer periods. A follow-up study showed that beginning Quranic students learn quickly how to use chanting as a way of "keeping track" of Quranic verse. Only later do more advanced students learn to "chunk" passages into units to aid remembering. The exceptionally high scores of the Michigan students were probably a function of the ideal testing conditions of the laboratory, test-taking experience, and a highly selected population of college sophomores.

In general, the combined results of the two memory experiments support the hypothesis that experiential factors, such as formal schooling and living in an urban environment, may influence the development of control processes or strategies in memory. The results of the recall experiment showed that verbal rehearsal appeared to be used regularly only by older schooled subjects—both in Morocco and Mexico. These data, reflecting the stable use of rehearsal strategies by about age 13, are consistent with data collected among American school children. For the recognition experiment there was little evidence of ontogenetic change in use of strategies. Of equal importance was the fact that certain features of memory were *not* evidently influenced by the experiential contrasts of this study. Specifically, it seemed that structural features of memory were least affected: a relatively fixed-capacity short-term store was found in all groups; and forgetting rates were also found to be relatively invariant. Furthermore, family and demographic background data collected about each subject were found to be of little help in predicting memory performance when schooling and urbanization were controlled.

A number of conclusions may be drawn from these memory experiments. It seems clear that the methodology itself enables the investigator to distinguish between components of memory that are culture-specific and those that seem more or less universal. Knowing that memory strategies develop as a function of cultural experience such as schooling and urban life (as opposed to a more biological or maturational view) does not, however, allow us to define precisely the detailed learning experiences that promote cognitive growth. In other words, we know some of the clusters of experiences sufficient for cognitive growth, but we do not know the particular events or experiences that are necessary for its production.

## CONCERNS ABOUT A THEORY OF CULTURE AND COGNITION

Ever since social scientists first concerned themselves with the study of cognition, there have been proponents of the two opposing poles: the universalists and the cultural relativists. There have also been, of course, proponents of all kinds of intermediate positions. At least since the famous case of the "wild boy" of Aveyron at the beginning of the 18th century (Lane, 1976), scientists have debated the origins of differences in human cognition and its relative plasticity. In more recent years there has developed an increasing tendency to focus not only on the larger theoretical (or ideological) perspectives, but also on the difficult question of determining the validity of any method for measuring cognitive abilities.

One influential theoretical approach has been that of the rediscovered work of Soviet psychologists. Vygotsky and his student Luria worked to create a theory of cognition based on sociohistorical factors, in the manner of Marx's analysis of the role of the individual in the dialectical process of creating human society. This perspective led Luria to undertake some of the early cross-cultural work on cognition and the special effects of literacy on rural peasants in postrevolutionary Russia (Luria, 1975). The approach is one that is necessarily ontogenetic and diachronic—there can be little understanding of group differences between adults without an understanding of the social forces that shaped their youth.

Vygotsky and his students took this analysis further and opposed simpler views of measuring general "intelligence." They believed that the dialectical interaction between the individual and society must create patterns of abilities that are unique, as was the child's own cognitive socialization. In Vygotsky's words, "the mind is not a complex network of *general* capabilities, but a set of specific capabilities. . . . Learning . . . is the acquisition of many specialized abilities for thinking." (1978, p.83). The work of Cole and his colleagues (for example, Cole and Scribner, 1974) follows this general point of view. They propose that human beings are likely to possess the same "basic component cognitive processes," and that any observed differences in performance on experimental tasks are a function of: (1) situational determinants; (2) varying "functional systems" of cognitive processes; and (3) differences in the "applicability" of a given process to a given task.

The notion of functional systems emphasizes how the individual's abilities are organized in ways that are specific to and applicable to particular task content or domains. The term *functional systems* is not easily understood and is obscured by our lack of a clear understanding of the interface between domains of knowledge and cognitive processes. Historically, psychologists have attempted to avoid the question of individual differences in knowledge by creating tasks that were often unrelated to the individual's everyday cognitive tasks. Thus we would rarely if ever find "Can you remember Grandfather's age?" among the tasks asked a child in an intelligence test, even though it might be typical of home-based cognitive activities. Yet familiarity, as such, is not always the key element in success, as is evidenced by a variety of cross-cultural studies (see Wagner, 1981).

One novel approach is to shift the emphasis away from the search for abstract cognitive skills to an in-depth analysis of the particular *domains* of cognitive activities. Domains—such as skilled map drawing, chess playing, or bicycle riding—may have inherent structures that require cognitive skills organized not only in domain-specific ways, but also requiring a stage-developmental sequence of acquisition. This approach, which has recently been espoused by Feldman (1980), allows for an understanding of the cognitive requirements of a given cognitive domain and therefore provides the investigator with a deeper understanding of the relationship between the child's cognitive skills and the task domains that the child has to master. Furthermore, the approach enables us to go beyond cognitive tasks associated with schools and laboratories, and deal with cognitive activity in the everyday life of children.

# CONCLUSION

This brings us back to our earlier discussion of the role of ontogenetic views of culture and cognition, and the separate contributions of diachronic and synchronic perspectives to a theory of the socialization of cognition. The necessity of ontogenesis is clear if we accept the proposition that the child's mental abilities develop in close interaction with society. This diachronic view of the socialization of cognition assumes that the mind is a product of the particular activities that each society has to offer. We may also argue that a synchronic view of performance must be considered in any comparative assessment of cognitive abilities: situational and task domain variables are so persistent that they must be taken into account. A focus on the particular domains of cognitive activity provides one avenue for discovering how cognitive skills are acquired in specific contexts and may lead to a more comprehensive understanding of cognitive development.

The research described in this paper demonstrates the complexity of interaction between variables such as social experience, physical environment, and chronological age. The studies also show the vital role that a developmental perspective plays in the study of culture and cognition. All comparative studies have the inherent difficulty of determining which independent variables may be the "cause" of differences in the dependent measures, but the ontogenetic approach enables us to compare trends of behavior and forces us to consider the possible origins of the behavioral differences that we observe in individuals and in members of different cultures.

# 6

# Nutrition and Preschool Mental Development

*John W. Townsend*
*Robert E. Klein*
*Marc H. Irwin*
*William Owens*
*Charles Yarbrough*
*Patricia L. Engle*

Although two-thirds of the all Third World children under five years old are believed to suffer from chronic mild-to-moderate malnutrition (Béhar, 1968), little is known about the relationship of this condition to intellectual development. Ignorance concerning the effects of chronic malnutrition persists despite the accumulation of studies investigating the relation between malnutrition and mental development (Brŏzek, 1978; Pollitt and Thompson, 1977; Warren, 1973).

The majority of such studies have either employed animal subjects or involved children hospitalized following episodes of severe malnutrition. Studies performed with rodents (for example, Franková, 1974; Levitsky and Barnes, 1972) and primates (for example, Belkings, and Hegsted, 1977; Zimmerman, Geist, Stroebel, and Cleveland, 1974) report learning deficits in animals that have been experimentally malnourished, particularly when malnutrition has been accompanied by a reduction in social stimulation. These findings are of limited value, however, since important differences between animal species exist both in the effect of timing and in the behavioral effects of malnutrition, making interspecies generalization difficult.

Studies of clinically malnourished children have also been of only limited value. Although these studies have generally reported deficits in mental test performances among previously hospitalized children, the trauma of hospitalization and separation from parents may itself have disrupted normal mental development. Furthermore, studies of hospitalized children have commonly been retrospective in design. Recuperated children have been observed several years after hospitalization, when interim nutritional status, home environment, and cognitive development can only be inferred retrospectively. In addition, the prevalence of severe or clinical malnutrition is relatively rare (5 percent of children under 5 years), and studies of severe malnutrition fail to address the much more common and potentially more significant public health problem of chronic mild-to-moderate malnutrition.

The problems involved in studying the relationship of chronic protein-energy malnutrition to cognitive development are formidable. First, experimental assignment of children to a food-deprivation condition is precluded on ethical grounds. Second, as several investigators have documented (for example, Champakan, Srikantia, and Gopalan, 1968; Chase and Martin, 1970; Evans, Moodie, and Hansen, 1971; and Stoch and Smythe, 1967), undernutrition is almost always accompanied by poverty, illness, and various forms of social deprivation, each of which constitutes a plausible alternative explanation for observed deficits in cognitive development. In addition, it is extremely difficult to monitor total food ingestion in everyday environments. Finally, while chronic malnutrition tends to occur in rural, semiliterate settings in developing countries, available instruments for measuring mental development have mostly been developed for use with middle-class children in the United States and other developed countries.

Several investigators have attempted to deal with these problems by selecting groups of middle-class children with extraordinary nutritional histories. Lloyd-Still, Hurwitz, Wolff, and Schwachman (1974), for example, studied middle-class children who were malnourished during the first 6 months of life due to cystic fibrosis, bowel obstruction, or protracted diarrhea. They found that these children showed no cognitive deficits in later childhood. However, it is possible that such children received considerable social support and special care during their early childhood years. Winick, Meyer, and Harris (1975) studied Korean orphans with varying nutritional histories during the first six months of life who were adopted into middle-class homes in the United States. They found persisting effects of early malnutrition on cognitive development (that is, up to 10 IQ points by age 12) in these children. However, among the children studied who were adopted prior to 2 years of age, even the most severely malnourished had above-average IQ scores due to their enriched adopted home environments.

As Warren (1973) has argued, a preferable strategy for studying the effects of chronic protein-energy malnutrition is a longitudinal prospective intervention design. Though costly, such a design permits a form of experimental manipulation consisting of increasing the variability between children's diets by providing food supplementation. Such a design also makes possible the prospective measurement of home dietary consumption and of social factors which were confounded with malnutrition in previous studies.

Four prospective investigations that have employed nutritional interventions have been undertaken (Chávez and Martínez, 1977; Klein, Irwin, Engle, and Yarbrough, 1977; McKay, Sinisterra, McKay, Gómez, and Lloreda, 1978; Mora, Clement, Christiansen, Ortíz, Vuori, Wagner, and Herrera, 1977); two of these had cognitive stimulation programs in addition to their nutritional interventions (McKay et al., 1978; Mora et al., 1977). All except McKay et al. tested their subjects during infancy, and all report that nutritional supplementation during infancy was positively associated with improved development test scores (Chávez, Martínez, and Yaschine, 1974; Klein et al., 1977; Mora et al., 1977). In addition, Chávez, Martínez, and Bourges (1972), Chávez and Martínez (1977), and Mora et al. (1977) report increased levels of activity and demand for attention on the part of the well-nourished infants. They also report correspondingly higher levels of caretaker-infant interaction, a finding of considerable theoretical importance, since increased levels of environmental stimulation and exploratory behavior may well be the mechanisms by which improved nutrition can affect intellectual and behavioral development.

In addition to these behavioral and cognitive differences between well and poorly nourished infants, Mora et al. (1977) also report that babies with supplementation show lower levels of irritability and higher levels of visual attention and habituation to repeated visual stimuli at 15 days of age. They report that at 4 months the stimulation program produced higher levels of caretaking behavior on the part of the mother and lower levels of apathetic behavior at 4 to 8 months among supplemented children. In these analyses apathy was negatively related to scores on the Griffith's Infant Development Scale. The long term implications of these behavioral and developmental differences associated with early nutritional status are still a matter for speculation.

In the study by McKay et al. (1978), chronically undernourished preschool children were provided with a program of nutrition education and health care activities for varying periods of time. The authors report that cognitive ability improved among the children in the treated groups and that these gains in cognitive test performance were greater among children who entered the program at younger ages. Further, they report that the gains were still evident at the end of the first year of primary school, a year after the treatment had ended. The authors do not estimate the proportion of the gains in test performance associated with the nutritional component of the treatment, though it would appear from their results that it could not be very great.

The present chapter describes the findings of the oldest and largest of the longitudinal perspective studies of malnutrition and mental development, the Institute of Nutrition of Central America and Panama (IN-CAP) study of chronic mild to moderate protein-energy malnutrition and preschool mental development in rural Guatemala, which was recently completed.

## NUTRITION RESEARCH IN GUATEMALA

Four Ladino villages in eastern Guatemala were included in the study. Of the four villages, the two larger and the two smaller were matched on a number of demographic, social, and economic characteristics. This was done because factors associated with village size (for example, available social stimulation) might contribute to children's mental development independent of nutritional factors. Baseline data on home diet, anthropometry, and mental test performance collected prior to the initiation of the nutritional intervention indicated that the villages matched by size were comparable. Then, one village within each matched pair was randomly assigned to the "Atole" supplementation condition, in which a high protein-energy drink was made available to all residents twice daily at a central dispensary. This beverage resembled a popular local corn-based gruel, known as *atole*. The remaining villages were assigned to a control, or "Fresco," condition in which a low-calorie cool

**Figure 6–1**    *Guatemalan children from four villages participated in the nutritional supplement program.*

drink was similarly made available to all residents. *Fresco* is the local term for a refreshing drink. Individuals were free to consume as much of the beverage as they wished.

The Atole supplement contained 163 kilocalories (that is, thousand calories) per cup, of which 46 kilocalories were derived from protein sources. In contrast, the Fresco supplement contained 59 kilocalories per cup and no protein. From October 1971, both beverages contained enough vitamins and minerals to assure that these nutrients would be adequate in recipients' diets. Fluoride was also added at that time to combat caries. In all villages, mothers and children were encouraged to consume the supplements.

From the beginning of the project, free preventive and curative medical care was available at a clinic in all four villages, staffed by an auxiliary nurse, with weekly supervision by a physician. The occasional cases of severe, or clinical, malnutrition that came to the attention of project personnel were immediately referred to the clinic for medical attention and nutrition rehabilitation.

From March 1969 until March 1977, prospective longitudinal data on children's physical growth, home diet, daily supplement consumption, and cognitive development were collected. Biweekly morbidity surveys that collected data on the frequency and severity of symptoms of illness were initiated for children in June 1970. Data were similarly collected on supplementation, home diet, and morbidity for all pregnant and lactating women. Each of these measures is described below in greater detail.

## Setting and Subjects

The study villages are located in the department of El Progreso, in eastern Guatemala. The climate of this area is hot and dry, the terrain rugged, and arable land scarce. Most families in the villages are farmers who plant corn, beans, and a few vegetables. Some families supplement their income by providing migrant farm labor or urban day labor.

Life in the communities studied is characterized by poverty, malnutrition, and illiteracy. The median family income when the study began was $200 ± $50 per year. Infectious diseases and chronic mild to moderate malnutrition are endemic, with more than 80 percent of children below 7 years old having been identified as being malnourished to some degree in 1968 to 1969. Though each community has a public elementary school, adult functional illiteracy is high, and school-aged children of the present generation average less than two years of attendance before dropping out. Additional ethnographic information on the villages can be found in Nerlove, Roberts, Klein, Yarbrough, and Habicht (1974) and Mejía-Pivaral (1972).

In 1968 the total population of the four communities was approximately 2600. Two of the villages, one in the Atole condition and one in the Fresco condition, were larger, each having a total population of about 800 residents, while the other two were smaller, each having a total of about 500 residents in 1969.

The subjects in the study were all pregnant and lactating women and all children under 7 years of age in March 1969 who were living in the villages when the study began. In addition, those born or migrating into the communities from that date until March 1973 were also recruited into the study. Data collection continued for this sample until February 1977, but no newborns were added after March 1973. Measurement for mental tests included over 95 percent of children who were present in the villages at their scheduled time of testing.

The total number of children for whom some data are available (for example, morbidity or supplementation) is 1,623. Preschool psychological test data are available for 1,235 children. Data analyses described here are for the 550 children who were born between March 1969 and February 1973, for whom home dietary and supplement intake were measured since gestation, and for whom we are best able to characterize nutritional and illness history. This subsample provides the clearest test of the effect of the early nutritional intervention on mental development of children from 3 to 5 years of age.

## Independent Variables

Daily Atole and Fresco supplement consumption by children under 7 and by pregnant and lactating mothers was measured to the centiliter and recorded daily in the supplementation center. Supplement intake is expressed in kilocalories per day during a given time period (for example, 12 to 24 months, 24 to 36 months). It should be noted that energy totals contain kilocalories derived from protein sources. The actual volume of supplement consumed at the community level was measured with a net reliability of over 0.99.

In addition to measuring supplement ingestion, records were maintained on attendance at the center, since such visits might have provided social and intellectual stimulation that could, in its own right, affect mental development. Concern about the possible confounding effects of attendance was the principal reason for the inclusion of the Fresco control condition.

The home diet surveys reported in this paper were conducted twice during pregnancy for mothers, quarterly for children from 15 to 36 months of age, and every 6 months thereafter until the children were 60 months old. Dietary surveyors interviewed mothers and pregnant women about their previous day's food intake (that is, type and amount of food ingested) as well as about the food intake of their children. The specific nutrient intake was then computed from food composition tables (Wu, Woo, and Flores, 1961) and was summarized in terms of calories, proteins, and various vitamins and minerals. In addition, the length of lactation was determined for each child.

In the analyses discussed in this paper, the Atole and Fresco groups are compared within village size categories (where village matching was most adequate). Although not reported here, all dependent variable comparisons were accompanied by total energy and total protein intake comparisons to insure that the groups being compared in fact differed in nutritional status as a result of the intervention.

## Dependent Variables

The principal outcome variables in the study were children's performance on tests in the INCAP Preschool Battery. The variables reported in the present paper are derived from the tests listed in Table 6–1.

These tests were chosen to assess a broad spectrum of intellectual abilities including reasoning, verbal processes, learning, memory, and perceptual–analytic skills. A few noncognitive abilities were also measured (for example, motor control by the Draw-a-Line Slowly Test and persistence by the Impossible Puzzle Persistence Test).

The battery was administered during 3 sessions within 2 weeks of each child's birthday. Ten of the tests were administered at 36 and 48 months, and all of the tests were administered at 60 months. The tests added to the battery in 1970 and 1971 were developed to assess additional areas of theoretical importance and to include subtests of recognized IQ tests such as the Wechsler Preschool and Primary Scale of Intelligence and the Stanford-Binet.

The tests in the Preschool Battery were adapted for use in the research setting from the psychometric literature by a team of bilingual North American and Guatemalan psychologists, and a Guatemalan cultural anthropologist (Klein, 1971). Efforts to validate the test battery indicate that performance on tests in the battery improves with age, predicts age of school attendance as well as school performance, and is positively associated with measures of family economic resources and intellectual stimulation available in the home. Test scores are also associated with adult villagers' ranking of study children on an indigenously defined dimension related to the Western concept of intelligence (Nerlove et al., 1974; Klein, Freeman, Spring, Nerlove and Yarbrough, 1976).

The structure of the battery can be described from two perspectives. First, the intercorrelation matrix of the preschool battery tests evidence the general low interdependence of test scores. For example, at 5 years of age, Pearson $r$ correlations between tests range from $-0.35$ to $+0.72$, however less than 5 percent were greater than $\pm 0.40$. Second, the results of factor analyses up to 5 years of age reveal largely test specific factors (such as a memory factor consisting of Memory for Digits and Memory for Sentences and a conservation factor consisting of three conservation tasks). An important exception is a perceptual analysis factor emerging at age 5 that includes tests such as Embedded Figures, Block Designs, Memory for Designs, and Incomplete Figures. Although missing data rates vary by test (principally due to test difficulty), they are similar across

**Table 6-1** Tests in the INCAP Preschool Battery, Scoring Method, Test–Retest Reliability; Ages at Which Each Is Administered, and Year Added to the Battery

| TEST | SCORING METHOD | r* | AGES ADMINISTERED | YEAR ADDED TO BATTERY |
|---|---|---|---|---|
| Embedded figures I | Items correct | 0.66 | 3 | 1969 |
| Embedded figures II | Constructed score | 0.48 | 4 to 7 | 1969 |
| Memory for digits | Constructed score | 0.78 | 3 to 7 | 1969 |
| Picture vocabulary naming | Items correct | 0.74 to 0.95 | 3 to 7 | 1969 |
| Verbal inferences | Items correct | 0.62 to 0.96 | 3 to 7 | 1969 |
| Draw-a-line slowly | Distance/Time | —— | 3 to 7 | 1969 |
| Impossible puzzle persistence | Time | —— | 3 to 7 | 1970 |
| Knox cubes | Series correct | 0.54 | 3 to 7 | 1971 |
| Memory for objects | Items correct | 0.42 | 3 to 7 | 1971 |
| Matching familiar figures | Items correct | 0.47 | 5 to 7 | 1969 |
| Memory for designs | Constructed score | 0.77 | 5 to 7 | 1969 |
| Incidental learning | Items correct | 0.43 | 5 to 7 | 1969 |
| Conservation of area | Non-conserver (0) | 0.34 to 0.84 | 5 to 7 | 1971 |
|  | Transition (1) |  |  |  |
|  | Conserver (2) |  |  |  |
| Incomplete figures | Items correct | 0.28 to 0.92 | 5 to 7 | 1971 |
| Elimination of odd picture | Items correct | 0.73 | 5 to 7 | 1971 |
| Block designs | Constructed score | 0.73 | 5 to 7 | 1971 |
| Animal house | Constructed score | 0.75 | 5 to 7 | 1971 |

*Test–retest reliabilities are reported for the tests. The reliabilities ($r$) are estimates of population reliability ($p$) from several reliability substudies conducted from 1969 to 1975. Where a range of reliabilities is reported, the results of individual substudies could not be combined (Snedecor and Cochran, 1967). The number of cases varies between 90 and 297, except for Animal House, where $N = 44$. All correlations are significant at at least the 0.01 level.

treatment conditions. In analyses described here, scores for individual tests are reported.

Preschool mental testing took place in each community in an adobe testing house similar in construction to village houses. Testing was done by Guatemalan women qualified as elementary school teachers, under the supervision of a Guatemalan psychologist. The testers were observed for comparability of procedures twice a year in urban child care facilities and were rotated among villages within supplement type every 9 months. Mean intertester reliability for tests in the Preschool Battery was above 0.95. Test–retest (one-week interval) reliabilities have also been calculated for the cognitive tests and are presented in Table 6–1.

## Potentially Confounding Variables

If a child was ill on the day scheduled for mental testing, the session was rescheduled. Nevertheless, morbidity data were collected to demonstrate that chronic illness does not confound any observed associations between food supplementation and mental development. Morbidity data were collected during standardized biweekly home interviews in which mothers were asked to recall any symptoms of illness of their preschool children in the past 2 weeks. Morbidity is reported in the present paper as the percentage of days the child was seriously ill with anorexia, apathy, diarrhea, fever, or common infectious diseases.

Measures of social stimulation in the home were collected to demonstrate that the level of stimulation in the child's home environment did not confound observed associations between food supplementation and cognitive development (see Elardo, Bradley, and Caldwell, 1975; Honzik, 1971). The stimulation indexes include the amount of material stimulation available in the home (Material Stimulation), which is based on the number of toys, pictures, books, and other conceivably stimulating material objects in the child's home. Several intellectual characteristics of the mother, including measures of her vocabulary (employing an adapted version of the Wechsler Intelligence Scale for Children vocabulary subtest), literacy (determined by a brief test), years of school passed, and modernity (employing an adaptation of the Overall Modernity Scale designed by Inkeles and Smith [1974], a scale that includes measures of whether the mother read newspapers, traveled outside her community, had knowledge of current events, and so on) were also measured. The extent of the father's schooling (years passed) was also determined. All these variables were measured once, during late 1974 and 1975.

Test–retest reliability (one-week interval) of the parents' intellectual characteristics averaged over 0.90, and the interviewers were trained to a level of 90 percent reliability on observation of material objects in the home.

In addition to these measures, an index of family economic status was collected for each family in the four communities. This variable, House Quality, is an index of family wealth (correlations for measurements taken over a 2-year-period > 0.90) based on the size and type of construction of the family's house. Although the quality of housing varies, families typically live in two-room houses constructed of adobe, with one room serving as a kitchen and the other as sleeping quarters for the entire family. Sanitary facilities are absent. Data on house quality were collected in 1968, 1972, 1973, and 1974 and summed across these four measurements. Because of village differences in climate and availability of building materials (for example, the small Fresco community has many houses made of cane due to its warmer climate), this measure was standardized within villages.

## Impact of the Nutritional Supplement

Village comparability in mental test performance within matched pairs of villages was determined prior to initiation of the study. Thus, to conclude that the nutritional intervention resulted in better mental test performance, it is necessary to demonstrate that the nutritional intervention effectively increased the normal diet of children, and that within the matched pairs of villages, Atole village children's test performances from ages 3 to 5 years were superior to those of Fresco village children.

Additionally, if an association between Atole supplementation and test performance is found, it is still necessary to rule out other plausible explanations for such an association. For example, it must be demonstrated that improved nutritional status resulting from the intervention was not systematically related to factors which covary with better mental test performances, such as higher family economic level, more stimulating home environments, and lower morbidity rates.

For pregnant mothers, both the Atole and Fresco supplements increased energy intake substantially. The median energy increment from the supplements was approximately 92 kilocalories per day, and the mean ranged from 64 to 114 kilocalories per day in the various treatment groups. Total energy intake for pregnant mothers, or kilocalories from both protein and energy sources in their home diet and supplement combined, was equivalent in all but one treatment comparison. The exception involved mothers of boys from large villages, where a 300 kilocalories per day difference in total energy favored the Atole village (1620 versus 1326 kilocalories per day). Because of the large protein contribution of the Atole supplement, total protein intake of mothers was generally about 7 grams per day higher in both Atole villages.

Children are generally breast-fed until 17 months of age, and they begin consuming supplement, particularly Atole, as early as 3 months of age when their mothers bring them to the center. For this reason, supplement consumption of mothers and children is highly correlated early in life for both energy and protein ($r > 0.60$ during the first 15 months of life). Children's intake is used in this chapter to interpret the relationship between nutrition and mental test performance.

Although Atole children consistently received more energy from supplementation, only in the large communities do Atole children show significantly higher total energy intakes than Fresco children. Children in the Atole villages consistently demonstrate higher protein intakes and, as can be seen in Table 6–2, are also significantly both taller and heavier than Fresco children for every comparison at ages 3, 4, and 5 except those involving boys from the smaller villages. This group differs from others in that the Atole boys were weaned earlier and, as will be noted below, suffered more episodes of illness than their Fresco counterparts. The failure to find evidence of significant differences in height, weight, and total protein and energy intake between Atole and Fresco boys from smaller villages suggests that there should be no Atole versus Fresco differences in mental test scores for this group.

Table 6–3 presents mean mental test score by village size, sex, and treatment for those tests that demonstrate treatment effects. With the exception of a Draw-a-Line-Slowly test, higher scores indicate better performance. As Table 6–3 indicates, test performances of Atole children are generally superior to those of Fresco children. Significant main effects for treatment within village size (with sexes combined) are seen on 10 tests for at least one age. Sixteen of the significant contrasts result from superior performance by children in Atole villages, and one from superior performance in the Fresco condition. Within large village pairs, 6 of 7 significant effects favor Atole children. All 10 significant effects favor Atole children in the smaller village pairs. Tests that demonstrate no significant treatment differences include Memory for Sentences, Memory for Designs, Matching Familiar Figures, Incomplete Figures, Block Designs, Animal House, and Conservation of Material.

Table 6–3 also indicates which matched village comparisons (large Atole village versus large Fresco village, and small Atole village versus

**Table 6–2** *Indicators of Nutritional Status for Children*

| Measurement | Age | LARGER VILLAGES | | | | SIGNIFICANT EFFECTS (SEXES COMBINED) | SMALLER VILLAGES | | | | SIGNIFICANT EFFECTS (SEXES COMBINED) |
|---|---|---|---|---|---|---|---|---|---|---|---|
| | | BOYS | | GIRLS | | | BOYS | | GIRLS | | |
| | | FRESCO | ATOLE | FRESCO | ATOLE | | FRESCO | ATOLE | FRESCO | ATOLE | |
| | | (N≈68) | (N≈69) | (N≈52) | (N≈54) | | (N≈48) | (N≈42) | (N≈49) | (N≈55) | |
| Height (in centimeters) | 3 | 84.7 | 87.2[b] | 83.3 | 86.2[b] | b | 85.8 | 86.3 | 82.9 | 85.6[b] | b |
| | 4 | 92.0 | 94.3[b] | 90.7 | 93.5[b] | b | 93.2 | 93.5 | 91.1 | 93.7[b] | b |
| | 5 | 98.3 | 100.2[b] | 97.2 | 99.5[b] | b | 99.2 | 99.6 | 98.2 | 100.0 | — |
| Weight (in kilograms) | 3 | 11.6 | 12.5[b] | 11.0 | 12.0[b] | b | 11.8 | 12.3[a] | 10.6 | 12.0[b] | b |
| | 4 | 13.4 | 14.2[b] | 12.8 | 13.6[b] | b | 13.5 | 14.1 | 12.7 | 13.9[b] | b |
| | 5 | 15.0 | 15.7[a] | 14.5 | 15.3[b] | b | 14.8 | 15.4 | 14.2 | 15.4[b] | b |

Cell *N*s are approximate because different numbers of children participated across years and tests.

Letters (a, b) refer to *p* values from tests between Atole and Fresco within smaller and larger village pairs and within village size: a. *p* < 0.05, b. *p* < 0.01.

small Fresco village) are significant. As expected from the nutritional data, only one village comparison is significant for boys from small towns. However, 19 comparisons involving the other 3 groups are statistically significant, with 17 of these 19 significant village differences favoring Atole children. Tests that commonly evidence treatment differences are Picture Vocabulary Naming, Knox Cubes, Elimination, and Draw-a-Line-Slowly. Three of the significant village contrasts favoring Atole occur for boys in the large villages, 6 occur for girls in the large villages and 8 occur for girls in the small villages. Although not statistically significant, it appears that the most consistent effect occurred among girls from the smaller villages.

Since many of the same children appear in the cross-sectional analyses at different ages, comparisons at ages 3, 4, and 5 reported in Table 6–3 are not independent, and it is therefore difficult to determine appropriate significance levels. In addition, not all children tested at 3 years old were tested at age 5, since approximately one-fourth of all children studied since conception had not reached 5 years of age by the time the study ended. To deal with these problems, a series of statistical analyses was made on measures obtained from the same children as they grew older. As with the cross-sectional analyses, the repeated measures also reflect both greater height and weight and higher mental test performances among Atole children. Thus the effects of Atole are seen both cross-sectionally for each age group and with repeated measures on the same individuals across time. This validation adds confidence to our interpretation that the results seen are due to the Atole treatment.

Looking at test performance within the Atole condition, scores of children ingesting greater amounts of supplement are typically superior to those for lower-ingesting children. In addition, mean scores of low-ingesting Atole children are in general comparable to those of children in the Fresco villages. Thus the association between supplementation and mental test performance seen in Atole versus Fresco comparisons, though less strong, is replicated in Atole villages, where children were free to select their own level of supplementation.

However, before a causal relationship can be assumed, it must be demonstrated that other factors that covaried with mental test performances in study children did not also covary with supplement ingestion. Unless logically eliminated, such factors would constitute plausible alternative explanations for nutrition–mental-test-performance associations.

One such factor is the effect of social stimulation associated with attendance at the supplementation centers. Analyses investigating the effects of familiarization with the project staff that compare preschool test performance of children born from 1962 to 1969 during the first versus

**Table 6-3**  *Mean Mental Test Performances By Sex and Treatment, Within Larger and Smaller Village Pairs*

| TEST | AGE | LARGER VILLAGES | | | | SIGNIFICANT EFFECTS (SEXES COMBINED) | SMALLER VILLAGES | | | | SIGNIFICANT EFFECTS (SEXES COMBINED) |
|---|---|---|---|---|---|---|---|---|---|---|---|
| | | BOYS | | GIRLS | | | BOYS | | GIRLS | | |
| | | FRESCO | ATOLE | FRESCO | ATOLE | | FRESCO | ATOLE | FRESCO | ATOLE | |
| | | (N=65) | (N=65) | (N=50) | (N=50) | | (N=45) | (N=40) | (N=40) | (N=50) | |
| Embedded figures I, II | 3 | 10.4 | 9.7 | 10.5 | 11.0 | — | 9.6 | 9.9 | 9.2 | 9.9 | — |
| | 4 | 2.6 | 3.0 | 2.7 | 3.5[a] | b | 2.6 | 3.2 | 2.9 | 2.7 | — |
| | 5 | 4.6 | 4.4 | 5.6 | 5.4 | — | 3.9 | 4.6 | 4.1 | 4.1 | — |
| Memory for digits | 3 | 9.3 | 12.2[a] | 13.2 | 12.8 | — | 9.2 | 10.1 | 9.7 | 14.7[b] | a |
| | 4 | 20.7 | 20.7 | 23.8 | 23.4 | — | 24.2 | 22.0 | 21.2 | 21.0 | — |
| | 5 | 35.0 | 31.4 | 39.0 | 33.2[a] | b | 36.2 | 34.5 | 32.7 | 32.1 | — |
| Picture vocabulary naming | 3 | 7.5 | 7.7 | 8.9 | 9.2 | — | 6.4 | 7.7 | 6.2 | 8.4[b] | b |
| | 4 | 12.6 | 13.9 | 13.9 | 15.9[a] | b | 12.5 | 13.5 | 12.3 | 15.9[b] | b |
| | 5 | 18.1 | 18.2 | 18.1 | 19.8 | — | 16.5 | 17.6 | 15.8 | 19.1 | — |
| Verbal inferences | 3 | 2.3 | 2.3 | 2.5 | 2.5 | — | 1.9 | 1.9 | 1.2 | 1.8 | — |
| | 4 | 3.4 | 3.5 | 3.8 | 3.1[b] | — | 3.1 | 3.1 | 2.9 | 3.3 | — |
| | 5 | 4.5 | 4.4 | 4.6 | 4.8 | — | 3.7 | 4.7[b] | 3.6 | 4.2 | b |
| Knox cubes | 3 | 0.5 | 1.0 | 0.5 | 0.5 | — | 0.3 | 0.5 | 0.9 | 0.3 | — |
| | 4 | 1.2 | 1.6 | 1.6 | 1.7 | — | 1.2 | 1.5 | 1.0 | 1.1 | — |
| | 5 | 3.7 | 5.0 | 4.0 | 4.5 | — | 3.4 | 4.6 | 2.7 | 4.2 | — |

| Measure | Age | | | | | p | | | | | p |
|---|---|---|---|---|---|---|---|---|---|---|---|
| Memory for objects | 3 | 1.8 | 2.1 | 2.3 | 2.7 | – | 2.0 | 1.8 | 1.5 | 2.0 | – |
| | 4 | 3.3 | 3.3 | 4.0 | 4.4 | – | 3.5 | 3.4 | 4.1 | 4.0 | – |
| | 4 | 4.8 | 5.5 | 6.0 | 6.5 | a | 5.1 | 5.3 | 5.9 | 6.2 | – |
| Impossible puzzle persistence | 3 | 6.6 | 7.0 | 6.8 | 8.0 | – | 6.7 | 7.1 | 5.6 | 7.8[a] | – |
| | 4 | 8.9 | 10.5 | 9.2 | 10.8 | a | 10.3 | 9.1 | 10.1 | 11.5 | – |
| | 5 | 14.9 | 14.5 | 13.2 | 14.9 | – | 11.7 | 13.3 | 13.4 | 12.9 | – |
| Draw-a-line slowly | 3 | 1.0 | 1.0 | 1.1 | 0.9[a] | – | 1.0 | 0.9 | 1.2 | 0.9[b] | b |
| | 4 | 0.8 | 0.5[b] | 0.7 | 0.5[b] | b | 0.6 | 0.5 | 0.8 | 0.6[b] | b |
| | 5 | 0.5 | 0.3[a] | 0.5 | 0.3[a] | b | 0.3 | 0.4 | 0.4 | 0.3 | – |
| Incidental learning | 5 | 1.8 | 2.0 | 1.9 | 1.8 | – | 1.5 | 1.9 | 1.4 | 1.8 | a |
| Elimination | 5 | 5.1 | 5.2 | 5.0 | 6.1[a] | – | 4.6 | 5.2 | 4.6 | 5.3 | a |
| Conservation of area | 5 | 0.5 | 0.4 | 0.6 | 0.4 | – | 0.4 | 0.4 | 0.2 | 0.5[a] | – |

With the exception of the Knox Cubes test and Verbal Inferences at 3, where cell $N$'s are about 20, approximate $N$'s for ages 3 and 4 are listed at the head of each column. $N$'s at age 5 are somewhat smaller, since only some three-fourths of the children in the fully longitudinal sample had reached age 5 by the end of the study.

Letters (a, b) refer to $p$ values from tests between Atole and Fresco within small and large village pairs, and within village size: a. $< 0.05$, b. $< 0.01$.

the second year of the program (before high-supplement-ingestion levels confound such comparisons) show no significant differences.

Nevertheless, the supplementation centers did function to some degree as community social centers, and it is possible that the social stimulation they provided mothers and children during the 4 hours of daily operation affected the mental development of children who would normally have been confined to less stimulating home environments. Because attendance at the centers was a necessary condition for supplement ingestion, there is a very high correlation ($r > 0.75$ for all sample groups) between frequency of attendance and amount of supplement consumed.

The design of the longitudinal study was intended to control for effects of attendance at the centers on test performance by the inclusion of Fresco villages that provided a nutritionally insignificant beverage to children in centers similar to those dispensing Atole. However, for the Fresco villages to function as effective controls, equivalent attendance levels must have occurred in both Atole and Fresco conditions, or some threshold of attendance-related stimulation must have been achieved in the Fresco villages. It was originally hypothesized that two or three visits to the supplementation center per week would probably provide most of the stimulation the center had to offer.

In fact, by 5 years of age, both Fresco and Atole children were typically exceeding this attendance rate, although Atole children from 2 to 3 years of age were averaging about 112 days of attendance to the centers per year, or about 28 more days of attendance per year than Fresco children. Between 3 and 4 years of age, the Atole versus Fresco difference in average attendance was 18 days to the center per year, and from 4 to 5 years of age attendance rates were equivalent (that is, about 130 days of attendance per year). Thus it is unlikely that stimulation associated with attendance per se can explain the associations seen between supplement ingestion and mental test performance in the Atole versus Fresco village contrasts.

Similarly, self-selection (that is, the fact that children or their mothers decided how much of the treatment they wished to ingest) cannot account for these treatment differences. Although self-selection to levels of supplement ingestion undoubtedly occurred within villages, communities and not individuals were randomly assigned to the Fresco and Atole conditions. Such an explanation cannot account for between-community differences in test performances.

Nevertheless, it is possible that the observed association between indicators of nutritional status and test performance could have resulted from higher economic status or higher levels of home stimulation in Atole than Fresco communities. Such variables as House Quality, amount of material stimulation available in the home, and paternal intellectual characteristics are consistently and positively related to psychological test performance (Klein et al., 1977).

Although parents' heights, which provide a crude index of long term economic condition, are equivalent for Atole and Fresco villages, the major index of family economic level employed in the longitudinal study, House Quality, cannot be compared across villages, due to differences in climate and availability of building materials. However, we have compared the House Quality of high-supplement-ingesting children (that is, above 50 kilocalories per day) within the Atole condition. These comparisons indicate that the economic conditions of families of more poorly supplemented children were virtually identical to those of children who consumed more Atole supplement.

Table 6–4 presents means by village size, sex, and treatment for other potentially confounding variables, including material stimulation in the home, parental intellectual characteristics and child morbidity. It will be noted that although families in smaller villages provided less material stimulation in their homes, there were no significant differences between Atole and Fresco groups in material stimulation. Furthermore, indexes of parental intellectual characteristics are consistently higher in Fresco villages. For example, of the nine statistically significant village comparisons involving mother's vocabulary, mother's years of schooling, literacy, modernity, and father's schooling, seven favor Fresco villages. Thus community differences in intellectual stimulation available in the home cannot explain the superior mental test performance of children in the Atole condition.

Child morbidity has also been shown to relate negatively to physical growth (Martorell, Lechtig, Yarbrough, Delgado, and Klein, 1976). Although children were not tested if they were ill on the day of a scheduled testing session, it is possible that differential morbidity rates over time for Fresco versus Atole villages could have confounded the observed nutrition–mental-test-performance association. Of the five significant village comparisons in Table 6–4 involving serious illness, three indicate that Fresco children were ill a greater percentage of the time and two indicate that Atole children were ill a greater percentage of the time. However, cases in which Fresco children were more often ill are confined exclusively to the large village block, and no morbidity variable shows greater incidence in the Fresco condition for girls from small villages, where the most consistent impact of the supplementation program on mental test performances occurred. We thus conclude that differences in

**Table 6–4** *Mean Scores On Potentially Confounding Variables (Stimulation and Illness), by Village Size, Sex, and Treatment*

| | LARGER VILLAGES | | | | SIGNIFICANT EFFECTS (SEXES COMBINED) | SMALLER VILLAGES | | | | SIGNIFICANT EFFECTS (SEXES COMBINED) |
| | BOYS | | GIRLS | | | BOYS | | GIRLS | | |
| | FRESCO | ATOLE | FRESCO | ATOLE | | FRESCO | ATOLE | FRESCO | ATOLE | |
| | (N=68) | (N=69) | (N=52) | (N=54) | | (N=48) | (N=42) | (N=49) | (N=55) | |
|---|---|---|---|---|---|---|---|---|---|---|
| Material stimulation | 20.2 | 25.6 | 41.0 | 79.0 | – | –138.4 | –88.4 | –114.8 | –63.3 | – |
| Mother's vocabulary | 7.0 | 4.9b | 7.0 | 4.4b | b | 5.6 | 6.3 | 5.6 | 6.5 | b |
| Mother's schooling | 1.2 | 1.2 | 1.8 | 1.2a | – | 1.5 | 1.0 | 1.4 | 1.0 | b |
| Mother's literacy | 2.0 | 1.8 | 2.5 | 1.8b | b | 2.0 | 2.3 | 1.9 | 2.1 | – |
| Mother's modernity | 0.6 | 0.5a | 0.6 | 0.4b | b | 0.5 | 0.6a | 0.5 | 0.5 | b |
| Father's schooling | 1.2 | 0.9 | 1.8 | 1.5 | – | 2.5 | 1.0b | 2.4 | 0.7 | b |
| Serious illness (15–36 months) | 26.4 | 19.0a | 23.5 | 15.5b | b | 16.0 | 23.9a | 17.9 | 19.1 | – |
| Serious illness (36–60 months) | 13.7 | 9.5 | 14.1 | 7.2a | b | 4.4 | 14.3b | 10.6 | 11.4 | b |

Letters refer to tests between Atole and Fresco, within small and large village pairs: a. $p < 0.05$, b. $p < 0.01$.

morbidity levels cannot adequately explain the observed association between nutritional supplementation and mental test performance.

## SUMMARY AND DISCUSSION

The INCAP longitudinal study was undertaken to test the hypothesis that chronic mild-to-moderate protein-energy malnutrition is a contributing factor in children's failure to reach their full potential for mental development. To test this hypothesis, one member of each of two pairs of demographically matched rural villages suffering from endemic chronic mild-to-moderate protein-energy malnutrition was randomly assigned to an experimental condition in which a high-energy–high-protein beverage was made available on a voluntary basis. The other member of each pair of villages was assigned to a control condition in which a low-energy beverage containing no protein was similarly made available.

Children in each pair of villages were equivalent on indicators of nutritional status and mental test performance prior to the intervention. Total energy and total protein intake increased significantly among children and pregnant women in the Atole villages. In Fresco villages, as intended, total energy and protein intake did not increase significantly among children, though total energy intake did increase significantly among pregnant women.

Mental test performance was superior among children in Atole villages at ages 3, 4, and 5. This pattern of results was seen for all groups except boys from the smaller villages, the only Atole group for whom a nutritional status advantage of the Atole village did not result from the nutritional intervention.

As we have noted, most studies of the relationship between malnutrition and mental development have been plagued by inability to discard the possible confounding role of social and economic factors associated with poor nutrition. In the INCAP study, the estimated intellectual stimulation in the home environments of Fresco children was equal to or greater than that available to Atole children. Furthermore, within the Atole villages, family economic level was equivalent or higher for low as compared to high-supplement-ingesting children. Since other plausible alternative explanations for the observed association between supplement ingestion and mental test performance, such as social stimulation provided by attendance at the supplementation centers or self-selection to high-supplement-ingestion levels, are controlled by the study design, we conclude that chronic mild-to-moderate protein-energy malnutrition indeed contributed to poorer mental test scores of children whose total nutrient intake was lower in the present study.

The size of the contribution of malnutrition to poorer test performances in the data we have presented is modest. Differences in mean test performances between paired Atole and Fresco village children, where statistically significant, range from one-third to one-half a standard deviation. This effect appears to be consistent with the probable contribution of supplementation to mental test performance in the most comparable study to have published findings to date, the Cali intervention study (McKay et al., 1978). Direct comparison is not possible, since the design of the Cali study does not permit the separation of effects of supplementation from those of the intellectual stimulation program, health care, and instruction in personal hygiene that accompanied it.

With respect to the treatment mechanism through which the Atole supplement affected mental development, the INCAP study was not designed to allow estimation of differential effects of protein and energy. This is a consequence of the widespread assumption at the time of the study's inception that malnourished children suffered most severely from protein deficits, a belief that is no longer as widely held (for example, Scrimshaw, 1978). It is now generally thought that malnourished children in Latin America suffer both protein and energy deficits. Nevertheless, some evidence in the INCAP study offers a provocative clue concerning the relative importance of protein and energy in mental development. This is the observed absence of an Atole village advantage in total energy intake among girls from the smaller villages. For this group, significant differences did occur in both total protein intake and growth in height and weight. Furthermore, it is among this group of children that the most consistent effects of Atole supplementation on mental test performances are seen. Thus a reasonable hypothesis is that the provision of protein was largely responsible for the improved mental test performance of supplemented children. Additional evidence from this longitudinal study also suggests that provision of protein rather than energy is responsible for the substantial observed effects of the Atole supplements on physical growth (Martorell et al., 1976).

By including a wide variety of tests of cognitive functioning, the planners of the INCAP study hoped to be able to identify which specific mental abilities were affected by chronic malnutrition. Largely because the Preschool Battery data up to 5 years lacks a simple factor structure, this was more difficult to achieve than anticipated. It is possible, of course, to treat each test as a measure of a distinct set of abilities determinable from the test's contents. In doing so, we note that association of supplementation with test performance is spread across a wide range of mental abilities. Measures of vocabulary, which are among the best predictors of overall mental ability among U. S. children (McNemar, 1942; Edwards, 1963) and are also among the most reliable and valid measures in the Preschool Battery, are frequently associated with improved nutrition.

We have noted the high incidence of chronic mild-to-moderate protein-energy malnutrition among children growing up in developing countries. What do the results of the INCAP study suggest about the effects of this condition on the lives of these children? Since it has only been possible to follow children from conception to 5 years of age, we have no information concerning the later lives of children who participated in the longitudinal study. However, some indirect evidence is available from children born prior to the initiation of the study who were followed to 7 years old and who now range in age from 9 to 16. Substudies performed with these children reveal that their Preschool Battery test performances generally predict both how intelligent they were judged to be by village adults and how well they eventually perform in school (Irwin et al., 1978). Thus, lower test scores of chronically malnourished children suggest that these children may ultimately be less competent in the tasks of adult life.

# 7

# The Validity of "Cultural Differences Explanations" for Cross-Cultural Variation in the Rate of Piagetian Cognitive Development

*Raphael M. Nyiti*

Among the fundamental issues that have dominated cross-cultural developmental research designs for many years is that of universals in human cognition. Failure to resolve this issue in the past may have been due to many reasons, but the most serious one was a lack of psychological theories with universal validity.

In recent years there has been a growing recognition that Piaget's theory of cognitive development offers serious hope for shedding light on this issue. Proof for this assertion stems from the fact that it has been the single most widely used theoretical context for cross-cultural research during the past 20 years. However, because of cross-cultural variations in rate trends for the acquisition of cognitive abilities and transition from lower to higher cognitive stages, there has been a general tendency among cross-cultural Piagetian researchers (Dasen, 1972a, 1974) as well as other social scientists (Mangan, 1978) to explain these variations as real and significant, reflecting cultural differences in the importance attached to different cognitive abilities.

The purpose of our research was to test the validity of the "cultural differences explanation" in view of the fact that the majority of cross-cultural Piagetian studies seem to suffer from at least two major methodological problems: (1) inadequate knowledge of the child's language and culture; and (2) the use of standardized rather than open interviews. In open interviews, examiners do not limit themselves to asking each child a single standard set of questions. Rather, after beginning an interview with a standard question they feel free to create, on the spot, follow-up questions designed to verify the thought processes underlying the child's responses.

Inadequate knowledge of the child's language and culture creates communication barriers between the child and the examiner. Thus the child's deficiency may be a deficiency in comprehending certain words and questions rather than a general lack of competence with the concepts under investigation. In an effort to cope with communication barriers in cross-cultural Piagetian studies, many researchers have used potentially questionable methods such as interpreters (Dasen, 1972b; de Lemos, 1969), the child's second or third language (Dasen, 1972b, 1974; de Lemos, 1969; Vernon, 1969), or nonverbal methods (Heron and Simonsson, 1969; Heron and Dowel, 1973). When Piaget's clinical method is applied by an examiner who is not only fluent in the subject's language but also a native of the child's culture, many of the alleged differences in the ages at which the attainment of concrete operational stage has been reported in the literature seem to disappear (Kamara and Easley, 1977; Kiminyo, 1977; Nyiti, 1976).

The second problem, as stated above, arises from the tendency for cross-cultural Piagetian researchers to use standardized rather than open interviews to collect data (Dasen, 1972b, 1974, de Lemos, 1969; Vernon, 1969). The disadvantages of using a standardized method have been discussed by Piaget (1929) and Piaget and Inhelder (1947). According to these authors, such a method is inadequate for exploring children's thought processes. It does not permit an in-depth evaluation of how the child views his environment or of the child's potential for logical thinking. By posing to the child questions that have been prepared in advance with no follow-up questions, as is often the case with standardized interviews, there is a clear implication that the responses the child is to give are limited by the questions themselves. This kind of procedure implies also that the examiner knows ahead of time what he expects from the child and believes himself capable of interpreting the responses. With respect to this last point, the tendency is generally to content oneself with evaluating the responses as right or wrong without trying to analyze the thought processes the children evoke to arrive at their conclusions. In contrast, in the open interviews in which the examiner discusses the task with the child over and over, thus bringing in many perspectives, the children are given as much chance as possible to manifest their cognitive structures or underlying thought processes. The disadvantages that the standardized interviews have for the European children are magnified many times in those cultures in which a standardized procedure is an unfamiliar method of social interaction.

The study reported here was designed to repeat Piaget's original study in a manner consistent with Euro-American replications so that results would be comparable. In these replications we find, for instance: American children have been examined by an American in English (Elkind, 1961); English children have been examined by examiners in English (Lovell & Ogilvie, 1960; 1961a, 1961b); in Zambia, European children have been instructed in tasks in English by English-speaking examiners (Heron and Simonsson, 1969); in Australia, English children have been examined in English by an English-speaking examiner (Dasen, 1972b; 1974); and French Canadian children have been examined in French by French Canadians (Laurendeau and Pinard, 1972). In all of these studies the children and the examiner belong to the same social group in terms of language, culture, and ethnicity. The same cannot be said of the Piagetian studies in non-European cultures, where the majority of the studies have been conducted by Euro-American researchers. Here the child and the examiner belong to different groups linguistically, culturally, and ethnically. Therefore, it is possible that the performance of the children from non-European cultures reflects not so much the inadequacies of these children's environments as much as methodological problems described above.

## PIAGET'S THEORY

Many talk about Piaget, but few read him. His views are widely misinterpreted and misunderstood, so perhaps a brief summary of the principal features of his theory will be in order at this point.

For a better understanding of Piaget's theory of cognitive development we must understand what he means by cognitive structures. To Piaget, cognitive development or logical thinking is the elaboration of structures or logical relations that one uses to construct and interpret the environment. To draw an analogy in everyday language, we say that the structure of an object comprises its parts and the way they are arranged. Thus the structure of a molecule would be its atoms and their arrangement. Equally so, cognitive structures are schemes of mental operations that enable one to perceive, think, and act. Piaget uses logical and mathematical models to infer the presence of a structure through the actions or operations performed by the child.

The term operation has a dual meaning. Logically and mathematically it refers to the transformations implied in such terms as $+$, $-$, $\times$, $\div$, $<$, and $>$. Psychologically it refers to the mental activity involved in carrying out such transformations. When Piaget speaks of concrete operations he means that the child is able to perform mental actions he has previously carried out in actuality. Thus the operation is the central idea in Piaget's system. It is an internalized action that modifies the object of knowledge. For instance, an operation would consist of joining objects in a class to construct a classification, or ordering things to form a series. Operations, however, have to be equilibrated. To understand Piaget's concept of equilibration we must understand first his concept of behavior as a functional interaction between a child and his environment; the two aspects are interrelated. Accordingly, a response represents a particular case of interaction between the external world and the child, which may assume the form of overt behavior (action) or internalized behavior (thought), and constitutes an instance in the process of achieving adaptation or the balance of thought and experience. The process of adaptation is achieved through two mechanisms: assimilation and accommodation. Assimilation refers to the act of integrating one's perception or conception of a new experience with an object or event into an already existing system of logical categories, which constitute a previous cognitive structure in relation to the present object or event. Accommodation, on the other hand, refers to the act of transforming previous cognitive structures or making new structural arrangements to provide a better fit or match (between thought and experience) to the demands of the external world.

Equilibration therefore represents a regulatory mechanism by means of which assimilation and accommodation are kept at pace in the course of ontogenetic development. Thus, Piaget suggests that equilibration is a cognitive counterpart of autoregulation in the organic process of embryogenesis. Embryogenesis is the development of the embryo's many systems, especially the central nervous system, which is not only the regulatory organ upon which all the others depend for their development, but also the instrument of cognitive functions. In the case of cognitive development, embryogenesis ends only in adulthood because it is inseparable from the physical development of the child. The maturation of the nervous and endocrine systems, especially, continues until the age of 16. This is not to suggest that ready-made cognitive functions are written into the nervous system from the beginning, but rather that its maturation opens up new possibilities in the child. It is thus the equilibration that assures that cognitive development proceeds toward the end state (adult competence) at a rate neither too abrupt nor too lethargic for the organism's survival. The last point explains why Piaget and his collaborators have devoted their entire research program to discovering the successive stages in the development of cognition.

Piaget (1972) distinguishes four main stages, the sequence of which he believes characterizes the course of cognitive development of all members of the human species from infancy to adolescence. These are, in order of their emergence: sensory motor, preoperational, concrete operations, and formal operations.

## Sensory Motor Stage: 0 to 2 years

This is the preverbal stage, and generally speaking it is a period when the child performs only overt actions and develops practical knowlege that will constitute the bases of later representational thought. This is the time of the construction of the first invariants, such as the schema of object permanence. It is easy to observe that a young infant does not have object permanence. If an object disappears from sight, no attempt will be made to find it.

## Preoperational Stage: 2 to 7 Years

Characteristic of this stage is the appearance of the symbolic function, and therefore of thought, in terms of preoperational representations. Although the child can imagine the actions he wishes to perform, and consequently can think of those he has already performed, he cannot describe them in words. Level of understanding is strongly limited by egocentrism, and personal analysis pervades the child's reasoning. In that sense, for example, psychological relations between motive and action take the place of causal and logical relations. With the absence of deductive reasoning, intuition plays the most important role. Thought is tied to perception, and no concept of reversibility—which is the psychological criterion of conservation—is possible. As a result, sensory motor actions cannot be translated into operations.

## Concrete Operations Stage: 7 to 12 Years

It is during this stage that the first operations appear. As stated earlier, an operation is an internalized action that modifies the object of knowledge, and therefore can be considered as a reversible mental process that grows out of overt physical activity. In this stage the child can perform such operations only with perceived or imagined objects and not yet with symbols, that is, only in a concrete level of reasoning.

According to Piaget, classifying and ordering in a series are the fundamental operations that precede the complete development of formal logical reasoning to be achieved in the next stage. During this period some conception of "invariance" and reversibility is gradually achieved. Research carried out in this field in Geneva by Piaget and his co-workers shows that the conservation of substance appears first (7 to 8 years); then the conservation of weight (9 to 10 years), and finally the conservation of volume (10 to 12 years). Like the stages of development, the appearances of the various conservations follow sequentially.

## Formal Operations Stage

The period of concrete operations is surpassed when the child develops the capacity to perform formal or hypothetical–deductive operations—in other words, when the child can accomplish at a symbolic level the logical operations that in the previous stage he could perform with things actual or imagined. To this extent he can isolate variables as well as combine them. His thinking is not limited by perception and action so that he can consider data hypothetically, and draw implications from purely hypothetical statements.

## Factors Underlying Development

Piaget (1969) describes four general factors that he postulates as necessary for the transition from lower to higher cognitive stages, namely: maturation, experience, social interaction and transmission, and equilibration.

*Maturation*

Piaget, like Gesell, believes that maturation plays an important role in development, since development is a continuation of embryogenesis, but disagrees with Gesell's assertion that maturation by itself is enough to explain the transitions. For Piaget, as has already been pointed out, maturation of the central nervous system, which is the instrument of the cognitive functions, consists essentially of the opening of new possibilities. Fulfillment of such possibilities depends on functional exercise and on a minimum of experience.

*Experience*

This is also a basic factor in cognitive development, though Piaget insists that experience by itself cannot explain transitions in development. There are two types of experience: physical and logico-mathematical. Physical experience consists of acting upon objects with the purpose of drawing or abstracting from them a knowledge of their physical properties, such as when the child discovers a weight difference between two objects of equal volume. This is by no means a simple recording of just what happens but constitutes either an assimilation or accommodation as described earlier.

Logico-mathematical experience consists of acting upon objects with the purpose of abstracting knowledge not from objects themselves but from coordination of one's actions performed on objects, such as when the child discovers empirically that the sum of objects in a group is independent of their spatial arrangement. In logico-mathematical experience, knowledge is abstracted from actions rather than from objects. During the course of development these actions become internalized as operations of thought and consequently provide the structures of logico-mathematical experience. As Beth and Piaget (1966) explain, logico-mathematical experience is the basis of universal laws of thinking. They describe this point as follows:

> In fact, actions such as combining (or separating), ordering (in one direction or in the complementary direction), putting into correspondence, etc., actions which form the starting point of the elementary operations of classes and relations, are not simply actions capable of being performed on external objects: they are primarily actions whose schemes express the general co-ordination of all actions, for every action (from simple reflexes to actions which are learnt such as picking a flower or lighting a pipe) presupposes at least one of the coordinations consisting of the ordering of successive movements or the combining of elements, etc. This is why such schemes have a completely general significance and are not characteristic merely of one or another of the actions of a single individual. (p. 235)

What this statement implies is that all actions can be considered as expressing certain general features both in the sense that there are general (logical) laws by which coordinations are effected and in the sense that they are common to all mankind, hence independent of cultural milieu.

## Social Interaction and Transmission

Piaget points out that this factor is fundamental but insufficient because society does not act on the developing child simply by environmental pressures. The child is not, vis-à-vis either the social or physical environment, a blank sheet of paper on which a ready-made knowledge is written. If social transmission and interaction are to have any effect on development, the child has to attain some degree of maturation of brain processes, and hence the necessary cognitive structures. Social action is ineffective unless there is active assimilation by the child.

## Equilibration

As described above, this is the most central and fundamental factor in Piaget's theory. It keeps development oriented toward the end states of adult competence. Flavell (1970) elaborates this point very well when he remarks:

> There are . . . certain characteristic properties of childhood intellectual changes which I believe no theory that considers only environmental inputs could ever explain. One is the very fact that cognitive change is inevitable—guaranteed to occur—in neurologically-intact growing children the world over. Another is that the changes we witness between birth and maturity are of immense scope and significance; they are truly big changes, both quantitatively and qualitatively. Furthermore, the evidence suggests that at least the major landmarks in the child's cognitive evolution emerge in a fixed order; there is, in other words, considerable intrinsic directionality and individual uniformity in the developmental progression. And finally, the changes that occur are largely irreversible, that is, the cognitive structures and operations that eventually emerge are essentially permanent, essentially unextinguishable. (p. 248)

In this statement Flavell is corroborating Piaget's view of equilibration as an underlying autoregulatory mechanism that gives development its inevitability, magnitude, directionality, within-species uniformity, and irreversibility. This is not to reduce the role played by the other three factors in the developmental process, but to suggest that their influence is regulated by equilibration.

In sum, Piaget's theory emphasizes that cognitive development is dependent on the underlying presence of a biological growth process that develops as a consequence of maturational changes and of the child's interaction with his physical and social environment, and is not due to the specific cultural milieu. This brings us back to the question of whether alleged cross-cultural variations in rate of Piagetian cognitive development are genuine and significant, reflecting cultural differences in values placed on cognitive concepts; or whether the rate of development is the same, and only the performance, from which the rate of development is inferred, is different, due to the methodological problems outlined earlier.

## SUBJECTS

Children were selected from two Canadian cultural groups: Europeans (white English-speaking Canadians) and Micmac Indians from the Eskasoni Reserve in Cape Breton Island. A total of 48 Indian and 39 European children, aged 10 to 11 years, approximately 20 at each age level, were selected randomly for testing. The Indian children lived in a reserve about 28 miles from Sydney, the nearest city. All were attending the federal government school in the reserve at the time of this study. Their school curriculum is much the same as that followed by all schools in Nova Scotia. These children speak vernacular (Micmac) as their language at home, but English is the medium of instruction in school from grade 1. Of their teachers, 95 percent are English-speaking Europeans. Only recently were Indian teacher aides introduced in the school to assist with language problems in early grades. While there is a small-scale industry involving woodwork, handicrafts, and oyster farming, the majority of the 1,585 residents in the reserve live on social welfare. Even if they work they have no direct intercourse with a European-type industrial, commercial, and technological culture.

The European children were from Sydney, a city of about 35,000 people. They came from a wide range of economic backgrounds, including wage-earning, salaried, and professional groups. These children were matched with the Indian children in terms of age, sex, and grade in school.

## INTERVIEW CONDITIONS

### Language

The European children were interviewed in English by an English-speaking European. The Indian children were divided into two groups. Children in Group 1 were interviewed first in English by an English-speaking

European and then in Micmac by a Micmac Indian. In Group 2, children were first interviewed in Micmac by a Micmac Indian and then in English by an English-speaking European.

Both the European and the Indian children were interviewed during the school hours in buildings near their respective schools. In Sydney interviews were held either in the school library when it was not in use or in a vacant classroom that happened to be away from noise and other distractions. At the Eskasoni Reserve a building adjacent to the school was used for the interviewing sessions. It too was free from noise and other distractions.

## Interviews

For the European children the examiner was a student from the department of psychology at the College of Cape Breton. For the Indians the examiner was a member of the reserve school committee and a teacher aide.

## Tasks

Each subject was seen individually and was given Piaget's conservation tasks. The interviewing was flexible—that is, instead of using a standardized interview the examiners rephrased the questions or added new ones as the situation demanded. Suggestions and countersuggestions were frequently used by both examiners to check the authenticity of the child's responses. Most of the interviews lasted about 30 to 40 minutes per child, and all were recorded in their entirety on audiotapes for translation (Micmac to English) and analysis. The tasks used were essentially those described by Piaget and Inhelder (1947, 1969) on the conservation of substance, weight, and displacement of volume. The tasks are described below. They were presented in the order listed, and for each task the child was required to give reasons for his judgment or prediction.

*Substance*

The child was shown several balls made of modeling clay and was asked to choose two that he thought were the same size or equal in amount of clay. When the child had done this and was convinced the two balls had the same amount, the examiner rolled one ball into a wiener-shaped object and then asked the subject to indicate whether the wiener had more, less, or the same amount as the ball.

*Weight*

The experiment consisted of establishing, first, the equality of weight between two balls of clay by weighing them on the scale and then getting the child to agree that both weighed the same. When this was done, one of the balls was flattened into a pancake-shaped object. The child was asked to give his judgment as to whether the pancake weighed more, less, or the same as the ball.

*Volume*

Two glasses of water were shown and the child was asked to verify if water levels were the same. Then he was asked to choose two balls of equal size from several presented to him. When this was accomplished he was asked to predict the water levels if one ball was dropped into each of the glasses. Whether or not the subject predicted correctly, one ball was dropped into each glass of water to establish equality of displaced volume. After the child had agreed that both balls would displace an equal volume, one ball was rolled into a wiener shape and he was asked to predict whether the new object (wiener) would displace more, less, or the same volume as the ball.

## CLASSIFICATION OF DATA

The criteria used for classifying data on conservation are described below.

### Conservers

A. The child was classified as a conserver for the experiments on conservation of substances and weight if he gave an equality judgment with conviction (indicated, for example, by resistance to countersuggestions) and justified it by giving reasons or arguments such as:

1.  Only the shape has been changed, not the quantity.
2.  Nothing has been added or taken away.
3.  The ball and the wiener were the same before.
4.  A change in form doesn't matter because the substance and weight are still the same.
5.  The wiener is longer but it is thin.
6.  The ball is fatter but it is short.

7.  You have just rolled the ball into a wiener.
8.  You can roll the other ball into a wiener, too.
9.  You can roll the wiener back into a ball again.
10. The wiener has the same clay as before.

B. The child was classified as a conserver for the experiment on volume if he gave a judgment indicating a conviction of equality of displacement of water and justified it by at least one of the following reasons:

1.  Both the ball and the wiener take up the same room or space in the water.
2.  The ball and the wiener contain the same quantity of clay.
3.  The ball and the wiener were the same before.
4.  A change in shape is not important so long as both contain an equal amount of clay.

C. The child was also classified as a conserver if, to begin with, he denied conservation but in the course of probing changed his position and gave equality judgment with conviction and justified this by expressing one of the reasons outlined above.

## Nonconservers

A. The child was classified as a nonconserver for the experiment on conservation of substance and weight if he denied equality of substance and weight and was shown by probing to justify this by perceptual centering, usually on one of two dimensions of an object, for instance, length or thickness:

1.  The wiener has more (or is heavier) because it is longer.
2.  The ball has more (or is heavier) because it is fatter.
3.  The ball has more (or is heavier) because it is pressed together, that is, it is compact
4.  The wiener has less (or is lighter) because it is thinner.
5.  The ball has less (or is lighter) because it is shorter.

B. The child was classified as a nonconserver for the experiment on volume if he denied equality of displacement of water and justified his judgment by reasons such as:

1.  The wiener displaces more water because it is longer.

2.  The ball displaces more water because it is fatter.

3.  The ball displaces more water because it drops to the bottom of the glass.

4.  The ball displaces more water because it is heavier (it sinks).

5.  The ball displaces more water because it is round.

6.  The wiener displaces less water because it stays straight in the glass.

7.  The wiener displaces less later because it is thinner.

8.  The wiener displaces less water because it is lighter (it does not sink as well as the ball).

C. The child was also classified as a nonconserver for the experiment on conservation of substance, weight or volume, if, to begin with, he gave equality judgment, but in the course of probing changed his position and denied equality and justified it by consistently appealing to nonconservation reasons outlined above.

## Transition

The child was classified as being in the transition stage for any one of the experiments if he gave evidence of such operations as identity, reversibility, and compensation that must be taken into account in the transformation of quantity, but under slightly changed conditions vacillated between the consideration of these operations and the strong influence of perceptual data; or if he became weary of giving the same reasons to support his judgment for inequality, that is, if he were consistently nonconserving but sometimes gave length as a reason and sometimes thickness.

## Uncertain

The child was classified in the uncertain category for any one of the experiments if:

1.  The responses did not give sufficient evidence to indicate conservation, transition, or nonconservation in terms of the criteria outlined above. Such responses included some like:

    a. I don't know.

    b. No response. (Subject gave no response at all.)

    c. It just looks the same.

     d. Mine is a wiener, or mine is a ball.

     e. You have rolled it.

     f. It feels that way.

     g. It looks like that.

     h. I just think so.

2. The child's responses indicated conservation but appeared to have been influenced by clues provided by probing or statements put to him, unknowingly, by the examiner. A change from nonconserver to conserver in this case raised a question as to whether the change reflected true conviction of the child.

## RESULTS

Qualitative analysis of results indicates that both the European and Indian children develop along similar lines. Both groups gave similar types of responses and explanations whether it was for nonconservation, transitional, or conservation stages. The attainment of conservation followed a similar pattern in both groups, conservation of substance being the easiest, that of weight intermediate, and that of volume the hardest. However, one fundamental difference between the European and Indian children appeared when the examiner was European and the language English. Compared to the European children, most Indian children gave very short verbal explanations or made incomplete statements that quite often kept the examiner guessing and waiting. This made it necessary for some responses to be classified as "uncertain" because the necessary evidence to classify them into Piaget's three stages was either uncertain, insufficient, or lacking completely. But when the interview was conducted by an Indian and in Micmac, their explanations were similar to those of European children.

    Quantitative results and statistical significance are presented in Table 7–1. This table shows the percentage of success on conservation tasks by the European and Indian children when interviewed by a European examiner in English and by an Indian in Micmac. As can be observed from the table, the Indian children lagged behind their European counterparts and were classified more frequently as "uncertain" than the European children when the examiner was European and the language English. But when they were interviewed by examiners of the same culture and language, there were no significant differences in performance between the European and Indian children, as shown by statistical anal-

**Table 7-1** *Percentage of Success on Conservation Tasks by 10- and 11-Year-Old European Children (EUR)Interviewed by a European Examiner in English (E) and Indian Children (IND) Interviewed Either in English (E) or by an Indian Examiner in Micmac (M)*

| | 10-YEAR-OLDS | | | 11-YEAR-OLDS | | |
|---|---|---|---|---|---|---|
| GROUP | EUR (N=16) | IND (N=16) | IND (N=26) | EUR (N=23) | IND (N=22) | IND (N=22) |
| LANGUAGE | E | E | M | E | E | M |
| **TYPE OF QUANTITY** / STAGE OF CONSERVATION | | | | | | |
| **Substance** | | | | | | |
| Nonconservers | 0 | 31 | 12 | 0 | 9 | 0 |
| Transition | 12 | 8 | 0 | 4 | 23 | 5 |
| Conservers | 88 | 46 | 84 | 96 | 50 | 90 |
| Uncertain | 0 | 15 | 4 | 0 | 18 | 5 |
| | $X^2 = 10.36^*$ (EUR/E and IND/E) | | $X^2 = 5.72$ (EUR/E and IND/M) | $X^2 = 12.32^{**}$ (EUR/E and IND/E) | | $X^2 = 1.07$ (EUR/E and IND/M) |
| **Weight** | | | | | | |
| Nonconservers | 19 | 42 | 15 | 0 | 32 | 0 |
| Transition | 0 | 15 | 12 | 9 | 9 | 9 |
| Conservers | 75 | 31 | 73 | 91 | 45 | 86 |
| Uncertain | 6 | 12 | 0 | 0 | 14 | 5 |
| | $X^2 = 8.47^*$ | $X^2 = 3.54$ | | $X^2 = 13.89^{**}$ | $X^2 = 1.08$ | |
| **Volume** | | | | | | |
| Nonconservers | 50 | 54 | 65 | 30 | 40 | 36 |
| Transition | 13 | 11 | 8 | 22 | 18 | 14 |
| Conservers | 37 | 8 | 23 | 48 | 28 | 45 |
| Uncertain | 0 | 27 | 4 | 0 | 14 | 5 |
| | $X^2 = 8.96^*$ | $X^2 = 1.97$ | | $X^2 = 4.81$ | $X^2 = 1.59$ | |

df = 3, $^*p < 0.05$, $^{**}p < 0.01$.

yses in the table. On all concepts, the percentage of success at both age levels is about the same for both groups. Only a small proportion of any group succeeded on the conservation of volume; it seems that this concept is not fully developed by the age of 11 years. Piaget (1969) and Lovell and Ogilvie (1961) are among the few that have ever reported success on conservation of volume for the period covered by this study.

## DISCUSSION

While neither Canadian sample varied qualitatively from the Genevan norms, the rate of development of the Indian sample lagged behind both their European counterparts and the Genevan norms when the culture and language of the examiner were different. This is consistent with the findings of the majority of cross-cultural Piagetian researchers. However, the picture is quite different when the culture and language of the examiner are the same. The children's performance is not only equal to that of their European counterparts but follows the Genevan pattern. This is consistent with a minority of studies in the literature (Kamara and Easley, 1977; Kiminyo, 1977; Nyiti, 1976). In the latter studies the subject and the examiner were of the same ethnic, cultural, and language backgrounds.

With the exception of a few investigators (Lloyd, 1971a, 1971b, Price-Williams, 1969), cross-cultural Piagetian researchers, when studying people from traditional cultures, have rarely adopted the attitude suggested by Cole et al. (1971) that people with whom one is working always behave reasonably and when their behavior appears unreasonable it is to one's self, one's procedure, and one's experimental tasks that one should look first for an explanation. This attitude is obviously maintained when studying children from their own social groups. For instance, Dasen (1974), having found that his European subjects had failed to achieve conservation of weight at ages 10 and 11 years, not only searched the protocols and retested the children but tested additional samples to determine the reasons for the failure.

Perhaps because of expectations, we find no similar concerns directed toward native children in Australia, Papua–New Guinea, Zambia, Senegal, or Uganda, whose performances make them appear to be retarded in their mental development. We find little consideration of the fact that using a foreign language with children from a different linguistic and cultural background is like using a clinical method, which is largely verbal, with a group of mentally deficient children, knowing very well that these children's verbal abilities are limited. Nor is sufficient consideration given to the effects the ethnic background of the examiner and standardized interview might have on the performance of these children. Rather, we find their "retardation" attributed to lack of contact with Europeans and European culture. The writers present their arguments as if *European* is synonymous with *progressive* and European culture is a symbol of progress.

In most traditional cultures, standardized procedures are not familiar forms of social interaction; hence children and even adults are not as sophisticated in taking tests or answering questions from an interviewer as are Europeans. The consequences of administering standardized interviews to such people is well explained by Brislin (1976) when he states that:

> The performance on the test can be due to any of these factors: real competence which the test is designed to measure; unfamiliarity with the test materials; nervousness in the presence of the test administrator (who is white); indifference at working on a test whose relevance is not obvious; total boredom; purposeful efforts to sabotage the research; ingratiation tendencies, leading to responses the test-taker thinks the administrator would like to see. (p. 29)

It is being recognized that the findings of many cross-cultural Piagetian studies may have been distorted by methodological problems such as those examined here. For example, Dasen suggests:

> When applying a Piagetian task intra-culturally but even more so cross-culturally, the result represents a "performance level" that may or may not reflect the "competence" for the operations which the task is supposed to measure. A lot of care is needed to insure that the performance level is equivalent to competence level. (Dasen, 1977, p. 10)

The present study attempted to eliminate as much as possible the distorting effects of methodological factors on the data collected from the Indian sample. The result showed that the Indian children attain conservation, hence concrete operations, at about the same rate as has been reported for European children studied by Piaget and other European researchers. This suggests that before accepting cultural differences as a valid explanation for cross-cultural variations in the development of intellectual operations or attributing them to the child's environmental conditions or cultural bias in Piaget's theory, one ought to ascertain first that the studies used to draw this conclusion are methodologically sound. As it stands now, most cross-cultural Piagetian studies suffer from such serious methodological problems that their findings offer limited information.

# CONCLUSION

If we are to draw any conclusion from the findings of the present study, it will be that the development of cognitive structures described by Piaget is not a direct product of cultural milieu but rather of progressive coordination of a succession of actions that the individual carries on with objects, events, or situations in his physical and social environment. The actions that are coordinated are not restricted to characteristic actions of the individual in particular circumstances. Rather, they are results that can be obtained by almost anyone carrying out the same actions, thus expressing the universality of the logical operations or laws by which such coordinations are accomplished.

A useful step toward understanding this conclusion is to recognize the distinction that Piaget (1972) makes between psychosocial and spontaneous aspects of the child's cognitive development. The psychosocial aspects refer to what the child receives from others—for example, etiquette, values, beliefs, and technical skills—and learns by physical abstraction from special experiences with objects and events in the physical and social environment. Psychosocial development is, in short, the cognitive acculturation of the child and therefore can be expected to vary from one society to another. The spontaneous aspect refers to the development of cognition itself or the general instrument of learning. This is what the child learns or discovers by himself through the force of his own power of reasoning or logico-mathematical thinking—for example, when he learns that the result of an addition of a group of objects is independent of the order followed. This type of learning is not acquired by means of physical abstraction from objects in one's environment but rather by formal abstraction from general coordination of actions and operations performed on objects by the individual.

While the prime motivation for psychosocial development originates from without, that is, from the child's social environment with some specific end points in view, spontaneous development results from an intrinsic drive of a psychobiological field toward an end state or more stable equilibrium, which is reached only at maturity (between 15 and 16 years of age). The stages described by Piaget represent forms of equilibrium. Each stage is characterized by a qualitatively different cognitive structure that determines the manner in which what is presented to the child's senses is assimilated or learned during that stage.

Thus it appears that psychosocial development or the acculturation of the child is not possible before the spontaneous development of cognition. The latter provides the necessary condition for the former and not vice versa. It is obvious, as Furth (1970) points out, that the development of cognitive structures takes place "within a concrete person who lives in a specific physical and social environment from which he learns specific things and toward which he has personal attitudes and motivation" (p. 80). But what the child learns and the manner of his learning depend largely upon the developmental status of his cognitive structures, which is determined not only by the physical and social environment in which he lives but also by biological maturational factors.

Piaget regards cognitive development as presupposing a close collaboration between the maturation of the central nervous system, physical and logico-mathematical experience, social interaction and transmission, and equilibration. Thus the effect of any one of these factors on the child's developing cognition will be difficult to decipher. For instance, when the rates of acquisition and stage transition are found across widely divergent cultural groups, it is not useful to attribute this finding exclusively to biological maturational factors. While such an explanation may explain the epigenetic processes of development in terms of inevitability, magnitude, directionality, within-species uniformity, and irreversibility, it underestimates the effects of physical and social environment.

It is equally useless to attribute cognitive development to differences in physical and social environment, because that approach ignores the child as an active psychobiological field capable of spontaneous construction of operational structures. For example, it is sometimes claimed that children from non-European cultures lack toys and are therefore passive and apathetic. This attitude is clearly ethnocentric because, as has been noted already, what the child needs for Piagetian cognitive development is not a special kind of physical object, but a variety of objects to act on. Bits of wood, stones, mud, sand, and even cows' and goats' feces would do just as well as European toys when it comes to building up operational structures.

In summary, it appears that cognitive structures described by Piaget are universal and represent a necessary condition for any successful acculturation. It has been noted that they are not products of any one particular cultural milieu and therefore are not acquired by means of external pressure but rather by formal abstraction from general coordination of the individual's own actions on objects and events. Implicit in the coordination of actions is the spontaneous construction of general rules or laws, general in the sense that (a) they apply to any object whatever, and (b) they are common to all individuals carrying out the same actions. Thus the infant at the sensory motor stage constructs such rules but remains implicit in his overt actions on objects. At later stages, however, when actions are internalized and operations emerge, the child becomes capable of consciously applying and treating such rules as systems of logical classification, serialization, spatial and temporal coordinates, and causality. This is not to suggest that differences in the physical and social environment in which the child lives do not produce cultural differences in thinking. They do, but only in terms of physical abstraction or learning from specific experiences and objects in the environment. In other words, each environment provides children with certain physical and social objects and events that act as a source of reality, hence values, attitudes, motivations, and so on. But to comprehend reality of any kind, children everywhere must, on their own, proceed by formal abstraction to discover the general rules that they then apply to judge and evaluate (that is, assimilate) certain objects or events as related to, implying, or contradicting certain realities in their physical and social environment. Thus, while children in different cultures may have to deal with different realities, they all apply the same operations or processes of thought, especially those of an elementary logico-mathematical system. Therefore, we doubt that there is much validity in the "cultural differences explanation" for cross-cultural variation in the rate at which children acquire the cognitive structures described by Piaget. The differences that have been found may be due to methodological problems of the types raised in this study.

# 8

# Animistic Cognition: Some Cultural, Conceptual, and Methodological Questions for Piagetian Research

*Tom Ciborowski*
*Douglass Price-Williams*

Piaget's research and theorizing regarding the concept of animism was first introduced to the English-speaking world in 1929 in his book *The Child's Conception of the World*. This pioneering work took little heed of possible cultural and social variables that can play a crucial role not only in the development of animistic thinking, but in the development of all aspects of cognitive processes. Piaget (1966) was aware of this shortcoming and commented on the significance of cross-cultural work for his own theories. More recently, however, a volume edited by Dasen (1977) is of particular interest since it includes pertinent cross-cultural data that indicate the influence of cultural and social variables on cognitive development. In Dasen's book, Laurendeau-Bendavid investigated animistic ideas such as the concept of life and the movement of clouds in both Rwandan and French Canadian children. A review of such investigations takes us direclty to a consideration of precisely what is meant by the term *animism*.

In a 1972 reprint of *The Child's Conception of the World*, Piaget defined animism as "the tendency to regard objects as living and endowed with will," thus virtually equating the concept of animism with the idea of consciousness. We will return to Piaget and other conceptions of animism after presenting his stage model. Piaget traced the development of animism through four major stages. Stage I (6 to 7 years old): The child regards all things as conscious. Stage II (8 to 9 years old): The child regards all things that move as conscious (for example, a bicycle). Stage III (11 to 12 years old): Only things that move of their own accord are considered conscious. Stage IV (about 12 years old): Consciousness is restricted solely to humans and animals. Piaget's formulation hinges on the differentiation of consciousness, beginning with an all encompassing "life-belief" that gradually becomes more articulated and restricted as the child develops and acquires more knowledge about the world.

Animism has been described in Gould and Kolb (1964) as "the belief in the existence of a separable soul-entity, potentially distinct and apart from any concrete embodiment in a living individual or material organism." This description can be traced to Tylor, the noted anthropologist who originated the concept of animism. In contrast to this description is the view of the anthropologist Marett, who coined the term *animatism*. Animatism refers to the belief in the animation of natural objects by some impersonal force, such as the Polynesian idea of *mana*. It seems apparent that Piaget's (1972) conception of animism is substantially more in line with Marett's animatism than with animism as defined by Tylor.

A number of investigators of animism within non-Western cultures found that the subjects drew sharp distinctions among the various denotations and connotations of the concept of being "alive." For example, Dennis (1943), in his early studies with the Hopi, found that such things as rivers, fire, and the wind are "alive" in one sense, but *not* in the same sense in which people are alive. The Hopi language, in fact, possesses specific words that sharply distinguish this difference in meaning. Working in West Africa, Jahoda (1958) discovered that certain common objects have two different names. One name for such an object was reserved for ordinary, everyday use, while the other name was used when the object was part of a traditional story or myth—in the latter case the object was endowed with qualities characteristic of living things. The ready availability of certain kinds of terms and their precise meaning was thought to be crucial for the study of animism by Mead (1932), who worked on this topic among the Manus.

In light of the above differences in definition, one needs to begin cleaning away the conceptual bush before embarking on a trail toward an understanding of animism. With this viewpoint we began our study of animistic cognition among rural Hawaiian children and observed that animistic stories in collected myths of the Islands (for example, Beckwith, 1970; Westervelt, 1963; Kalakaua, 1972) were repeated by contemporary Hawaiians. We examined the daily field notes of anthropology students who had worked on a variety of topics for more than 3 years among our subject population. We searched for evidence of *spontaneous* animistic or "superstitious" remarks by both adults and children, but such remarks are not easily elicited. Even in very rural areas, adult Hawaiians are cautious and sophisticated enough to shield their beliefs and comments on such matters from outsiders. Examination of the field notes revealed numerous instances of what could very loosely be called superstitions, but we found *no* animistic instances in the sense of attributing life or consciousness to inanimate objects either by adults or by children. The examination of the field notes was only a cursory beginning, undertaken to establish some indication of the contemporary conceptual background of our subject population.

Our quasi-experimental inquiry of animistic cognition was twofold. First, we conducted a series of three related investigations in which we asked the children simply to *name* some things that were alive and some things that were dead. Second, we conducted a Piagetian type study of causality of specific topics and phenomena culturally relevant to Hawaiian children. Except for the last study in our three investigations, all research was conducted in Pidgin (Hawaiian Islands dialect), a major dialect of English that shares many of the features of other Creole variants of English (Carr, 1972). All the children in our subject population were verbally skilled in Pidgin. We will first present the details and findings of our three related investigations and then present the outcome of our study of causality.

## INVESTIGATIONS ONE AND TWO: DISTINCTIONS BETWEEN "ALIVE" AND "DEAD"

### Subjects

All the children lived in a relatively isolated area located on the island of Hawaii and were predominantly Hawaiian in ancestry. The children were divided into 5 groups for each of the investigations. In the first 2 investigations, the ages of the 5 groups were: 4 to 5 years, 6 to 7 years, 8 to 9 years, 10 to 12 years, and 13 to 15 years. In the third investigation the children's ages corresponded to their grade levels, thus: kindergarten (5 years), first grade (6 years), third grade (8 years), fifth grade (10 years), and eighth grade (13 years). In the first investigation a total of 30 children participated, 6 for each of the 5 age groups. Twenty different children, divided in groups of 4, participated in the second investigation, and in the third investigation a total of 30 children participated.

## Procedure and Results

All three of the related investigations were conducted by a Hawaiian assistant who was fluent in both Pidgin and Standard English. The assistant, who was familiar to all the children, asked each child, in Pidgin, to tell her some things that are alive and some things that are dead, or *make* (the equivalent Hawaiian word). Each child's responses were tape-recorded and transcribed into Standard English by the assistant. The percentages of living and dead things (according to Piagetian definitions) reported by the children were calculated.

The first investigation revealed two major findings. First, when the children were asked to name things that were "alive," the majority responded with things corresponding to Piaget's Stage IV. The percentages for the five age levels were 33, 78, 63, 76, and 68. Thus, even children as young as 6 or 7 responded at least as well as the older children tested. According to Piaget (1972), this stage or level of attainment is not hypothesized to occur until about the age of 12. The second major finding was that when asked to name things that are dead, or *make*, many of the children responded with items that are alive. A developmental pattern emerged and is shown in Table 8–1.

**Table 8–1**  *Percentage of Items Reported When Asked to Provide Examples of* Make *(Deal) Things in Investigation I*

| AGE | "ALIVE" (STAGE IV) | MAKE (DEAD) |
|---|---|---|
| 4 to 5 years | 100.0 | — |
| 6 to 7 years | 92.3 | — |
| 8 to 9 years | 63.2 | 28.0 |
| 10 to 12 years | 56.8 | 30.0 |
| 13 to 15 years | 24.0 | 52.0 |

Note: Most rows do not sum to 100 percent since the small percentage of Stage I, II, and III responses are not shown in the table.

This table shows that as the children grow older, the percentage of "alive" Stage IV items they reported, when asked to name dead or *make* things, declined. A substantial part of this decline is reflected in the increase in the percentage of items reported as dead. Our surprising findings led us to question the basic procedure of our investigation. Interviews with a number of knowledgeable Hawaiians revealed an unexpected outcome.

Apparently, the words dead and *make* are not equivalent. In fact, the Hawaiian word *make* does not represent for these children, in any clear way, a permanent state such as death, but rather represents a possibility or potentiality of dying. The word *make* means for our sample something that is (or might be) alive, but will (or might) die at some unspecified time in the future. This is the way the word is currently used by the Hawaiian children in our sample, despite the fact that authoritative sources such as the respected *Hawaiian Dictionary* (Pukui and Elberg, 1971) and *Nana I Ke Kumu* (Pukui, Haertig, and Lee, 1972) define the word *make* as equivalent to the word dead.

With a new understanding of the word *make*, we focused our second investigation on what things the children would classify as dead. This was accomplished by conducting extensive interviews with many Hawaiians in an effort to obtain a clear and unambiguous set of instructions. The final set of instructions we arrived at was: "Can you tell me some things that are really dead? Can you tell me some things that have no life, or never have life?" The instructions were translated into Pidgin without using the word *make* and were used in our second investigation. As in the first investigation, the children also were asked, in Pidgin, to name "alive" things. Responses to the question "really dead" are shown in Table 8–2.

**Table 8–2**  *Percentage of Items Reported When Asked to Provide Examples of "Really Dead" Things in Investigation II*

| AGE | "ALIVE" (STAGE IV) | "REALLY DEAD" |
|---|---|---|
| 4 to 5 years | 100.0 | — |
| 6 to 7 years | 81.5 | 11.1 |
| 8 to 9 years | 71.1 | 28.9 |
| 10 to 12 years | 17.4 | 56.6 |
| 13 to 15 years | 7.7 | 76.9 |

*Note:* Most rows do not sum to 100 percent since the small percentage of Stage I, II, and III responses are not shown in the table.

## Discussion

Two major findings emerged from the second investigation. First, the revised set of instructions significantly affected the pattern of responses of the two older age groups. The percentages of alive Stage IV responses were 17.4 percent and 7.7 percent respectively, when the older children were asked to name dead things. However, the change in instructions had practically no effect on the performance of the three younger age groups. One possible interpretation of this finding is that the younger Hawaiian children possess a different comprehension of death (or what is dead) than children in the continental United States. The work of Nagy (1959) has shown that the concept of "dead" in the continental United States is generally understood by the age of about 8. It is not until Hawaiian children reach the age of about 11 and have had extensive exposure to formal classroom schooling do they begin to show a "Western" understanding of what is dead.

The second major finding of our second investigation was the very high rate of Stage IV responses when the children were asked to name things that were "alive." Even the very young children performed at a level much earlier in age than the levels stipulated by Piaget. This result is supported by the work of Kastenbaum and Aisenberg (1972), who concluded that children abandon 'animistic' thinking somewhat earlier than Piaget proposed. The differences between our results and those of Piaget (1972) could perhaps be attributed to the fact that different procedures were used. Also, Piaget was primarily interested in causality, while our study initially sought only to elicit items regarding what is alive and what is dead.

A third investigation was performed in which the context was changed by using Standard English and a different set of instructions.

# THE THIRD INVESTIGATION:
# A CHANGE IN LANGUAGE

## Procedure and Results

Since the actual instructions that were used best illustrate the procedure, the instructions will be given in full. The Hawaiian word *haole* refers to a Caucasian person.

> Hello. We are going to play a little game. Let's make believe that I am a *haole* teacher from the Mainland. I have just moved to Hawaii from the Mainland. Let's make believe that I am a *haole* teacher and that I know nothing about Hawaii, so we can't talk in Pidgin. I am going to ask you two questions. First, I want you to tell me some things that are alive. And remember that we are making believe that I am a *haole* teacher. OK. That's very good. Now I want you to tell me some things that are dead. Things that are *not* alive. And remember that we are making believe that I am a *haole* teacher. OK.

All the children's responses were tape-recorded and then transcribed. The same measures of performance were used as in the two previous investigations. The responses of the children who were asked to name "alive" things are shown in Table 8–3.

The most striking feature of the data is the extremely high percentage of Stage IV items that the children produced. In fact, the highest percentages were obtained for the younger children. Also shown in Table 8–3 are the percentages of plant-type responses (flower, tree, and so on) the children gave. A separate category is necessary since such items are not classifiable according to Piaget's four stages. It is interesting to note that the category of plants arose when the investigation was conducted in Standard English, although we have no ready explanation for this development.

The responses of the children who were asked to name dead things are shown in Table 8–4.

## Discussion

The intent of the third investigation was to determine if a change in the context and the dialect of experimentation would alter the pattern of apparent animistic beliefs of rural Hawaiian children. Comparing the data of the present investigation to the first two investigations, we observe that the effects of changing the context and the dialect were primarily restricted to the older grade levels. The revised set of Pidgin instructions was substantially more effective, and the responses were more similar to what would be obtained with Mainland children. An important finding of the third investigation, however, was that it replicated the finding of the Pidgin investigations: when asked to name things that are alive, the rural Hawaiian children predominantly named items consistent with Piaget's Stage IV.

The overall results of our three investigations yielded a pattern of animistic thinking by rural Hawaiian children that differed sharply from

**Table 8–3**  *Percentage of Items Reported When Asked to Provide Examples of "Alive" Things in Investigation III*

| AGE | "ALIVE" STAGE IV | PLANTS |
|-----|------------------|--------|
| 5 years | 91.4 | 6.9 |
| 6 years | 98.5 | — |
| 8 years | 91.3 | 8.7 |
| 10 years | 72.5 | 24.6 |
| 13 years | 66.0 | 9.4 |

*Note:* Most rows do not sum to 100 percent since the very small percentage of Stage I, II, and III responses are not shown in the table.

the developmental sequence obtained by Piaget. As indicated earlier, however, the disparity in findings may be attributable at least in part to procedural differences. Piaget's investigative procedure used his well-known clinical method, while our approach simply elicited examples of alive and dead items in a direct manner. Given the fact that such different procedures were used, it seemed imperative that we investigate animistic thinking using a procedure that closely approximated Piaget's. We then would be in a much better position to attempt to resolve the disparity between our findings and those of Piaget. We limited our investigation primarily to topics that were culturally relevant to our subject population. Hence we focused on some specific culturally relevant topics such as Hawaiian canoes, waves, tides, and lava.

## A CULTURALLY SPECIFIC INVESTIGATION

### Subjects and Procedures

A total of 22 previously untested children of predominantly Hawaiian ancestry participated in the present study. There were 5 first-graders, 7 third-graders, 5 fifth-graders, and 5 seventh-graders. The ages were respectively, 6, 8, 10, and 13 years. The children were tested individually after a lengthy warm-up period by a Hawaiian assistant using Pidgin dialect and by one of the authors. At the beginning of testing all of the children, save for one first-grader, appeared relaxed and eager to participate.

A large glass bowl of water was placed before the child, who was presented with a small (5-inch) authentic replica of a Hawaiian fishing

**Table 8–4**  *Percentage of Items Reported When Asked to Provide Examples of "Dead"
Things in Investigation III*

| AGE | "ALIVE" STAGE IV | "DEAD" |
|---|---|---|
| 5 years | 91.2 | 7.1 |
| 6 years | 58.5 | 18.9 |
| 8 years | 80.9 | 17.6 |
| 10 years | 49.4 | 39.5 |
| 13 years | 54.6 | 40.9 |

*Note:* None of the rows sum to 100 percent since the very small percentage of Stage I, II,
and III responses are not shown in the table.

canoe. The canoe was complete with an outrigger (*ama* in Hawaiian)
connected to the canoe with two metal strips (*lona* in Hawaiian). The
child first was allowed to handle the canoe and then was asked whether
the canoe would "stay on top" or "go to the bottom" if it were placed on
the water. The child was also asked to justify the answer. The canoe was
then carefully placed on the water and the child was asked to explain the
result and to justify the explanation.

Since almost all of the children had extensive direct experience with
tides and waves, the child was then asked about the cause of tides. He
or she was also asked whether the tide "knows" or does not "know"
when it is coming in or going out. The child then was asked what makes
the waves, along with the question of whether a wave "knows" when it
hits the shore and breaks. In all cases the child had to justify the answers.

Finally, the child was allowed to handle a small fist-sized piece of lava
rock and a small sharp knife with a very fine point. The child first was
asked whether the lava rock was "alive" or "dead" and then was asked
whether the lava rock would "feel" the prick of the sharp knife. The child
had to justify his or her response.

## Results and Discussion

Three caveats must precede the presentation of our findings. First, despite repeated and patient coaxing by the investigators, some children
steadfastly justified their responses with a simple "I don't know," or
variations of the phrase "That's the way it is." Second, the use of the
clinical method, and the verbal protocols it elicits, does not produce
easily quantifiable data that lend themselves to unambiguous analyses.
Finally, we must view our findings with some degree of caution since,
due to the limited availability of subjects, a comparatively small number
of children were tested.

*The floating of boats*

This topic is particularly relevant since the children in our sample are quite familiar with boats and fishing activities. The boat with which they have extensive direct experience is the modern Hawaiian outrigger canoe. This canoe is identical to those used by Hawaiian fishermen in antiquity save for the fact that today the stern is squared off and an outboard motor is attached. Piaget (1972) described four stages in the child's development of understanding of how boats float. They are: Stage I, in which the child (less than 5 years old) explains floating in terms of some moral necessity; Stage II (closely linked to Stage I), in which the child (5 to 6 years old) explains floating by equating the heaviness (weight) of the boat with strength—the boat is stronger than the water and "pushes" it down; Stage III, in which, as Piaget puts it, the 7-to-8-year-old child's understanding involves a struggle between the weight of the boat and the weight of the water; and Stage IV, in which the child (about 9 years old) mentions that the wood is lighter than the water and approaches the concepts of density and the displacement of water.

With the first-graders and four children from the higher grades, we found it nearly impossible to make an assignment to one of Piaget's stages. Almost all the children in our sample, save for four third-graders and one fifth-grader, explained the capacity or ability of the canoe to float in terms of either one or two structural features of the Hawaiian canoe. That is, the bulk of the children said that the canoe floated because of the *ama*, the outrigger connected to the body of the canoe by means of the two poles called *lona*. The remaining children in this category claimed that the canoe floated because of the *lona*. One first grader, four third-graders, and one fifth-grader could give no reason why the canoe floated, despite repeated coaxing and some suggesting by the investigators. Not one child in our sample stated that a Hawaiian canoe floated because of the outboard motor that is very commonly attached to the stern. This is important since many children in Piaget's investigations said that flotation was due to a motor (engine) or the movement of oars. It would appear that the real-life experiences of the children with Hawaiian canoes played a strong role in shaping their understanding of how boats float.

*Tides*

Three of the first-graders said that the tide "knows" only when it is coming in. Another said it "knows" when it is coming in and going out. Yet another said the tide doesn't "know" since it has "no brain." Five of the third-graders stated that the tide "knows" when it comes in and out, while two others said the tide doesn't know when it is "high or low."

Among the fifth-graders, three children said the tide "knows" when it comes in or out ("comes high or low"). One child steadfastly refused to answer, and one child said the tide does not know when it comes in or out since "you don't know when the tide will come up or not." Among the seventh-graders, three children claimed the tide doesn't know when it comes in or out, and one of them justified his answer by stating that the "tide don't know where land is, so the water just bring the tide." The two remaining children claimed that the tide does know when it is high or low. The children who attributed some quality of consciousness to tides were about evenly divided between those who could give no reason and those who justified their belief primarily on the basis of the power or efficacy of the tides to either "move the stones" (pebbles on the beach), "throw a rock" or "pound the ground."

*Waves*

Piaget (1972) described three stages in the child's development of understanding regarding the causality of waves. At Stage I, 4-to-5-year-olds see waves as caused by animistic and artificialist forces (people, man, and the like); they can also be caused by oars, movement, and water. At Stage III, 5-to-8-year-olds see waves as caused primarily by the wind—but, paradoxically, the waves are seen as causing the wind. At Stage III, 9-year-olds see waves as caused by the wind and allegedly understand the sophisticated concept that waves have no movement of their own, but rather are "energy" or "force" propagated through the water in a wave form. The three stages are listed here not with an eye toward a comparison of our findings with those of Piaget, but rather as an indication that the stages may not be applicable to our subject population due to strong cultural and experiential factors. Piaget investigated the causality of comparatively docile Lake Geneva waves, while the children in our sample experience substantial ocean waves that break violently on jagged rocks close to their homes. In fact, the area in which the children live was nearly destroyed by tidal waves on several recent occasions. Although large waves are viewed with some degree of trepidation, many of the children in our sample engage in surfing and hence view waves as a long-standing cultural source of recreation.

In terms of animistic beliefs we found the following: except for one first-grader and one third-grader, all the children in the first three grade levels said that a wave "knows" when it hits the beach, and all but one of the seventh-graders said that a wave does *not* "know" when it hits the beach. It would appear that the Hawaiian children up to ages of about

10 or 11 attribute some form of consciousness to waves. When pressed for a justification of how (or why) a wave "knows" when it hits the beach, however, the first-, the third-, and the majority of the fifth-graders could give no reason despite considerable coaxing, although several children in the latter group said that waves are alive.

*Lava*

Before each child was asked whether a piece of lava rock would "feel" the sharp point of a small knife, they were asked whether the rock was "alive" or "dead." Among the first-graders, three children said it was alive, one child said it was dead, and one child said she didn't know what a lava rock was. Among the third-graders, four children said it was alive, two children said it was dead, and one child couldn't decide whether it was alive or dead. Among the fifth-graders, only one child said the rock was dead while all the other children claimed that it was alive. Finally, three seventh-graders said that the rock was alive while two children claimed that it was dead.

We expected that the children who said the lava rock was alive would also say that the rock would feel the point of the knife, and, conversely, that those children who said the rock was dead would say that it would not feel the knife. To our surprise, this expectation did not hold up in all cases. Of the three first-graders who said the rock was alive, two said it would feel the knife but one said that it would not. The young girl who didn't know what a lava rock was said that it would not feel the knife, but the one first-grader who said the rock was dead claimed that the rock would still feel the knife. Despite repeated coaxing and prompting, none of the first-graders could explain in what way the rock was alive or dead, nor could they say why they believed the rock would or would not feel the knife.

All four of the third-graders who said the rock was alive said it would feel the knife, while one child who said it was dead didn't know if it would feel the knife. But the other third-grader who said the rock was dead insisted that it would still feel the knife. The remaining third-grader who couldn't decide if the rock was alive or dead also couldn't decide whether it would feel the knife. We found that the children who said the rock was dead (or couldn't decide if it was dead or alive) could give no reason for their belief. Of the four children who said the rock was alive, two said they couldn't explain it, one claimed that the lava rock was alive, because it derived "life from the mountain," while the remaining child said it was alive "only if can move." This last justification is very important, since ethnographic investigations have revealed that ancient Hawaiians apparently believed that lava rocks not only moved of their own accord but grew as well.

Two of the fifth-graders stated that lava was alive because of Pele, the ancient Hawaiian volcano goddess. While both of these children said that the lava rock was alive, and one claimed that it would not feel the knife "cause it not alive" and the other child said it would feel the knife since Pele was still in the rock! Two other children who attributed life to lava indicated that this was due to volcanic activity. One child said that the "volcano erupts and lava get hot," while the other child simply said "'cause it erupts." Importantly, both of these children stated that the rock was dead and would not feel the knife since it was "broken off from alive rocks," and it would be alive "only if it move." Except for the lone fifth-grader who said that a lava rock was not alive"'cause it dead," it would appear that old Hawaiian cultural beliefs as well as some sort of volcanic activity were influential in shaping the animistic conceptions of the fifth-graders.

Of the three seventh-graders who attributed life to lava and lava rocks, one child said it was due to Pele, another said "cause the thing never be dead," and the last qualified his belief by saying that lava was alive "only when hot." Despite their belief that lava was alive, all of these children claimed that the lava rock would *not* feel the knife and two children apparently contradicted themselves and said it was because the rock was dead ("it's hard"; "it has no legs"). The two seventh-graders who said that the lava rock was dead qualified their beliefs by claiming that it actually was alive prior to becoming "hard"; or, as one child said, the rock was dead "only after it cools." The seventh-graders' responses not only show some influence of cultural beliefs on their conceptions of animism, but also indicate that heat and movement due to volcanic activity play key roles in their understanding as well.

## GENERAL DISCUSSION

Quite apart from specific cultural examples, Piaget's notion that the child progresses chronologically from an all-embracing life-attribution to a naturalistic phase in which life is attributed only to plants and animals has received criticism in the literature. The criticism revolves around the fact that while children may attribute life to inanimate objects, this fact does not of itself necessarily suggest a kind of thinking qualitatively different from that of adults (Klingberg, 1957; Klingensmith, 1953; Huang and

Lee, 1945). Concepts of animism among children have encountered difficulties of interpretation. For example, Looft (1974), in studying the concept of animism among 7-year-olds in a U.S. midwestern city, found that there was an incomplete and confused understanding of concept of "living." Also, in a study of first-grade children (Berzonsky, 1973), it was noted that the animism factor is quite specific to direct questioning about life-attribution, and is relatively independent of operational thought, conceptions of physical causality in general, and Piagetian-type problem solving.

Most psychological research of childhood animism omits background or cultural knowledge of the kind that we are interested in here and notably omits or blurs the traditional anthropological distinction between animism and animatism discussed previously. This is especially true in the case of Piaget's four-stage theoretical model.

Considering the first three of our investigations, one might infer that the prevailing awareness of encompassing life in the form of animals, people, and plants among Hawaiian children is perhaps so strong as to eclipse the usual distinction between living and dead. It also tends to eclipse the kinds of distinctions that Piaget makes with his Stages II and III (both based on movement). However, there are some consistencies in the data: as we reach the higher age levels, there is an approximation to data found in studies of children in the continental United States. Also, when we clarified the concept of what *dead* means in the second investigation, we obtained a clear decrease with age of animal and people responses, and a clear increase of "dead" things. Nevertheless, although these Stage IV (alive) responses decrease with the "really dead" question, they are very high through age 9, and drop off sharply in the 10-to-12-year-age range. One plausible conclusion we can make is that for these Hawaiian children, the distinction of living versus dead tends to become firm at about the age of 11 or 12.

Turning to the findings of our investigation of causality regarding specific cultural topics, we find that a tentative observation can be made. Whether the topic was floating boats, waves, tides, or lava, we encountered a substantial amount of recalcitrance on the part of the children (particularly in the younger age groups) to supply verbal justifications for their beliefs. Despite this verbal reluctance, however, a general theme in the verbal protocols was detected. The theme revolved around the strong influence of cultural and experiental factors that affected the children's causal thinking. In the case of boats, many children singled out the structural features of the canoe and totally omitted any reference to a motor or engine, a pattern of justification that differs sharply from

Piaget's (1971) investigations. The verbalizations regarding tides and waves also tended to indicate the influence of experiential factors. The clearest evidence for the influence of cultural beliefs on animistic thinking was seen in the children's conceptions regarding the living–dead dichotomy of lava. A number of children even stated that the living aspect of lava was directly attributable to a traditional Hawaiian goddess.

Certainly, any investigation of animistic cognition would have to incorporate the cultural and experientially based beliefs of the population studied. To exclude these important factors would be to exclude powerful influences that underlie, and contribute to, children's conception and understanding of the world around them.

# 9

# Cognitive Aspects of Informal Education

*Patricia Greenfield\**
*Jean Lave*

## INFORMAL AND FORMAL EDUCATION COMPARED

In recent years anthropologists and cognitive psychologists have turned up as associates in the study of "informal education" because of a common interest in culture and its relation to cognition. In the field of psychology (as in the culture at large) the terms *school* and *formal education* long served as descriptors of those institutions that we think of as "education." But as anthropologists and psychologists expanded their research to include other cultures, the terms that were adequate in this culture were not appropriate descriptions of educational institutions in other cultures.

---
*This paper was an equal collaboration. A coin flip determined the order of the author's names.

Anthropologists have argued that all varieties of educational activities should be included in the educational domain, including much more than formal schooling. By this view, for example, apprenticeship to learn a craft or become a master navigator, is part of education. Learning to play pool by hanging around the pool room and practicing is part of education. Learning to sew, to play games, and even to master basic self-management skills in early childhood are informal educational experiences. Formal education includes other kinds of schools besides Western schools, including bush schools, Quranic schools and Sunday schools.

"Formal education" and "informal education," considered as two poles in a typology, have opposite characteristics. Our analysis draws on Lave (no date), Fortes (1938), Mead (for example, 1928, 1930, 1943), Cohen (1971), and Scribner and Cole (1973). The dichotomy shown in Table 9–1 has served a useful role in expanding our conceptualization of education beyond the boundaries of our own culture. But the distinction is an idealized one. Too often the dichotomy has been applied as if all forms of education in a culture could be described by one term—"culture x has informal education." But this is clearly overgeneralization. For example, in the Vai culture in Liberia, forms of education include Western-style schools, bush schools, Quranic schools, apprenticeship, training to farm, and tutorial transmission of a syllabic script. This and other examples also make it clear that educational formality is more a continuum than a pair of opposites. In addition, all societies in the world provide several different types of education to their members, and these types differ in how formal they are.

Let us contrast examples of formal and informal education from American culture. Formal schools in this culture are highly institutionalized: schooling takes place in special buildings, at times that take precedence over other activities and is conducted by special personnel, specially trained. Training is an end in itself—one learns to read, write, and do arithmetic in order to know how to read, write, and do arithmetic. The curriculum and principles for teaching are explicit and quite highly systematized.

In contrast, learning to cook takes place in the kitchen, a space designated for cooking activities but not explicitly for educational ones. The person who teaches cooking is probably doing so because he or she is a parent or older sibling, not because of prior attendance at a cooking school. The purpose of learning to cook is to be able to contribute to the family welfare, or to one's own. A person may learn by waiting expectantly in the kitchen when hungry, watching the cook of the day, and helping out by chopping things or setting the table. What is learned is

**Table 9–1**  *Some Idealized Characteristics of Informal and Formal Education*

| INFORMAL EDUCATION | FORMAL EDUCATION |
| --- | --- |
| 1. Embedded in daily life activities. | 1. Set apart from the context of everyday life. |
| 2. Learner is responsible for obtaining knowledge and skill. | 2. Teacher is responsible for imparting knowledge and skill. |
| 3. Personal; relatives are appropriate teachers. | 3. Impersonal; teachers should not be relatives. |
| 4. Little or no explicit pedagogy or curriculum. | 4. Explicit pedagogy and curriculum. |
| 5. Maintenance of continuity and tradition are valued. | 5. Change and discontinuity are valued. |
| 6. Learning by observation and imitation. | 6. Learning by verbal interchange, questioning. |
| 7. Teaching by demonstration. | 7. Teaching by verbal presentation of general principles. |
| 8. Motivated by social contribution of novices and their participation in adult sphere. | 8. Less strong social motivation. |

probably as much influenced by menu plans and grocery specials as by considerations of which step or stage the apprentice cook is currently at. Also in this culture, people do not sit around at parties or at work discussing how to teach cooking.

Certain consequences should follow from these different sets of circumstances, according to the formal–informal analysis. When something is learned informally, the balance of responsibility for the transmission of knowledge is apparently tipped in the direction of the learner: There is little formal teaching, as learning is a by-product of activity that is primarily aimed at meal preparation. But the learner in informal learning situations is likely to be highly motivated, for several reasons. For one thing, all women, and more recently many men, in American culture are expected to know how to cook. If it is the learner's assumption, shared with relatives, friends, and neighbors, that the learner will of course learn $x$, the learner is likely to be highly motivated to learn, or at least not inhibited by choices, doubts, or questions about whether learning $x$ is worthwhile.

A second source of motivation is the close relationship you are likely to have with your teacher, and the fact that learning often occurs in the context of a one-to-one interaction. A third source of motivation is the social contribution that learners make in the course of learning. In the cooking example, cutting up the onions that go into the stew is a genuine contribution to the family dinner. In contrast, learning a multiplication table is not going to have immediate practical consequences for anybody. All the points made here about cooking in this culture have been made by anthropologists concerned with informal learning in other cultures.

One further contrast made by anthropologists is between culture transmission centered around the preservation of tradition and culture transmission oriented toward change and innovation. This is a very complex issue. If the subject matter is strongly valued and part of cultural tradition, we assume that great emphasis will be placed on exact learning of what is being taught, not on teaching the child to develop novel examples or new interpretations of old ideas. For example, we don't encourage children in Sunday school to make up new Bible-like stories or offer novel interpretations of them. Formal education in Western schools not only teaches new ways of doing things, but may also encourage cultural discontinuity and change because, like all other forms of education, it reflects cultural values.

The effects of "formalness" must be disentangled from the effects of cultural values. To do so, one must search for formal education in the context of traditional values or informal education in a cultural context that fosters change.

Anthropologists, and also psychologists, have taken the view that education in small, farming–craft cultures is mainly informal while education in large industrial cultures is mainly formal. The cooking example, above, illustrates the existence of informal education in a large industrial culture. Anthropologists and psychologists have often assumed that formal Western schools, when exported to countries where members of small societies can attend them, reflect Western values concerning tradition, change, and educational practices. But Gay and Cole (1967), as well as Erchak (1977), question this assumption, suggesting that values taught in Liberian schools may differ from those taught in American schools. Thus a value taught to Kpelle children in Liberia in informal educational situations—respect for authority—is also taught in school in that society. In parallel fashion, informal education in industrial countries may well differ from informal education in small farming–craft cultures in manifesting characteristics of school-based learning. It is our view that more empirical research needs to be done to establish the characteristics of each educational situation.

# EDUCATIONAL PROCESSES AND
# THEIR COGNITIVE CONSEQUENCES

Hypotheses about the impact of the two idealized poles of educational formality on cognitive skills have focused on the role of teaching–learning techniques in shaping cognitive skills and on the role of learner motivation. Among teaching–learning techniques, the role of language in instruction and learning has received special emphasis.

We know very little about the diverse educational experiences that are supposed to lead children to different approaches to cognitive tasks. One clear indicator of our ignorance is the practice of contrasting schooled to nonschooled subjects in experiments. "Nonschooled" covers a variety of types of education of different degrees of formality for different subjects, but these types are generally not specified. The picture produced by experimental investigation is one in which schooled experimental subjects in cultures around the world are usually more successful than unschooled subjects on experimental tasks. In general, subjects who have been to school are more likely to generalize from one experimental problem to the next and more likely to formulate general rules to explain their answers (Scribner and Cole, 1973).

## Learner Motivation and Instructional Techniques

These positive effects of formal schooling are especially interesting since, in comparisons of the idealized modes of teaching, informal learning and teaching strategies look much more effective than formal ones. One commonly accepted rule of good education is that active learning is more successful than passive learning. Anthropologists have documented cooperation and participation as of great importance in informal learning (for example, Fortes, 1938; Hogbin, 1946; Read, 1960). If cooperative participation is a major part of the learning process, informal education should have strong effects. Participation in daily activities that involve use of skills is both a good teaching–learning technique and highly motivating to the learner. Such opportunities are, however, rare in school. Thus it is quite puzzling why informal education doesn't appear to have more powerful effects than formal education on cognitive performances in experimental contexts.

The apparent superiority of school-based performances is to some extent an artifact of cross-cultural experimental design (Cole, Sharp, and

Lave, 1976). Cole and colleagues argue that the tasks used in cross-cultural research on the effects of schooling tend to be drawn from Binet and others, who were seeking tasks that would be good predictors of school performance. Thus school children will perform better on these tasks as a result of their greater familiarity with them, not because school is a more effective form of education.

On the other hand, Scribner and Cole's (1978) research among the Vai in Liberia showed that literacy acquired in a Western-style school produced skilled performance on a wider variety of tasks, including unfamiliar ones, than literacy acquired either informally or in a Quranic school. The problem of course is to distinguish between two sources of skilled performance: on the one hand, schooling as a social institution, and on the other, literacy learning in school.

This research opens the possibility that differences in performance are due to differences in teaching and learning techniques. A study by Kaye and Giannino (1978), focusing on the strengths and weaknesses of imitative and observational learning, illustrates the possibility. Their study compared three methods of teaching 8-year-old boys and adult males how to open a puzzle box: trial and error, verbal shaping ("you're getting warmer/colder"), and simple demonstration. The box opened when the subject pushed a certain button on each side. A transfer task involved an identical-looking box that opened when the subject pushed a button on the front. The demonstration–observation method produced the most effective original learning but the least successful transfer to a new situation. In other words, successful imitation of a demonstration led to perseveration of the method even where it was ineffective. Thus education that relies heavily on observation and imitation by the learner may be the most effective way to teach a given task but the least effective for transfer to a new task. Trial-and-error learning, with or without verbal shaping, may have the opposite pattern of strengths and weaknesses.

## The Role of Language

Earlier thinking about the instructional role of language has tended to treat formal and informal education as dichotomous. On the one hand, people have argued for the special importance of verbal channels of communication in schools (for example, Bruner, 1964). Others have emphasized the comparative lack of verbal instruction and verbal learning in informal educational settings (for example, Cazden and John, 1971). Let us consider this second point here, for the analysis of interaction in school is beyond the scope of this chapter. Informal learning is supposed to involve demonstration by the teacher and observation by the learner, followed by cooperative participation. This method is possible because the learner has ready access to situations in which skilled adults are carrying out the activities being learned. With such intimate knowledge of what is to be learned, the rationale goes, teachers need provide little or no verbal explanation or direction in order for the child to understand.

Before reaching a general conclusion about the role of verbalization in informal education, it is necessary to separate out different formal and functional types of speech acts. It is also necessary to consider learner and teacher separately in approaching this question.

Commands seem to be important in informal education in pastoral and agricultural societies where children perform important economic tasks at a young age (Munroe and Munroe, 1972, 1975; Whiting and Whiting, 1975; Kirk, 1976; Harkness and Super, 1977). Positive commands become relatively rarer in the city, where the opportunities for children to perform important household chores decline (Graves, 1968). Often present with frequent commands in such societies is the high value placed on obedience (LeVine, 1963). In terms of language skills, obeying commands requires the development of comprehension rather than production skills, and may in fact be antithetical to an emphasis on self-expression (Harkness and Super, 1977). That is, verbal expression in response to a command often means a delay in carrying it out or, even worse from the point of view of obedience, the questioning of the command itself.

Whereas the use of explanation on the part of teachers seems to vary within small traditional cultures, questioning on the part of learners seems quite rare (Erchak, 1977; Fortes, 1938; Goody, 1980; Hogbin, 1946; Peshkin, 1972). For example, Kpelle parents in Liberia consider the asking of questions by children to be a very negative trait (Erchak, 1977). In terms of actual practice, Goody observed a very low rate of question asking by novice Gonja weavers in Ghana. Goody concludes that questioning may carry an implied challenge to the person questioned and that such challenges would be highly inappropriate from a low-status person (child, novice) to a higher-status person (adult, master). It is not clear how the rate of asking questions by unschooled novice weavers compares to the rate among Gonja children who attend Western-style schools. There is, however, evidence from Kenya that when mothers shift toward modern values they place greater value on the active encouragement of their 2- and 3-year-old children's language development (Harkness, 1975). The traditional Kipsigis socialization process encourages silence when in the presence of older or higher-status people (Harkness and Super, 1977). The more modern mothers also tended to be less dominant with their young children, and the children of less dominant mothers asked significantly more questions (Harkness, 1975). Hence, personal modernization on the part of mothers may lead, indirectly, to more active questioning on the part of children. Harkness is careful to point out, however, that more modern values are not necessarily associated with more education in the particular Kipsigis community where she worked. However, in a Maya Indian community in highland Guatemala, Rogoff (1977) found that mothers with more education, as well as mothers with more modern practices, used verbalization more and demonstration less in teaching their 9-year-old children to make a tinker-toy construction.

School is presumed to use verbal communication as the primary mode of teacher–learner communication because school activities are supposedly removed from the context of daily activities, and hence much of what is being taught is not present in the learning situation. It is on these assumed differences in verbal communication that psychologists have focused attempts to account for experimental performance differences between schooled and nonschooled subjects. But why should the use of language make such an enormous difference in cognitive performance? First of all, teachers may model verbal explanatory activity and encourage it on the part of learners. Also, Bruner (1964) argues that removing the learning situation from the situations of daily life (which school is assumed to do) makes it possible for learning to become an end in itself rather than a means to accomplish some practical activity. This separation from practical activity means that learning takes place more exclusively through language and symbolic activity. Yet it is clear to psychologists as well as to anthropologists that the language used by normal adults in all cultures requires fully developed language capabilities. Realization of this state of affairs has led to reformulations of the contrast between the use of language in informal and formal education situations in terms of degree of use of different modes of communication.

Our view is that it is insufficient merely to consider the amount of language; it is also necessary to consider the structure of its use. For example, the results of an empirical study of the development of concept formation in Senegal (Greenfield, Reich, and Olver, 1966; Greenfield, 1972) show how language use can vary as a result of formal schooling. In response to questions about why they had selected certain pictures or objects as most alike, unschooled (illiterate) Wolof children gave verbal reasons that were less redundant with their nonverbal communication than their schooled (and literate) peers. (Both groups were interviewed in Wolof, their first language, not French, the language of the school.)

For example, if a typical unschooled child grouped all the red objects together, he or she might well answer the question "Why?" by pointing to each object and repeating the Wolof word for "red." The typical school child, even from the same village, might well also point to each object in turn, but would also redundantly express the pointing gestures in a linguistic form, saying *"This one* is red; *this one* is red" and so on. While this research was not able to separate literacy effects from schooling effects, it is clear that unschooled children formed communications involving the nonredundant integration of linguistic and nonverbal elements, while school children used language more, even when it was redundant with nonverbally presented information.

## THE IMPACT OF INFORMALLY LEARNED PRACTICAL SKILLS ON COGNITIVE PERFORMANCE

Having discussed theoretical speculations about the ways in which different forms of education might affect the development of cognitive skills, we turn now to empirical research on relations between education and skills. We will concentrate here on informally learned skills.

Piagetian conservation tasks form a major part of the literature on relations between informal learning and skill attainment. But these studies (for example, Price-Williams, Gordon, and Ramirez 1967, 1969; Greenfield and Childs 1972, 1977; Adjei, 1977; Steinberg and Dunn, 1976; Harkness and Super, 1977; Durojaiye, 1972) investigate the effect of informally learned technical skills on performance in tasks that originated outside the cultures in question. There are very few studies in which a cognitive test has been generated from an analysis of a particular skill found in a given culture. The first such instance of this strategy occurs in Gay and Cole's (1967) research on the Kpelle of Liberia. Gay and Cole looked at the effect of rice farming, the central Kpelle subsistence activity for both men and women, on test performance in estimating quantities of rice. They compared illiterate Kpelle adults, Kpelle school children, American adults with little schooling, and American college graduate Peace Corps volunteers in training for service as teachers in Liberia. The illiterate Kpelle adults were by far the most accurate in their estimations, thus reflecting their extensive experience in measuring rice as it progresses in the cycle from farm to meal. Clearly, the cognitive test of rice estimation is closer in structure and materials to a frequently met technique in Kpelle life than the tests used in other studies. And the test superiority of the people who use this technique in everyday life is correspondingly greater than has been found in other studies. We take these findings as important guides for designing cross-cultural studies.

## Empirical Investigation of Zinacanteco Weavers

We began the work to be described here in order to test some of the prevailing ideas about the effects of informal learning on cognitive skills. And since much of the discussion revolves around the ability of different forms of education to produce generalized learning skills, both research efforts focused on the generalization of familiar skills to unfamiliar problems.

In Greenfield and Childs' (1977) work with girls learning to weave in an Indian village in Chiapas, Mexico, and Lave's (1977a, 1977b, no date) work on apprenticeship among tribal tailors in Liberia, we used very similar approaches. (This was no accident, since Lave drew on Greenfield and Childs' work in designing experiments in Liberia.) We both looked for subjects who displayed a range of school experience and a range of craft experience, and asked them to solve a set of problems that varied in degree of similarity to the situation in which they learned weaving or tailoring. The results were then analyzed to see whether skills used in weaving or tailoring tasks were used to solve unfamiliar problems.

Both of us found that it was necessary to spend many hours observing weavers or tailors at work, and both of us learned some of the craft skills ourselves before trying to design a series of problems that might appropriately tap both these learning experiences and the skills that might plausibly be expected to develop from them.

Greenfield and Childs worked in a highland Mayan village of Tzotzil-speaking Zinacanteco Indians near San Cristobal de las Casas in Chiapas, Mexico. With a population of about 8000, the Indians live in a typical Mayan settlement pattern: dispersed in small farming villages away from a central town, which is heavily populated only during the times of year when there are major religious festivals. These festivals are based on a syncretic religious practice combining Mayan and Catholic beliefs and rituals. The major crops are corn and beans, some raised for sale, and the major occupation is farming. Women do all the weaving, every adult woman being a competent producer of clothing. In all cases weaving is necessary to clothe one's family. Almost all clothing is hand woven, and weaving is therefore a frequent and important activity. Weaving is a sociable activity that takes place often in the late afternoon when other chores are done. Children thus have open access to weaving activities

**Figure 9–1**    *A Zinacanteco girl uses backstrap loom when first introduced to weaving.*

and observe a great deal of it. Weaving is carried out on a backstrap loom. One end of the loom is fastened to something rigid, such as a pole or tree, and the other end to the weaver, who maintains the tension in the warp threads by leaning back against the backstrap. By this process two types of cotton cloth are made, each with a different red-and-white striped pattern. In addition, a heavier type of cotton and wool cloth is made for wear in cold, rainy weather.

In Greenfield and Childs' sample, beginning weavers ranged from 8 to 11 years of age. Before they learn to weave they learn the simpler tasks of boiling warp threads and dyeing wool. After they learn to weave they still must learn to wind the warp threads and spin. By the time a Zinacanteco girl reaches the age of 13 or 14 she is able to do the work by herself.

To find out whether weavers can generalize their weaving skills to unfamiliar problems, Greenfield and Childs presented the weavers with a series of problems. Carefully designed sequences of problems are required in order to draw even tentative conclusions about subjects' abilities to apply skills learned in one situation to solve unfamiliar problems.

The researcher's first task, a complex one, is to design problems that gradually get more and more distant from the problem-solving require-

**Figure 9–2**    *The Zinacanteco woven patterns used in the experimental study.*

ments found in the everyday environment. Another difficult task in trying to assess cognitive consequences of everyday experiences experimentally is to characterize the cognitive skills used in the course of carrying out a given activity.

Experimental cognitive psychologists have recognized the importance of designing tasks that will minimize the variety of kinds of mental operations engaged by the task, so as to explore the cognitive characteristics of particular kinds of skills. Short-term memory or clustering in recall might be examples.* But we have chosen to focus on questions concerning the variety of skills brought to bear (or not) in the situations in which they are used in daily life, rather than on the nature of particular cognitive skills. It is partly this difference in research questions that led us to choose as the target skill "ability to generalize from familiar to unfamiliar problem-solving situations." This covers a large range of unspecified component skills rather than focusing on one of those skills. Greenfield and Childs' (1972, 1977) experiments with weavers in Chiapas, Mexico, illustrate this approach.

Greenfield and Childs presented the weavers with a series of pattern-

---

*Even tasks involving few cognitive operations can be influenced by education and other cultural factors. Wagner (1978) has interesting data from Morocco showing the impact of schooling, rural environment, and the occupation of rug selling on recognition memory for photographs of Oriental rugs (see also Chapter 5, this volume).

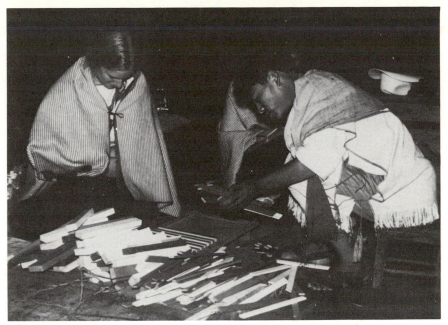

**Figure 9–3**     *Pattern representation task used with Zinacanteco children.*

representation and pattern-completion problems. First the weavers were asked to represent the familiar red-and-white striped cotton patterns of woven garments, but using wooden sticks in a frame to construct the designs. Pink and orange sticks were available, in addition to red and white. There were interesting differences between the female weavers and a group of Zinacanteco boys who did not know how to weave. By accurately representing the colors and the configurations of the two patterns, a substantial proportion of the girls used the sticks to represent the patterns as they are actually constructed with threads. In contrast, the boys generally used the sticks to represent the finished visual impression created by the garments at a distance, violating pattern configurations and even colors in the process. These results suggest that the weavers' knowledge of how woven patterns are constructed in Zinacantan affected their approach to representing the patterns in an unfamiliar medium.

Another interesting finding concerned the pattern-completion problems, where children were asked not just to represent familiar patterns but to continue novel patterns the experimenter had started. An example of this task might be a sequence of sticks that consisted of one white and one red, then one white and two reds. After two more repetitions, the subjects were asked to complete the pattern as it had been started. On these unfamiliar patterns, the nonweaving boys performed significantly better than the weaving girls, but there was not a significant difference between boys who had been to school and those who had not. (Because all Zinacanteco girls learn to weave, it was not possible to test a group of nonweaving girls of comparable age.) It suggests that the relevant educational experiences of the boys may be found in their preparation for the adult male role, a role that includes participation in the monetary economy beyond Zinacantan. This preparation includes trips to urban Mexican centers such as San Cristobal de las Casas and Tuxtla Gutierrez, where patterned fabric is not restricted to three major designs, as it is in Zinacantan. Thus boys have much greater opportunity than girls to observe varied cloth patterns, including the striped ones particularly pertinent to the experiment. The weavers' pattern skills do not seem to transfer to tasks involving novel, unfamiliar patterns. This fact is understandable when one considers that patterns are not among the things that Zinacantecos feel free to change or be innovative about.

But schooling did make a difference in representing the familiar woven patterns. The school boys, none of whom had weaving experience, resembled the weavers and differed from their unschooled age-mates: they too used the sticks as if they represented threads, maintaining the basic pattern configurations in their constructions. This was an unanticipated result, and we can only speculate about its cause. One possible explanation relates not to experience with patterns but to a more general skill: translation from one medium to another. The pattern-representation task differed from the continuations in requiring that a pattern existing in one medium (cloth) be represented in another (wood). It may be that Western schooling introduces this experience into an oral culture, for reading and writing involve translation between auditory and visual media.

In sum, in a situation quite different from the everyday context in which weaving takes place, that is, in a one-to-one relationship with an experimenter and using unfamiliar materials, the weavers are successful in generalizing their analytical skills in representing culturally defined woven patterns, a familiar task, but are not as successful as nonweavers in continuing novel patterns, an unfamiliar task. Since pattern continuation is in fact one type of pattern-representation task, this configuration of results suggests the possibility that generalization of an informally learned craft skill from everyday to new problem-solving situations is rather limited. On the other hand, it was also found that schooling, independent of weaving, had an influence on the pattern-representation task, perhaps because it involved translation from one medium to another. Here we see that more than one type of experience and more than one type of cognitive skill is relevant to a given task, a situation we shall meet again in Lave's data.

## Effects of Tailoring on Mathematical Skills

Lave conducted her study in the tailors' alley at the edge of the commercial district of Monrovia, the capital of Liberia. Here 250 master and apprentice tailors, most of them from the Vai and Gola tribes, ply their trade and learn their craft. After several months of observing in the shops, a set of four tasks was devised. The tasks were concerned with arithmetic skills. The problems the tailors were asked to solve ranged from very familiar to quite unfamiliar. The first task was to estimate the size, in inches, of the waistband of pairs of trousers, followed by size estimation of loops and strings, lengths of string, and finally sticks of wood. Some of the sizes were familiar ones, frequently encountered in the course of making trousers. Others were not customary sizes. It was hypothesized that the less familiar the materials (wood, string), configurations (straight lines instead of loops) and the sizes, the greater the generalization required and the more difficult the problems would be for the tailors.

The second task involved extrapolating an arithmetic function. The tailors associate certain hip and fly-length sizes with particular waistband sizes. In the second set of problems the tailors were asked to estimate the appropriate hip and fly-lengths, given a particular waistband size. The waistband sizes included several very familiar ones but also some very small and some extra large. Here the task was a familiar one, with content that varied from familiar to unfamiliar.

The third task involved arithmetic concepts. Tailors were asked to recognize and read numbers, identify a variety of units on a measuring tape (such as inches, yards, half- and quarter-yards) and do simple addition, subtraction, multiplication, and division problems. Some of these problems involved familiar questions and typical numbers encountered in tailoring work. Others were unfamiliar to tailors.

The fourth task was a proportions-matching task. On a 4" × 6" card was a drawing of a pair of trousers. (The drawing style was borrowed from a tailor who often drew pictures of trousers.) A line divided this portion of the card from the rest. On the other part of the card were three drawings of trousers. The figures were drawn so that only one matched the waist to length proportions of the stimulus figure. The object was to decide which figure was most similar in proportions to the

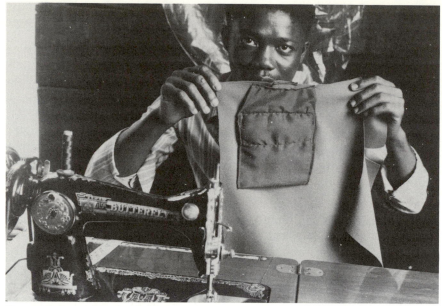

**Figure 9–4**    *A Liberian tailor.*

stimulus figure. Several demonstrations of the point and discussion with the tailors preceded the actual task. Three of the cards had drawings of trousers, and these were presumed to be most familiar to the tailors. Other cards had figures of squares, rectangles, triangles, trapezoids, and similar geometric figures.

Having decided on a framework for each experimental task, it was relatively easy to build sequences of problems that seemed on a priori grounds (and on the basis of months of observing and asking questions in tailor shops) to become progressively less familiar. It was also necessary, however, to consider the familiarity of the frameworks themselves, as well as the fact that many of the tailors and apprentices were going to school and had gone to school. To compare tailors with different amounts of schooling and different amounts of tailoring experience, it was also necessary to assess the familiarity of the experimental problems from the point of view of school problem-solving scenes as well as from the point of view of apprenticeship.

To assess the familiarity of problem frameworks, Lave first ranked the problems in terms of familiarity in the learning environment of the tailor shop, and then in terms of familiarity in the learning environment of school. Two of the tasks were very close to the form in which the same questions arise in the course of tailoring activity. Both the waistband

**Figure 9–5**    *A typical scene in a tailor quarter of Monrovia.*

estimation task and the extrapolation from waist size to hip and fly sizes
are challenge games played by the tailors themselves. One tailor finishes
a pair of trousers, tosses it to the master at the next machine and says,
"How big do you think it is?" The other master holds the trousers up
and makes a guess. The first master may disagree, and other tailors join
in to make their own guesses. Finally someone takes a tape measure and
finds out how big around the waistband actually is. As for hip and fly
extrapolations from waistband size, it is again the individual tailor who
has to make a guess and defend it on the basis of his own experience.
Neither estimation nor extrapolation is taught in Liberian grade schools.
Both of these tasks should be quite unfamiliar from the point of view of
school experiences.

The proportions-matching task is related to tailor work in some ways
but differs from it in others. First the similarities: Tailors make different
sizes of the same garment. They are likely to pay attention to proportions,
which usually should be invariant across garments of different sizes.
Therefore tailors ought to perform well on an experimental task that
involves noticing which two objects, irrespective of size, have the same
proportions. In particular, since they make lots of trousers, trousers
should be familiar content for tailors.

Now the differences: In the experimental task, pictures were drawn on
cards rather than using actual trousers as in the waistband estimation
task, or language, which is the customary medium of extrapolation

games. And the tailors were asked to choose which of three drawings with different proportions best matched a stimulus picture of a pair of trousers. Tailors do not routinely compare pairs of trousers to each other, examining their proportions. Nor are the tailors familiar with multiple-choice format. On the other hand, matching and multiple choice are characteristic school tasks, while comparing proportions is unfamiliar in the school context. In sum, from the point of view of tailoring, content is familiar and format unfamiliar, whereas the reverse is true from the point of view of school. Hence this task is relatively unfamiliar from both tailoring and school points of view.

In the fourth task, involving arithmetic operations, some problems were familiar from a tailoring point of view and others from a school point of view. This task involved some word problems, a very familiar format in school settings. On the other hand, some of the number-reading and doubling and halving problems involving waistbands and cuffs (circumference of trousers versus trousers laid flat on the table) were borrowed directly from tailors' questions to their apprentices. Within this frame, content was varied from typical trouser waist and cuff measurements to numbers approximately the same size, but ones that rarely come up in the course of making trousers.

Lave looked for frames in which the assumptions of the Vai and Gola tailors about the circumstances governing problem solving were approximately those to be encountered in the experimental situations. This is not to say that the experimental situation was thereby transformed into a native scene—far from it. But by "borrowing" situations from the daily activities of tailor shops and schools as the basis for testing the ability to apply past experience to a new problem, Lave hoped that the approximation to familiar scenes would be obvious to the tailors.

Statistical regression techniques were used to separate out the impact of tailoring experience (both specific tailoring skills and general tailoring experience) from the impact of school experience. The tailors and apprentices in the sample ranged from about 10 to about 40 years of age; from a few months of tailoring experience to 25 years; and from no schooling to 10 years of schooling.

The proportions-matching task, relatively unknown in either school or tailoring, was unaffected by either experience. The school-oriented arithmetic problems were affected by both tailoring experience and school experience, but more by the latter than the former. For tailoring-oriented arithmetic problems the reverse was true, and schooling contributed less than tailoring skills. For the estimation and extrapolation tasks, school had little or no effect and tailoring showed a major impact on the familiar problems; this effect decreased as the problem content (such as sizes and materials) became less familiar.

Conclusions from the research on tailors are two. First of all, when the experimental tasks are similar in form to the task that elicits those skills in daily settings, tailors and school pupils as well as weavers are able to bring their skills to bear on new problems and solve them successfully. Second, it appears that neither schooling nor tailoring skills generalize very far beyond the circumstances in which they are ordinarily applied. Thus, tailoring experience was not nearly as helpful in estimating the length of sticks of wood as in estimating the circumference of trouser waistbands. School, which had strong impact on word problems in arithmetic, had little impact on estimation, extrapolation, or proportions-matching tasks.

Tentatively, since there are few results on which to base conclusions, it seems that under some circumstances the ability to generalize cognitive skills to unfamiliar but related situations may be heavily constrained. It may well be that not only the familiarity of different task dimensions and problem-solving activity govern the ability to generalize, but also that integration of these dimensions in familiar ways is required.

The experimental work described in this chapter makes its contribution through exploring a little-used approach to comparative studies of the impact of educational experiences on cognitive skills. The more usual approach is to take tasks, most of which have been generated out of knowledge of school tasks and scenes, and administer them to people with different educational experiences. We have explored educational experiences other than school experiences and tried to devise tasks that were related to these other educational experiences in much the same way that most experimental tasks are relevant to school. The advantage of our strategy is that it allows us to directly assess some effects of non-school educational forms.

# A CLOSER LOOK AT TEACHING AND LEARNING

It is not sufficient to interpret experimental results in terms of idealized descriptions of formal and informal education. If we are going to establish valid connections between particular forms of education and particular kinds of cognitive skills, a necessary part of the enterprise is to build detailed descriptions of the relevant teaching and learning activities first.

Greenfield's work in collaboration with Childs, videotaping and analyz-ing instruction sessions between novice weavers and their teachers, is of special interest in this regard (Childs and Greenfield, 1980). They vid-eotaped 14 girls who varied from fairly expert to those who were starting their first weaving project.

## Informal Familiarity with Mature Practice Affects Initial Skill Level

Preliminary investigation of weaving activities revealed a marked contrast between novice weavers with different amounts of familiarity with the weaving process before they had tried it themselves. Greenfield found, in informal observation of a group of adult novice backstrap loom weavers in Cambridge, Massachusetts, who had not spent most of the afternoons of their lives in the company of weavers, that beginners were extremely inept. Zinacanteco girls not only observe weaving for years before doing it themselves, but also imitate weaving in play activities (Blanco and Chodorow, 1964; Cancian, 1974).

Not only have they had an opportunity to develop a concept of weaving techniques, they have also learned much about the finished product. In Nabenchauk, the Zinacanteco hamlet where Greenfield and Childs car-ried out their studies, girls frequently approached them to look closely at their Zinacanteco clothing. The girls' comments about the weaving and embroidery showed attention to details of construction so fine that they had escaped the notice of Greenfield and Childs until then. Thus Zinacanteco girls have an opportunity to develop a representation of the finished weaving products (although at what age this process starts is unknown). In contrast, the beginning adult weavers in Cambridge, lack-ing a preexisting representation of either method or finished product, had to use a trial-and-error approach to learning how to weave.

## Trial-and-Error Learning and Innovation

Novice weavers in Zinacantan displayed a much higher level of initial skill than those in Cambridge. Preexisting knowledge of "the right way" acquired through observation of expert models, plus help from the teacher when they encountered difficulties, allowed them to proceed in a relatively errorless fashion; that is, no evidence of a trial-and-error approach was observed. Kaye and Giannino's (1978) research led Green-field to hypothesize that trial-and-error learning may be associated with greater transfer of skill to new tasks than errorless learning. If so, then we have a possible explanation for the absence of transfer of pattern skill to novel patterns among Zinacanteco weavers: the original learning of the woven patterns was based on observational rather than trial-and-error learning. A further hypothesis is that trial-and-error learning is an educational hallmark of a weaving subculture that values innovation, for trial and error might pave the way for the discovery of new patterns and methods. This result would be intrinsic to the experimentation involved in the trial-and-error method.

We do not mean to minimize the role of cultural values in encouraging either innovation or conservation of tradition; such values are crucial. We are merely proposing that instructional strategies conform to these values and are one means by which societal values are actualized at the level of a concrete activity and its transmission from generation to generation.

The hypothesis of a connection between trial-and-error learning and innovation is further supported by two cultures in which weaving is important and in which pattern innovation is not only permitted but very much valued. One of these cultures, studied by Lisa Aronson, is the Ibo town of Akwete in eastern Nigeria. The other is, like Zinacantan, a Maya community, but is located in the highlands of Guatemala and was studied by Maria and James Loucky. Both sets of investigators suggest that girls learn to weave through the process of trial and error. Initially, miniature looms are set up, and the girls are given leftover scraps of material or grass to weave with. The nature of these materials supports the hypothesis that trial-and-error learning is only permitted in situations where it will not bring economic harm to the teacher. Later, when they start weaving real items on real looms, they are basically left alone—that is, there is no teacher hovering, waiting to intervene at the slightest sign of an error. Typically, the only people around are siblings who give advice but generally do not know how to weave themselves. Thus, in both Nigeria and Guatemala, weavers begin their craft by trial-and-error learning and finish by creating original designs.

In conclusion, the evidence available does indicate that cultural values promoting innovation are associated in the domain of weaving with the instructional technique of trial-and-error learning. Cultural values promoting the maintenance of tradition, in contrast, may be actualized in weaving instruction through observational learning.

## The Role of Scaffolding and Task Sequencing as Instructional Techniques

Educators have high regard for what is sometimes called "scaffolding" as an approach to instruction (Wood, Bruner, and Ross, 1976). Here the teacher designs instruction to fit the requirements of each learner, helping with the hard parts of the task, then backing off to let the learner do the parts that are within the range of his or her capabilities. Scaffolding closes the gap between task requirements and the skill level of the learner, thus creating what Hunt (1961) has called "the match." Yet effective instruction must operate in a "zone of proximal development," Vygotsky's (1977) term for the range of problems that learners cannot solve independently but can solve with the help of a teacher. If instruction is to push development forward, it cannot be limited to already acquired skills. Wood, Wood, and Middleton (no date) identify this "region of sensitivity" to instruction as lying in the gap between comprehension and production; the new skill component must be comprehensible although it has not yet been produced. This idea, applied to scaffolding, means that the teacher provides the minimum necessary scaffolding for the learner to produce new skill components that are understood but not yet performed. Wood, Wood, and Middleton have demonstrated experimentally that a scaffolding technique incorporating this pacing principle, which they call contingent instruction, is more effective in teaching 3- and 4-year-old children a difficult construction task than pure demonstration, pure verbal instruction, or alternation of demonstration and verbalization without reference to the learner's current skill level.

Analysis of the videotapes of Zinacanteco weaving shows that teaching and learning activity follow a scaffolding model in some respects. In the earliest stage of learning, the girls spend a bit more than half their time watching the teacher perform the weaving task. As they get more proficient, more and more of their interaction with the teacher is of a cooperative, participatory variety. Teacher intervention changes from taking over the weaving from the learner to participating cooperatively as learners gain more experience. Thus cooperative activity goes from 36 percent to 47 percent to 76 percent of total teacher intervention across levels of previous experience. And the amount of time the learner spends weaving independently goes from 7 percent for first-time weavers to 52 percent if the girl has already made one garment, to 58 percent if she has made two to four items, to 100 percent independent work for the expert. As the amount of cooperative participation and independent weaving goes up, the amount of observation, of course, goes down.

Since the major differences in the amount of teacher control of the weaving process are a function of previous weaving experience, and therefore of skill level, developmentally graded scaffolding seems intrinsic to the instructional process. Scaffolding means that the teacher provides just the amount of help required for the task to be successfully completed by the learner.

But there is another sort of developmental sequencing as well: providing easier tasks earlier in the learning process, so that the learner has a better chance of success even without teacher intervention. Thus items made in early stages of the weaving process are generally small, require few weaving cycles to complete, and require less strength on the part of the young weaver than larger garments assigned to the more experienced weavers.

Task sequencing seems to come into play wherever it is practical to introduce component skills in their order of difficulty. Thus the major processes of turning thread into finished garments are learned in roughly their order of difficulty. For example, Zinacanteco weavers learn to boil thread before learning to weave, but learn to weave before they learn to spin. This ordering is practical because each of these processes constitutes a separate task, with its own set of equipment, materials, and so on. Ordinarily only one of these processes would be carried out on a given day. These characteristics do not hold for the component parts of weaving itself, which are done in rapid succession to one set of materials on the same day. Because of these characteristics, it is important to learn to integrate the steps as well as learn each step in itself. It is therefore not surprising that within the process known as weaving, steps are introduced to the learner in the order that a mature practitioner carries them out, not according to order of difficulty.

Where some parts of a process are more difficult than others, the concept of scaffolding implies greater teacher intervention at the more difficult parts. In this way, task difficulty is always maintained within the ability range of the learner. Childs and Greenfield did find greater teacher intervention on the harder steps and less intervention on the easier ones. For instance, all teachers intervene more on the more difficult first cycle of weaving than on an easier later cycle.

It is interesting that among the tailors a similar two-level system of teaching exists. The major chunks of the process—cutting, sewing, and finishing—are learned from simplest first to most difficult last. This is the reverse of the order in which a mature practitioner carries out the tasks. But within each chunk, steps are taught and practiced in the order in which they will be carried out in mature practice, without regard to their relative difficulty.

It seems likely that there are conflicting pedagogical goals here. Both weavers and tailors demonstrate that they are quite capable of reordering the sequence of segments of mature practice to make them more accessible to novices. If they choose not to do so *within* a given chunk, it may well be because it is less practical and because the function of practice for the novice is to integrate component skills into a smooth sequence of interrelated steps. If the learner needs to learn how to carry out such sequences, then this learning is best served by practicing the correct sequence, even if it means initial difficulties for novice learners and perhaps a greater need for careful scaffolding activity on the part of the teacher. It would be interesting to know whether difficulty level is controlled within a chunk through scaffolding in Liberian tailoring as in Mexican weaving.

Anthropologists have claimed that in informal education the balance of responsibility for the transmission of knowledge is tipped in the direction of the learner because there is little formal teaching. The phenomenon of scaffolding reveals just the opposite. For teachers to follow an implicit rule of doing the minimum required for learners to be successful, they must exercise careful attention and thoughtful effort in judging when to step in and when to refrain from interfering. Maintaining a constant level of difficulty for the learner is clearly a technique that places responsibility on the teacher. Explicit pedagogical theory is not necessary in order for a teaching person to take responsibility for knowledge transmission. In fact, one adult Zinacanteco stated that Zinacanteco girls learn to weave "by themselves." If this woman is typical, the Zinacantecos have very systematic methods of instruction while placing no ideological emphasis on the teaching role.

## Another Look at the Role of Language

What about the role-of-language hypothesis? One interesting finding was that extrinsic verbal reinforcement (praise or blame) is essentially never used in this teaching–learning situation, which results in "no-failure" learning. Far more important than immediate extrinsic reinforcement is the broadly shared understanding of Zinacantecos that all normal women weave major items of clothing for their families. Childs and Greenfield's videotapes provide dramatic evidence that extrinsic verbal reinforcement is not necessary to produce learning in this situation.

Another finding has to do with the uses of verbal communication by both teacher and learner. The teachers do what appears to be a good deal of talking: On the average they produce five to six utterances per minute. The teacher gradually reduces the amount of talking as the girl gets more expert. There is other evidence that the teacher is fitting her instructions to the level of the learner. While there are few questions and explanations in the teacher's talk at any stage of learning, the proportions of commands and of statements, which make up most of the talk, shift as the learner becomes more adept. At the earlier stage about 75 percent of the teacher's utterances are commands, 25 percent statements. These proportions change to about 50–50 as the girl becomes more adept. The girl, on the other hand, does very little talking at any stage of the process, compared to her teacher. Childs and Greenfield compared the proportion of utterances made by the one girl with some schooling to another girl with the same amount of weaving experience, but no schooling. The girl who had some schooling did talk more—the school girl produced 11 percent of the talk between learner and teacher, as opposed to 3 percent by the comparable girl who had not been to school. Whether the effect of going to school is to directly teach verbal communication skills, whether it has the effect of raising the girl's status, or whether it changes the definition of a low-status role, or all three, is an open question.

Greenfield and Childs were able to test two specific hypotheses about the uses of language in informal instruction: these have to do with interaction between verbal and demonstration modes of teaching. The first hypothesis was that instructional redundancy across modes would go down as learners got more skillful. That is, combined visual demonstration and verbal instruction would be used in the early stages, and either demonstration (such as measuring the width of the warp threads) or verbal instruction (for example, "Don't put it in like that") would be sufficient at later stages, when the learner could already be presumed to have both knowledge and practice at weaving. The data strongly support the hypothesis. As the learner becomes more expert, the proportion of teacher-initiated interactions involving both verbal and nonverbal elements declines steadily. Thus while demonstration and verbal intervention both decrease as the learner gains skill, redundancy between the two also decreases.

The second hypothesis was that the weaving teachers, in this relatively informal teaching–learning situation, would be skilled users of language, and that they would adjust the specificity of their verbal output to meet situational demands. For instance, if the teacher is herself sitting within the loom and showing the girl how to weave, she can use gestures and actions to make a vague verbal statement informationally specific (for example, "Do it like this," accompanied by a demonstration). The same verbal behavior at a distance of 10 feet from the loom would convey no information because no demonstration would be possible. The data show that the specificity of the verbal component of teacher messages in fact goes up as the physical possibility of supplementing with nonverbal information goes down. Thus teachers do indeed adjust the specificity of their linguistic messages in sensitive accord with the requirements imposed by their distance from the learner and her weaving.

## SUMMARY AND CONCLUSIONS

From the perspective of the formal–informal theory of crucial differences between educational forms, we have covered a very wide range of variation in this chapter. The three major varieties of education that have been discussed range along a continuum of increasing formality: (1) weaving, where teaching and learning go on in the context of general-purpose family relationships in the course of daily activities in the household; (2) tailors' apprenticeship, where teaching and learning take place in the context of ongoing daily activities but where these activities are full-time specialized craft and business activities; and (3) school, in which learning and teaching are strongly separated from the arenas of mature practice, and teachers are taught how to teach. As far as schooling is concerned, we have limited ourselves to discussing cognitive effects, but have not delved into questions concerning the nature of teaching–learning interactions within the classroom.

We conclude first that there exists a great variety of instructional techniques in informal learning situations. "Teaching by demonstration" is *not* a sufficient characterization of informal teaching techniques in either Zinacantan or Liberia. "Learning by observation and imitation" is *not* sufficient to account for learning activities in either the weaving or tailoring settings. Other techniques such as trial and error, verbalization, and cooperative participation also occur, depending on factors such as culture and learner's skill level. Often techniques are combined to yield scaffolded learning, which is an active, organized enterprise. Teachers present verbal instructions coordinated with demonstration and actual performance, and fit these to the needs of learners. Thus the stereotyped association of verbal instructional strategies with formal education, and nonverbal instructional strategies with informal education, is not appropriate. If language use in teaching has a major role in differential cognitive performances by those who have been to school and those who have not, it may well be a specific one.

Second, we reject the view that there is little pedagogical organization to learning when it takes place in the context of daily activities. Instruction of weavers and tailors is both systematic and adaptive. Both Zinacanteco weaving teachers and Liberian master tailors reorder the clearly separate chunks of their respective craft processes in order of task difficulty. In addition, the Zinacanteco weavers use scaffolded intervention to achieve developmental sequencing within chunks. This results in relatively errorless learning under circumstances where errors would cause considerable economic harm to the teacher's household. The Liberian master tailors allow some trial-and-error learning at the early stages, under conditions where errors would have little economic impact on the teacher. Like the weavers, they intervene in the learning process in carefully regulated fashion as the economic consequences increase.

Third, we conclude that each of the diverse educational forms we investigated can lead to generalization from existing problem-solving skills to problem situations that are related in definable ways. The limited nature of generalization skills is characteristic of all of the educational forms discussed here—including schooling.

Fourth, because of the mutual influence of educational settings on each other within a culture (for which we have cited evidence from other people's work rather than our own), it is necessary to dissociate educational techniques and consequences from the categories of formal and informal education. That is, it appears that informal education may take on qualities of formal education in some cultures, and the converse is probably also true. The implications of this adaptability and mutual influence are that school, apprenticeship, home craft training, and other general terms for educational forms each encompass a wide variety of particular values and instruction and learning techniques.

Research thus far indicates that each combination of techniques is adapted to some purposes and not to others, and that there is no single "best" method. If this is the case, then we should guard against the educational hegemony of particular techniques associated with formal schooling. Future education need not look only to the school for its inspiration. It can also draw upon the rich pedagogical heritage of informal education.

# 10

# Influences of Schooling on Cognitive Development

*Harold W. Stevenson\**

A profound change occurred in the lives of children when public education was established. Schools for the elite had existed for centuries, but only during the past hundred years has school attendance become a reasonable goal for the common child. The change has been nearly complete in most industrialized countries, where nearly all children attend elementary and middle schools. Among the world's developing countries, however, the transformation has been more gradual, and even now large numbers of young children remain out of school.

Attending school has certain disadvantages. For example, it means that children are away from their homes many hours every day. Older members of traditional societies lament the fact that the children are

*This study was a collaborative effort with Timothy Parker, Alex Wilkinson, and Beatrice Bonnevaux. We are grateful to Max Gonzales, our coordinator in Peru; our hosts in Peru, Pontificia Universidad Catolica del Peru; the Ministry of Education; our examiners; and the parents, teachers, and children.

removed from their surveillance. They ask how they can make wise decisions when they are deprived of everyday opportunities to observe the children. How can the skills and strengths of each child be assessed and the child guided into a proper vocation? Families worry about how they can make up for the labor lost while the children are in school. Despite such concerns, however, members of most societies have decided that the benefits of formal education exceed their disadvantages. Parents agree that schools educate their children more rapidly and more effectively than is possible at home, and throughout the world they are sending their children to school in ever-increasing numbers.

The purpose of this paper is not to discuss the value of schools in imparting knowledge and academic skills. Rather it is to ask whether attendance at school has other influences on children's development. There are reasons to believe that it should. Should not the need to remember so much information in school change children's memory abilities? Does not the constant solving of problems posed by the teacher generalize to nonacademic forms of problem solving? Are there not generalized skills that result from listening to the teacher describe task after task and from being required to maintain attention in class over long periods of time? The need to decode abstract symbols and material organized by rules and systems should lead to changes in the manner in which children conceptualize and organize their daily experiences. Children who attend school should learn strategies and techniques from their academic work that make it possible for them to perform more effectively in other tasks. In short, we might expect that schooling would influence the general development of cognitive processes.

At first glance it would seem easy to obtain data relevant to this expectation. A study could be done in a developing country where one could find children who are normal mentally, physically, and emotionally and yet are not in school. The performance of these children on a set of cognitive tasks would be compared with that of children who have attended school. The children's cultural backgrounds and years of experience would be made comparable by selecting children from the same locations and of the same ages. It would be important, too, in thinking about the design of such a study, to select cognitive tasks that involve activities not directly taught in school, for we are interested in cognition rather than in scholastic achievement. If differences emerge between the two groups of children in their scores on the cognitive tasks, we would assume that they are due to the effects of schooling.

The psychological literature contains a number of studies of this type, and they have recently been reviewed by Rogoff (1981). Performance in memory, learning, and other types of cognitive tasks typically has been found to favor the school children.

Can we be content, however, to assume that the differences between the groups can be attributed to attendance at school without considering alternative explanations? There may be other variables that differentiate two such groups of children. For example, the parents of children who attend school might differ in their level of education, interest in education, and number of material possessions (such as books and radios) from the parents of children who do not attend school. If this were the case, we would have to consider the possibility that the children's performance was influenced by these variables rather than or in addition to the variable of schooling. Before we conclude that schooling is the critical variable, we must determine the degree to which the other variables may influence whether children attend school and thereby may contribute significantly to the children's performance on cognitive tasks. We cannot succumb to the error of considering the co-relation between two variables as evidence of a causal relation between the two variables.

## THE INCAP STUDY

The longitudinal study by the Institute of Nutrition of Central America and Panama (INCAP) of the relation between nutrition and mental development in rural Guatemalan children makes it possible to assess some of these assumptions about the effects of schooling on cognitive development (see Townsend et al. in Chapter 6 of this volume). The same children were studied for long periods of time. Nearly 300 of the children were tested with the 18 tests in the INCAP Preschool Battery (Irwin, Engle, Yarbrough, Klein, and Townsend, 1978) before they were 7 years old, the age at which they could enter school. The battery contains a variety of tasks, such as verbal analogies, digit span, memory for designs, and Piaget's conservation of liquid quantity. If the children who subsequently entered school received higher scores on the cognitive battery *before they entered school*, we would have evidence of selective sampling. That is, children whose parents decide to send them to school may demonstrate greater potential for academic success than children whose parents decide to keep them at home. According to this view, the higher levels of performance on later cognitive tasks would be due to variables other than the child's attendance at school.

The evidence supported such an interpretation. Level of performance on nearly all the tasks in the Preschool Battery was higher for children who later attended school; nearly half the differences were statistically significant. Moreover, the children who attended school also lived in homes of better quality and received more frequent parental teaching before they entered school than did children whose parents kept them at home. Such results raise serious questions about whether it has been appropriate in past studies of schooling to attribute superior performance of schooled children to schooling, rather than to other characteristics of the children and their families. We may have been led to assume that cognitive development is hastened and changed by education, when such development may have occurred simply because the children were of higher intellectual ability and from better environments than children who did not attend school.

We need more information about the influence of schooling on cognitive development, but such information is lacking because of the limited scope of most studies of schooling. Rarely have children been tested before their entrance into schools, and in few studies has sufficient supplementary information about the children been gathered to make analyses of parental and environmental characteristics possible. A study we have been conducting in Peru does enable us to add useful information to this discussion.

## RESEARCH IN PERU

Our research deals with developmental changes and the influence of schooling and environmental conditions on children's cognitive development. It is the second large project we have undertaken in Peru during the past few years (Stevenson, Parker, Wilkinson, Bonnevaux, and Gonzales, 1978). We began the present study because of the provocative results obtained in the first project. Schooling appeared to have a consistently positive influence on the average level of performance on the memory and cognitive tasks used in the study. However, the influence on the individual child was not equivalent for all tasks. Performance on some tasks was apparently strongly influenced by attendance at school for some children, while for other children schooling appeared to produce high levels of performance on other tasks. In addition, patterns of performance on the various tasks varied for children who lived in the city and in the jungles of northeastern Peru. Our more recent project was planned so that we could obtain information to clarify some of these differences, and to enable us to assess the hypothesis that the differences associated with schooling were not due to other variables, such as quality of the home, education of the parents, and early parental teaching. We will discuss the parts of the study that are related to the second of those purposes.

## The Land

Peru can be divided into three major regions: the mountains, the jungle, and the coast. Lima, Peru's largest city, is a coastal metropolis whose population is increasing at a very rapid rate, in part because of the migration of families from the highlands. Most of the migrants are Quechua-speaking Indians, descendants of the Incas, Chancas, and other highland groups, who come to the city in search of better economic conditions. They settle in *barriadas*, shantytowns built on the dry, barren hills that surround Lima. Life in the city is difficult. Jobs are scarce, prices are high, and there is a loss of cultural roots as the Indians adopt Western modes of dress, start to speak Spanish, and begin the transition from *indigena* to *mestizo*; that is, from being a member of the indigenous Peruvian population to being Hispanicized.

The *barriadas* are desolate areas without trees or plants. The only water available is brought in barrels to the newer migrants who have settled in the higher levels of the hills. There is no sewage system, and the shanties are made of straw mats, cardboard, and pieces of tin and wood, scavenged from building and construction sites. On the lower, more established levels, there is water, electricity, and in some cases a sewer system. The *barriadas* are phenomena of the past 30 years or so, the period of the great migrations from the highlands.

The *barriadas* in which the children of our study lived were populated by migrants from Andahuaylas, a province in the highland department (state) of Apurimac. We deliberately selected these *barriadas*, for the three sites of our study all contained indigenous populations originally from the same highlands area.

Andahuaylas, the second location of the study, is in a remote part of the highlands separated from the coast and the larger highland cities by 15,000-foot passes that can be traversed only during part of the year. In the rainy season it is often impossible to get to Andahuaylas; bridges are washed out and roads are impassable. Quechua remains the dominant language, and the cultural heritage is strong. Native dress is worn, and holidays, rituals, and stories of the past are still observed and recounted. The primary occupations are farming and herding.

Lamas is the third location in which children of our study lived. This province is in the department of San Martin, in the jungle or rain forest of the northeast. Quechua-speaking Indians have lived in Lamas for nearly 500 years and have remained unassimilated into the local *mestizo* and Amazonian Indian groups. Originally these Quechua-speaking Indians of Lamas were also from Andahuaylas. It is believed they are descendants of a group that migrated to the distant jungle villages after they were defeated in a battle with the Incas. The Indians of Andahuaylas are from a group known as the Chancas, who lived in an area adjacent to the Inca empire. Other than their language, however, they have retained little of the highland culture. They are farmers and exist in a subsistence economy.

The children from Lamas, as well as those from Andahuaylas, live in small villages varying in size from a dozen or more families to several hundred people. Lamas is in a remote region of Peru, and access to many of the villages in both Lamas and in Andahuaylas is possible only by foot.

## Recruiting Subjects

For such a study it is easier to secure children who are in school than children who are not. Even so, recruiting children did not prove to be an unusually burdensome task. The bright, interesting test materials, the great variety of activities, the sustained attention of an interested adult, and the material incentives, such as pencils, pencil sharpeners, and candy, produced high levels of motivation for participating. One should keep in mind how unusually positive these experiences were for the children. Few had books or toys, and seldom were they the recipients of so much adult attention and support. After obtaining permission from the regional and local authorities, the examiners went to the village in search of potential subjects. All examiners were Peruvians and, when appropriate, were bilingual in Spanish and Quechua. Their visits often were preceded by those of local "scouts," young men of the area who were hired to assist the examiners by finding homes with children of appropriate ages. Once testing began, practically all children were very willing to complete the testing—even though this lasted for several hours.

## The Subjects

Although school attendance is compulsory for all 6-year-olds in Peru, only 53 percent of Peruvian 6-year-olds are in school. The percentage varies in different regions, but in each location we found many children who had not attended school. Children at two age levels were selected for our study: 6 to 8 years and 9 to 12 years. The first were enrolled in first grade (or were not in school) and the second were in first, second, and third grade (or had not been to school). About 60 children, half boys and half girls, were in each group, yielding a total of nearly 1100 children in the six groups tested in each of the three locations. With this design it is possible to compare the effects of schooling for younger and older children in grade 1, for older children who had been attending school for 1, 2, or 3 years, and to compare the younger and older children who had never been to school. The average age of children in the various groups at each age level was very similar. We were careful not to have children of different average ages in the different locations, in the school–nonschool groups, or in first, second, and third grades, for we did not want to confound age with these variables.

Spanish was the dominant language for nearly all the children tested in Lima. Quechua was dominant in Andahuaylas, and in Lamas the majority of the children were more fluent in Spanish than in Quechua. It was not difficult for the examiners to assess which language should be used for testing. Although we had constructed tests to determine the dominant language for each child, informal conversation in each language proved to be a more effective indicator.

## The Tasks

We attempted to construct a range of tasks that would reflect direct influences of school attendance on scholastic achievement and indirect influences on cognitive development. Tests in reading, arithmetic, and general information tapped classroom achievement. The cognitive tasks assessed a variety of processes involving rote memory, learning through observation and trial and error, and applying concepts in analogies, series, and seriation. There were 21 cognitive tasks. Such a large number was included because we believed it was impossible to characterize the influence of a variable such as schooling on the basis of only a few measures. It appears that much of the confusion that has existed in our understanding of the complex interrelations between prior experience and cognitive abilities could have been avoided if larger numbers of tasks and more adequate samples of subjects had been included in previous investigations. Thus when different investigators obtained different results—and have used a single, but different, task—it is impossible to know whether the variable under investigation is unstable in its effects or whether the effects are task-dependent. The use of a broad sample of tasks can avoid many of these impasses in interpretation.

We should point out, however, that we did not plan to give the entire set of tasks to every child in each group. When our examiners found that the children responded enthusiastically to the whole set of tasks, however, we saw no reason to omit any. All the tasks were constructed with these children in mind. Thus part of the appeal of the tasks was derived from their obvious relevance to the indigenous culture.

We cannot describe each of the cognitive tasks in detail here, but a list gives an indication of the range and types of processes involved. The tasks can be divided into two general groups. The first, memory tasks, included memory for series of numbers, series of pictures, bodily movements, and auditory patterns; free recall of items in a miniature farm scene; memory for pairings of items from the farm scene; and memory for a brief story. The second group involved observational learning of movements from one location to another made by the examiner; visual matching of objects depicted in photographs and line drawings; acquiring a concept; perceptual learning, in which the child matches photographs of human hands; map reading, in which the location of objects is determined by "reading" a map depicting the locations and objects; making pictorial analogies; completing series representing concepts such as number, size, and sequences of actions; reproducing patterns of objects involving single and double seriation; and reproducing from memory matrix patterns of colored dots.

## Other Information

We were able to conduct interviews with a parent of each child, usually the mother. Parents were cooperative, we believe, because of the excellent rapport obtained by each of our local project coordinators, and because the parents believed the information might have a positive influence on their children's educational opportunities. (There is possible reality in the latter belief, for our results are shared with the Peruvian Ministry of Education and others in Peru interested in the education of young children.) The parents knew, too, that we had permission of the ministry, as well as regional and local officials. The interview provides extensive information about the family and about parental beliefs, efforts, expectations, and hopes in rearing and teaching children.

## Why Parents Keep Their Children Home

When asked why their children were not in school, practically no mothers mentioned psychological characteristics of the child, such as the child's intelligence or scholastic aptitude. Although some mothers did say their children did not want to go to school ("He's afraid he won't learn and others will hit him" or "Our child says the teacher does not teach well"), most of the reasons were extraneous to the children.

The most common reason, given by 61 percent of the mothers of the children in Lima, was that the child was too young. (For illustrative purposes here we will use the information provided by the mothers of the 6- to 8-year-old children who were not in school.) The second most common reason was that the child's help was needed at home (10 percent of the Lima mothers). The same reasons were given in Andahuaylas and Lamas, but the importance of the child's helping at home was more strongly emphasized in the rural settings. The percentages related to age and helping at home were 39 percent and 32 percent in Andahuaylas, and 14 percent and 35 percent in Lamas. Children in Peru must be registered before school begins, and some mothers mentioned difficulties associated with registering their children, such as not having a birth certificate, being late ("She was too late for the registration period at the school"), or not being in the area ("Because he was with his father in another place"). This reason accounted for 8 percent of the absences in Lima and Andahuaylas. Distance from school was mentioned by 10 percent of the mothers in Andahuaylas and 5 percent of the mothers in Lamas. Reasons given by the remaining mothers varied widely, especially in the case of Lamas mothers.

These explanations seem reasonable, and if we were to rely primarily upon parental report we would find little basis for suggesting any selective factors to account for the differences in cognitive performance often found between schooled and nonschooled children. We can understand why, with limited information about the families, earlier researchers tended to assume that the characteristics of families whose children are in school do not differ notably from families of children who remain at home.

## Family Characteristics

The picture changes very markedly, however, when other data from the parent interviews are examined. Let us look first at parental education, a variable often associated with children's scholastic success in industrialized countries. The relation between schooling of the child and education of the parents is evident in Figure 10–1. The average numbers of years the mothers and fathers attended school are presented for the younger and older children who were not in school or who were enrolled

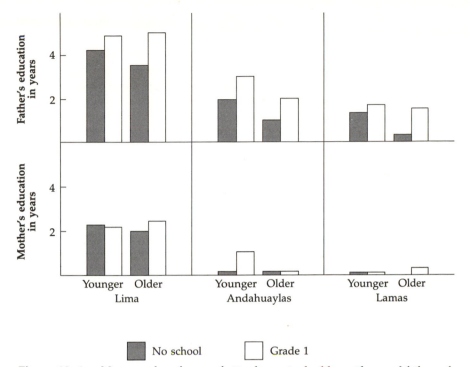

**Figure 10–1**  *Mean number of years of attendance at school by mothers and fathers of children who did and did not attend school. The data are plotted separately according to location and age of the children, 6 to 8 years (younger) and 9 to 12 years (older).*

in grade 1. Mothers attended school for only a small amount of time in all three locations, and their schooling was not highly related to their children's attendance at school.

For fathers, however, the relation is consistent and highly significant statistically. In all locations and at both age levels, fathers of children in school had more education than fathers of children out of school.

Another way in which the relationship between the fathers' educational attainments and children's attendance at school can be demonstrated is by looking at the father's literacy status. (For illustrative purposes we will use data from the older groups of children who were not in school and children who were in grades 1, 2, and 3.) Fathers of more than 90 percent of the children we tested in Lima could read, thus this was not a critical variable in Lima. In Andahuaylas, however, only 26 percent of the fathers of older children who were not in school could read. Of children we tested in grades 1, 2, and 3, the percentage of fathers who could read was, respectively, 55 percent, 61 percent, and 70 percent. Not only is there a difference (found also for the younger children) between fathers of children who do and do not attend school, but the percentage of literate fathers also increases as the number of years their children have been in school increases. A similar, even more pronounced pattern was found in Lamas. Only 16 percent of the fathers of nonschool children could read. Of the children who had been in school 1, 2, and 3 years, the percentages were 44 percent, 60 percent, and 74 percent, respectively. Children's attendance at school was highly related, therefore, to the literacy of the fathers. Fathers who were literate were more likely than nonliterate fathers to send their children to school, and to send them to school earlier.

A third variable, home environment, was evaluated by the interviewer. Rather than rely on subjective evaluations, the interviewer simply asked—or observed—whether items were present that we believed might reflect or contribute to a home environment that would stimulate cognitive development. Ten items were checked: the presence of electricity, any type of machine, radio, television, newspapers or magazines, books, children's books, toys, pictures, or portraits.

Urban and rural environments differed markedly. Homes visited in Lima had an average of about 7 of these items. Those in Andahuaylas and Lamas had averages of 2.5 and 1.4, respectively. The number of items differed between the homes of children who did and did not attend school in Andahuaylas. For the homes of older children not in school, the average was 1.1; for the homes of children in grades 1, 2, and 3, the averages were 2.4, 2.9, and 3.5, respectively. In Lima, where most homes had many of the items, and in Lamas, where most homes had very few items, differences among groups were smaller, but generally in the same direction. Thus if items such as these do indeed contribute to cognitive development, children who go to school would be judged to live in more stimulating home environments than children who do not attend school.

Mothers' responses to one more type of question will be considered. They were asked about things that were taught to the child at home by the parents, family members, or other adults. Questions were asked about teaching of colors, numbers, letters, money, seasons, riddles, Spanish, games, reading, and stories. Do children who go to school also receive more teaching at home than children who do not? The answer is yes, although the averages were not high for any of the children. For example, the average number of items taught older children who did not go to school was 4.1; and for children in grades 1, 2, and 3, it was 5.3, 6.1, and 6.1, respectively.

One conclusion is appropriate: Families of children who do and do not attend school differ in ways that may be important to the child's cognitive growth. Educational and literacy status of the father, quality of the home, and degree of out-of-school teaching are variables that differentiate families that do and do not send their children to school. These results, along with those of Irwin et al. (1978), strongly support the hypothesis that the superior performance on cognitive tasks found for children who attend school may be due to factors other than the child's experiences in school.

## Grouping the Tasks

The analyses we have made thus far appear to reduce the likelihood that schooling is an influential factor in cognitive development. Before we can accept this conclusion, however, we need to consider other factors. Although we have ascertained that several important environmental variables are significantly related to children's attendance at school, we do not yet know whether the variables bear significant relations to the cognitive tasks.

For these analyses we need, at least initially, to do something to simplify our data. Considering more than 20 tasks at this stage of our discussion is burdensome. We included this number to help us specify the kinds of cognitive functions that may be influenced by schooling or environmental conditions, but it would be helpful at this point if we could group the tasks into several coherent clusters. This grouping can be accomplished by means of a principal-components analysis, in which tasks are grouped so that all tasks within each cluster have a high relation to each other, but lower relations with tasks in other clusters. When this analysis was performed, four clusters emerged. The clusters and the tasks they included are as follows:

1.  *Contextual memory.* Tasks in this group appeared to tap the child's ability to remember information imbedded in meaningful contexts. They included general information, free recall of items in a farm scene, pairing of items in the farm scene, and memory for a story.

2.  *Spatial representation.* All of these tasks involved some form of spatial response. They included seriation, copying matrices, map reading and reproducing bodily movements in space.

3.  *Serial memory.* Children were asked to remember different kinds of items that were presented in serial order. This group included auditory memory, memory for bodily movements, memory for a series of pictures, and copying the simplest matrices.

4.  *Visual analysis and conceptualization.* The fourth group of tasks was somewhat less coherent than the others, but included tasks in which the child was required to make some type of visual analysis of material and respond to it in a conceptual manner. The tasks included concept learning, perceptual learning, completion of a meaningful series of pictures, analogies, and matching of pictures and objects.

Not all tasks appear in these four groups, but there is a sufficient representation to enable us to understand the general nature of the results.

## Correlations with Environmental Factors

A correlation coefficient was computed, indicating the degree of relation between the environmental factors we have considered and a value representing each child's performance on the tasks in each cluster. There were two separate sets of correlation coefficients in the three locations, one for the younger children who did or did not attend school, and one for the older children who were enrolled in grades 1, 2, or 3, or who did not attend school. There were over 400 children in the first analyses and over 700 children in the second. With sample sizes of this magnitude, a correlation coefficient of slightly less than 0.10 is statistically significant. The correlations that were obtained appear in Table 10–1.

Six variables were chosen for these analyses. Although others could have been included, and different kinds of breakdowns of variables could have been made, these variables (and two others that will be mentioned later) seemed particularly salient in reflecting the potential of the environment for stimulating cognitive development in the domains evaluated in this study.

The relevance of the geographical region in which the children lived was assessed in two ways. The urban–rural distinction involves the obvious contrast between children living in the urban environment of Lima and the rural environments of Lamas and Andahuaylas. A second variable contrasted the performance of children living in the two rural environments. Parental education, home quality, and home teaching are the same variables as those discussed earlier.

It is apparent that all variables except for home teaching were significantly related to the children's performance on the four clusters of tasks. While home teaching was related to children's attendance at school, it is infrequently related to children's performance. Why this should be the

**Table 10-1**  *Correlations between Environmental Variables and Children's Performance on Four Clusters of Cognitive Tasks*

| CLUSTER | GROUP | |
| --- | --- | --- |
| | OLDER CHILDREN | YOUNGER CHILDREN |
| CONTEXTUAL MEMORY | | |
| Urban–rural | 0.22 | 0.31 |
| Andahuaylas–Lamas | 0.55 | 0.42 |
| Father's education | 0.12 | 0.19 |
| Mother's education | 0.15 | 0.19 |
| Home quality | 0.23 | 0.28 |
| Home teaching | −0.02 | 0.09 |
| SPATIAL REPRESENTATION | | |
| Urban–rural | 0.42 | 0.36 |
| Andahuaylas–Lamas | 0.52 | 0.26 |
| Father's education | 0.24 | 0.18 |
| Mother's education | 0.20 | 0.20 |
| Home quality | 0.40 | 0.23 |
| Home teaching | 0.00 | 0.06 |
| SERIAL MEMORY | | |
| Urban–rural | 0.27 | 0.22 |
| Andahuaylas–Lamas | 0.51 | 0.35 |
| Father's education | 0.14 | 0.18 |
| Mother's education | 0.16 | 0.16 |
| Home quality | 0.24 | 0.22 |
| Home teaching | 0.00 | 0.09 |
| VISUAL ANALYSIS AND CONCEPTUALIZATION | | |
| Urban–rural | 0.30 | 0.25 |
| Andahuaylas–Lamas | 0.45 | 0.34 |
| Father's education | 0.13 | 0.10 |
| Mother's education | 0.12 | 0.17 |
| Home quality | 0.25 | 0.13 |
| Home teaching | −0.03 | −0.01 |

case is not clear. Perhaps the types of activities we included in our inquiries about teaching at home were insufficiently complex. There could be many reasons, none of which is immediately obvious to us as an explanation.

Generally, urban children performed at a higher level than rural children, and the performance of children from Andahuaylas was notably above that of children from Lamas. Amount of parental education and quality of the home were positively related to children's performance on the cognitive tasks. The effects were similar for the younger and older children, and the results for these children from Quechua-speaking backgrounds in Peru are generally in line with the results found in many studies of children in industrialized areas.

Correlation coefficients can be interpreted as indicating the degree to which variation in one factor is associated with variation in a second factor. That is, in technical terms, squaring the correlation coefficient gives us an indication of the proportion of variance in a variable such as the children's performance on the cognitive tasks that is related to the variance in a second variable, such as home quality. With this in mind, it is possible to say, for example, that between 4 percent and 16 percent of the variance in the children's performance is generally related to the variance in the quality of the homes in which the children resided— according to the manner in which we measured home quality.

Even though each individual variable may account for only a modest portion of the variance, a group of variables together may account for much higher percentages. We know, however, that factors such as home quality are related to other factors, such as parental education. Environmental factors are not independent of each other; thus we cannot add the percentages of variance derived from each variable as an indication of the total amount of variance for which we can account. Rather, a statistical technique is needed that will enable us to assess the cumulative proportion of variance that can be accounted for by the *independent* contribution of each successive variable. For example, having taken out the variance accounted for by geographical region, does parental education add significantly to the amount of variance for which we can account? The same question is then asked of the next variable, after the effects of geographical region and parental education have been included. Regression analysis enables us to do this. The variable is selected that has the highest correlation with the independent variable, each successive variable is then added, and an indication is given of whether the addition of successive variables results in a significant increase in the variance that can be accounted for.

Regression analyses were performed with the variables we have discussed and two additional variables: sex of the child and incidence of reward provided to the children by their parents. Mothers were asked in the interview about their modes of response to their children when various positive and negative acts were performed by the child. We could, of course, have added many more variables, but it seems to us that these variables covered a reasonably broad range of environmental characteristics. The cumulative (multiple) correlations are listed in Table 10–2.

Table 10 2  *Multiple Correlation Coefficient (R) Obtained Between Environmental Variables and Children's Performance on the Four Clusters of Cognitive Tasks*

| CLUSTER | MULTIPLE R | $R^2$ |
|---|---|---|
| CONTEXTUAL MEMORY | | |
| Younger children | 0.63 | 0.40 |
| Older children | 0.63 | 0.40 |
| SPATIAL REPRESENTATION | | |
| Younger children | 0.70 | 0.49 |
| Older children | 0.49 | 0.24 |
| SERIAL MEMORY | | |
| Younger children | 0.60 | 0.36 |
| Older children | 0.51 | 0.26 |
| VISUAL ANALYSIS AND CONCEPTUALIZATION | | |
| Younger children | 0.58 | 0.34 |
| Older children | 0.46 | 0.21 |

From the $R^2$ values, it is evident that environmental variables are generally related to one-fourth to one-half of the variability in children's performance on the cognitive tasks. Conversely, between one-half and three-fourths of the variability in children's performance must be accounted for by other variables, or perhaps by variables of the types we have included, but measured in a different manner. The correlations are as large as those found in studies of the relation of cognitive performance to environmental variables conducted in the United States. This fact is especially notable when we realize that the testing and interview conditions were typical of those found in field studies, where the physical setting is highly variable and it is impossible to control many situational variables.

## Schooling and Performance

It may appear that schooling, the variable of central interest, has been forgotten. This is not the case. It was necessary to establish the relation between other environmental factors and cognitive development before returning to a consideration of the influence of schooling.

What were the correlations between schooling and performance? For the younger children, who were grouped into those who attended school and those who did not, the resulting correlations were 0.17 (contextual memory), 0.17 (spatial memory), 0.09 (serial memory), and 0.17 (visual and sequential analysis). Four groups were formed for the older children, as they have been in the preceding analyses: children who had not attended school, and those enrolled in grades 1, 2, and 3. Correlations with performance on the four clusters of cognitive tasks were 0.20, 0.21, 0.19, and 0.09, respectively. The correlations are not large, but all are highly significant statistically.

Attendance at school was related in a positive manner, therefore, to children's performance in the cognitive tasks. Nonschool children's performance was generally below that of children who attended school, and correct performance increased on the cognitive tasks with increasing numbers of years in school.

A final, critical question can now be asked: Does schooling make a significant, independent contribution to children's performance on the cognitive tasks after the effects of sex, location, parental education, home quality, home teaching, and parental use of reward have been removed? Regression analyses indicate that it does. Even though the other variables were related to children's attendance at school and to children's performance on the cognitive tasks, schooling did have a significant, positive influence on children's cognitive development. For the present, then, we conclude that the effects found in earlier studies indicating the influence of schooling on cognitive development cannot be solely accounted for by selective sampling. Children who go to school do not attain their higher scores on cognitive tasks simply because important environmental variables differentiate these children from those who are kept at home.

Mechanisms whereby schooling exerts a positive influence on cognitive development remain unclear. Perhaps, as has been suggested, children in school learn strategies for organizing material and solving problems, and acquire modes of conceptualization that differ in their reliance on words and rules from those of nonschool children. We can gain an understanding of these mechanisms through fine-grained analyses of differences in the performance of school and nonschool children. Knowing what changes in cognitive processes occur through schooling may enable us to enhance and sharpen the whole educational process. Such research must be done soon, however, for it will become increasingly difficult to find children in the world who have never attended school.

# 11

# Cross-Cultural Comparisons of Personality Development in Mexico and the United States

*Wayne H. Holtzman*

Cross-cultural approaches are particularly appealing for the study of sociocultural factors in personality development. Different patterns of child rearing, variations in family life-style, contrasting value systems, sociolinguistic variations, and different social orders and their political or economic systems are but a few of the major environmental influences on personality development that require a cross-cultural approach if one is to study them under real-life conditions. In spite of the obvious appeal of cross-cultural approaches to personality development, conceptual and methodological difficulties encountered in such research have been so forbidding that, until recently, psychologists have generally left the field to anthropologists and social theorists.

Most of the early studies of personality development in different cultures were concerned primarily with testing evolutionary theory rather than with the study of personality development. The true beginning of modern cross-cultural research goes back more than 50 years to the work of Margaret Mead (1928), Bronislaw Malinowski (1927), and Edward Sapir (1927), who studied early child development and family patterns in different cultures. Usually these anthropological studies of culture and personality were intensive case studies of a single society rather than cross-cultural investigations in the real sense of the word.

The first attempts at truly pancultural research, based largely on the Human Relations Area Files, were undertaken by Whiting and his colleagues (Whiting and Child, 1953). Ethnographic data from a large number of societies were coded for one or two key cultural variables, such as the degree of overall infant indulgence and the type of household structure. Correlations were computed between two variables across many cultures, using whole societies as sampling units. Generalizations could then be based on statistical tests of significance, a method familiar to psychologists, although the raw data came largely from case studies of different cultures by anthropologists. Whiting and his colleagues soon discovered, however, that the information deposited by earlier investigators in the Human Relations Area Files was frequently missing or ambiguous, making accurate analysis impossible.

To avoid relying on ethnographic data of uneven quality collected earlier for other purposes, an ambitious program of new data collection was launched by Whiting (1963) to obtain more accurate firsthand information on child-rearing practices and personality development. Six different cultures were chosen as the first of what might eventually be as many as 100 societies examined in a standard manner to facilitate cross-cultural comparison. In cultures ranging from a New England village to an African tribe in Kenya, teams of field workers studied 24 mother–children clusters intensively, focusing in particular on patterns of aggression, dependency, and internalization of various mechanisms of behavior control. While the six-culture project proved to be a major advance, the results still left much to be desired. Essentially naturalistic, the data came from observation and interview, leaving still unsettled the problem of calibrating the human observer. Since observers often see human interactions quite differently, data from different cultures may not be truly comparable. The number of cases in each sample remains uncomfortably small because of the great expense of collecting such intensive data, and the level of quantification generally falls considerably short of the stability and power needed for definite results. Thus, the pancultural approach is limited in what it can add to our present knowledge of personality development because of the difficulty of collecting comparable measures from a large number of different societies throughout the world.

A more realistic approach is one in which a very limited sample of cultures is drawn from the world universe. By selecting cultures that maximize desired variation with regard to a dimension of special interest, more extensive data can be obtained on large numbers of individuals. The studies of children's moral values undertaken by Harold and Gladys Anderson (1961) in nine different countries of Western Europe and the Americas is an early example of this approach. Questionnaire data were collected from large numbers of children using the incomplete story method. In this technique, each child was given a series of incomplete stories and asked to tell how the story ends, thereby providing fantasy material that could be rated for honesty, responsibility, anxiety, and guilt. Average scores on these traits were compared across the nine countries, which were also ranked according to their presumed degree of authoritarian versus democratic political–social structure. Unfortunately, the obtained relationship between such traits and degrees of authoritarianism is impossible to interpret, since the countries under study differ in many ways other than the one singled out for attention. This problem points to a major dilemma in most cross-cultural research designs: Even if the research techniques are valid and the samples are truly representative, how do we know that the obtained differences in mean scores across nations are really due to the hypothesized cultural dimension, and not to any number of other dimensions confounded with it?

The most common type of cross-cultural study involves only two cultures. Here the possibilities for a misinterpretation of the cultural variables are even greater. As Campbell (1961) has pointed out, comparisons between cultures are generally uninterpretable because any of several cultural differences may provide alternative explanations of the findings.

The above picture, with respect to the difficulties of controlled delineation and replication of cultural factors in the study of personality development, is depressing. If investigators employ a pancultural approach in order to say something universal, they run a risk of including questionable secondhand data and of limiting themselves to a very small number of obvious personality variables, leading to a handful of unstable correlations, the interpretation of which is controversial. On the other hand, if an investigator focuses on only two cultures, the cultural factors per se may be completely uninterpretable in spite of demonstrated real differences in personality across the two cultures. Only if one is content with something less than the rigorous testing of universal hypotheses are there plausible alternatives.

Considerable subcultural variation exists within every large society. Indeed, some recent studies reveal greater cultural variation within the urban centers of different nations than across nations as a whole. A great deal can be learned about the interplay of culture and personality development by repeated measurement, using a variety of methods and adequate sampling of individuals within a single culture. Adding a second culture, selected because of contrasting features of particular interest, increases greatly the power of the research design.

The two-culture model is of special interest for several reasons. First, it is the simplest cross-cultural method and requires the least amount of special training in different cultures. Second, many psychological hypotheses concerning personality development can be tested, at least partially, by a careful selection of two contrasting cultures. Third, focusing on subcultural or within-culture variations such as sex, socioeconomic status, education, or family life-style adds an important dimension that greatly increases the power of the design when only two cultures are studied. Without such subcultural variation deliberately built into the research design, two-culture studies are generally uninterpretable because of the many unspecified differences which can provide alternative explanations of the findings and which cannot be ruled out.

For a two-culture study to be a valid comparison, satisfactory solutions must be found to the following three problems: (1) measurement and control of the cultural variables themselves; (2) delineation of sufficient subcultural variation to permit the systematic study of interactions between subcultural dimensions in the two cultures; and (3) achievement of semantic equivalence for individual assessment techniques. These problems and solutions to them can be illustrated by a recently completed longitudinal study of personality development of children in Mexico and the United States (Holtzman, Diaz-Guerrero, and Swartz, 1975).* Selected findings of special interest are presented to show the ways in which certain aspects of culture influence personality development.

---

*Much of the material in this chapter was adapted from W. H. Holtzman, R. Diaz-Guerrero, and J. D. Swartz, *Personality Development in Two Cultures* (Austin: University of Texas Press, 1975).

# DESCRIPTION OF THE AUSTIN–MEXICO CITY PROJECT

An overlapping longitudinal design was employed in the Austin–Mexico City Project so that a span of 12 years of child development could be covered in only 6 calendar years of repeated testing. The basic design is presented in Table 11–1. The 3-year overlap between groups is particularly powerful, since it is then possible to study curvilinear developmental trends and interactions longitudinally as well as cross-sectionally. Developmental trends are rarely linear when examined over many years of growth. Three points of overlap in age allow for much greater accuracy in splicing segments together in one overall age trend. Furthermore, assuming adequate sampling and careful matching at each age level, the effects of repeated testing per se can be isolated by this three-year age overlap so that the adjusted data reflect true developmental trends rather than artifacts of the methods employed. Taking a test several times often alters a child's performance due to practice or adaptation. The overlapped design allows one to correct for such practice effects.

The children in Austin were mainly drawn from six elementary schools and one junior high school. Austin is a sufficiently cosmopolitan city to be representative of "middle America," or what many have referred to as the broad working and middle classes that constitute the majority of

**Table 11–1**  *Overlapping Longitudinal Design for Six Years of Repeated Testing in Austin and Mexico City*

| GROUP | INITIAL AGE* | NUMBER OF CASES AUSTIN | NUMBER OF CASES MEXICO | SCHOOL GRADES COVERED |
|-------|------|--------|--------|------------------------|
| I | 6.7 | 133 | 150 | 1 2 3 4 5 6 |
| II | 9.7 | 142 | 143 | 4 5 6 7 8 9 |
| III | 12.7 | 142 | 150 | 7 8 9 10 11 12 |
| Total | | 417 | 443 | |

*The starting ages of 6.7, 9.7, and 12.7 years were chosen since most children in the public schools of Texas reach these exact ages at some time during the school year, September 15 to May 15. Actual time of testing took place within 30 days of the age specified in the table. (From W. H. Holtzman, R. Diaz-Guerrero, and J. D. Swartz, *Personality development in two cultures, a cross-cultural longitudinal study of school children in Mexico and the United States.* University of Texas Press, Austin, 1975. Copyright © 1975 by the Hogg Foundation for the Mental Health.)

American citizens. By restricting the Austin sample to English-speaking white families who seemed likely to remain in Austin for the six years of the study, the American culture was narrowed still further. It seems safe to say that the children and their families comprising the Austin sample were representative of the blue-collar, clerical, skilled-worker, and educated professional classes that comprise the Anglo-American value system characteristic of the American majority.

In Mexico City, extensive preliminary studies were necessary to obtain demographic information on which a detailed sampling plan could be based. Children were selected from one private and two public school systems. By oversampling from the private schools, a proportionately larger number of middle-class children were obtained in Mexico than would be characteristic of the population as a whole. Only in this way was it possible to obtain large numbers of individuals with comparable educational, occupational, and socioeconomic status across the two cultures. As in the case of the American families, only children with native-born parents and with some prospect of residential stability were selected for the developmental study, thereby narrowing the definition of culture to the emerging upper-middle class working classes in highly urbanized Mexico City.

The basic psychological test battery included many cognitive, perceptual, and personality tests given individually to each child once a year on the anniversary date of the initial testing. The techniques employed could be divided into three categories: (1) those that were applied uniformly throughout the six years of repeated testing—the basic core battery; (2) measures that were applied uniformly for all children in the second grade or above and tests that were employed two or more times though not uniformly—the partial core battery and supplementary repeated battery; and (3) other measures that were used once or twice but not successively across years. A list of the techniques employed in these three categories is presented in Table 11–2.

The kinds of data common to school children in both cultures can be divided into four major categories: (1) performance data by children in testing sessions; (2) ratings of the child's behavior, personality, or other characteristics; (3) variables dealing with the family and home environment taken largely from interviews with the mothers and observations in the home; and (4) attitudes toward child rearing and certain personal beliefs and values collected from the mother by use of a questionnaire. The four major classification or independent variables in the research design are culture, socioeconomic status, sex, and age of the child. The many significant relationships discovered between the test scores, rat-

**Table 11–2**  *Psychological Test Batteries and Related Measures*

CORE TEST BATTERY (ALL SAMPLES FOR 6 YEARS)

Holtzman inkblot technique
Human figure drawing
Vocabulary (WISC or WAIS)
Block design (WISC or WAIS)

SUPPLEMENTARY REPEATED

Test anxiety scale for children
Time estimation
Filled time estimation (Texas samples: fourth, fifth and sixth years)
Test behavior ratings
Object sorting test (first three years)
Embedded figures test (all samples age 9.7 or older)
Stroop color-word test (Texas samples age 9.7 or older for four years)
Visual fractionation test (all samples for two years)
Conceptual styles test (ages 7.7 and 8.7 only)
Perceptual maturity scale (last three years)
Word association test (last three years)
WISC or WAIS arithmetic and pictured completion (all samples: first, fourth, fifth, and sixth years)

OTHER MEASURES

WISC remaining subtests (age 6.7)
Family and home ratings from interviews with mothers
Parent-attitude survey (mother)
Academic summary (school record data)
Occupational values inventory (all samples, sixth year)
Personality research form (all samples, sixth year)
Survey of study habits and attitudes (Texas samples age 17.7, Mexico samples fourth and 5th years)
Manuel's reading test (Mexico samples fourth and fifth years)
Views of life and sociocultural premises (Mexico selected samples sixth year)

(From W. H. Holtzman, R. Diaz-Guerrero, and J. D. Swartz, *Personality development in two cultures, a cross-cultural longitudinal study of school children in Mexico and the United States.* University of Texas Press, Austin, 1975. Copyright © 1975 by the Hogg Foundation for Mental Health.)

ings, and other dependent measures, on the one hand, and these four independent variables both in isolation from each other and for any interactions among them, on the other hand, constitute the essential outcomes of the study that require interpretation. Intercorrelational studies as well as numerous analyses of variance were completed. Only a sampling of the findings concerning cultural influences on personality development can be presented here.

In most cross-cultural studies of personality development, it is not possible to control systematically major within-culture variation that often accounts for a great deal of the obtained variance in results. Where two cultures are markedly different, there is even a question as to whether enough overlap in such factors as socioeconomic status and life-style exists between the two cultures to permit systematic control. One of the major objectives of the present study was to control precisely for three key factors in such within-culture variation—sex, age, and socioeconomic status—to minimize the possibility of serious confounding of cultures and those within-culture classification factors that have been repeatedly demonstrated as influential in determining a child's performance on psychological tests.

Every effort was made to eliminate or at least minimize the likelihood that methodological artifacts could account for any obtained results. While cross-cultural matching on socioeconomic status cannot be perfect, because of differences inherent in the two cultures, the pairing of individual children cross-culturally on the index of socioeconomic status proved to be a fairly rigorous method of controlling for this important variable. Preliminary studies in Mexico also revealed that Mexican families with children in the private school system and the typical middle-class American families in the Austin sample had essentially the same level of father's occupation and education, size and quality of house, and prevalence of radios, television sets, automobiles, and refrigerators. Thus one can conclude that cross-cultural differences obtained in the present study are not confounded with social-class differences. Special studies were made of any possible bias due to the inevitable loss of some subjects over the six years of the study. Since no significant biases were found, it can be concluded that the distribution of social, cultural, and personal characteristics within each cell of the design remained constant throughout the six years of the study.

Matched cross-cultural samples were developed using the Socio-Economic Status (SES) Index, an overall socioeconomic index for the family based upon the education and occupation of the father in a modified version of R. J. Havighurst's procedure (Havighurst et al., 1955). Matching was accomplished on two levels of the SES Index, the three age groups, the two sexes, and the year of testing, so that the only obvious difference remaining was the primary cultural difference between children in Mexico City and those in Austin. Two levels of SES—"low" and "high"—were obtained. These two broad categories of SES encompass a lower class consisting mainly of blue-collar, clerical, and working-class families and an upper class comprised mainly of families with fathers who were highly educated professionals or businessmen.

A total of 203 matched pairs, one member of each pair being an American and the other a Mexican, were used in the design. In most of the cross-cultural comparisons, a four-way analysis of variance design was formulated. The four independent factors in the design consisted of two cultures by two SES levels by three age groups by two sexes.

The first time that a test was administered in each culture was the only instance employed in this particular analysis, leaving until later the question of repeated measures on the same test. While most variables employed in the analysis were obtained in the first year of testing, several were not introduced until later. For example, all of the data growing out of the parent interview and the Parent-Attitude Survey were collected in the fourth year of the study. We will now look at some of the specific findings.

# CROSS-CULTURAL SIMILARITIES AND DIFFERENCES IN PERSONALITY DEVELOPMENT

Similarities across two cultures in cognitive, perceptual, and personality characteristics can be just as important as the existence of significant differences. Out of more than 100 dependent variables, only 18 psychological measures from the children and items from the interviews with the mothers showed no differences whatsoever between Mexicans and Americans. These measures tended to be minor. Obviously, far more measures produced significant differences or interactions between culture and other variables. In most cases, social class, sex, and the age of the child proved to be significant factors related to the child's performance in both cultures. It is worth noting, however, that differences in performance due to social class are generally present for the Mexican children, though not for the American, resulting in significant culture–social-class interactions for many variables.

Before examining the findings in detail, it is important to note the extent to which the many personality measures show similar patterns of intercorrelations in the two cultures. The psychological meaning of a variable is defined in large part by the other variables with which it is correlated and the extent of the relationship. The pattern of interrelationships among variables defines a network of meaning. If the major dimensions underlying these intercorrelations are identical in the two cultures, one can interpret the results with a high degree of confidence that the meaning of the variables is similar in both cultures. On the other hand, if the patterns of interrelationships among the many variables in the Mexican samples are strikingly different from patterns involving these same variables in the samples of children from the United States, considerable doubt could be cast upon the interpretation of the results, since the meaning of the variables is quite different in the two cultures.

Extensive intercorrelation and factor analysis studies were carried out separately for the American and Mexican samples. In nearly every case, patterns of intercorrelations were remarkably similar in both cultures. Factor analysis of the Holtzman Inkblot scores for each of the age groups in each culture revealed five well-defined factors highly similar in each of the six groups. The dimensions underlying mental abilities as measured by the WISC and other cognitive tests also proved to be very similar in the two cultures. Even the 15 scales in the Personality Research Form yielded strikingly similar results, lending strong support to the hypothesis that personality measures have similar meaning and applicability in both cultures. Only findings of personality variables are highlighted here. For a detailed discussion of the extensive results obtained for the cognitive variables, as well as a more detailed presentation of personality findings, see Holtzman, Diaz-Guerrero, and Swartz (1975).

## Parental and Home Variables

Patterns of child rearing, family life-styles, and home environment have a profound influence on the personality development of young children. Variables dealing with the family and home environment were developed from interviews with the mothers and observations of the home that were conducted midway through the six-year longitudinal study. Items for the interview were drawn from a number of previous studies dealing with family and social background factors as they influenced developmental processes in children. Attitudes toward child rearing and certain personal beliefs and values were also collected from the mother by a specially developed Parent Attitude Survey containing 68 items. The mother was asked to indicate her choice among five categories ranging from *strongly agree* through *undecided* to *strongly disagree*. At the end of the 68 items were placed 15 traits identical to those used by the Lynds in their "Middletown" studies (1937) and repeated once again by Murphy and Moriarty (1976) in their studies of parental attitudes and values in Kansas in the early 1950s. The mother was asked to rate the importance of these personal traits as she valued them in her own child.

While space does not permit a discussion of the many significant interactions between culture and other factors in the analyses of data obtained from the parental interview and home-environment observations, a summary of the cross-cultural comparisons in which uniformly significant differences were obtained from the mothers is presented in Table 11–3. Let us now turn to an interpretation of the specific meaning of these cross-cultural differences and the content of the items for the samples in the study.

Intellectual stimulation of the child in the American home is generally greater than that in the Mexican household, and American mothers value curiosity in the child much more highly than do Mexican mothers. Socialization of the child in the American home is aimed at producing greater self-reliance or independence than is the case for children in the Mexican home.

When it comes to spoken languages, the Mexican families showed decided advantages over the American. Foreign languages (usually English in Mexico City) were spoken in half the Mexican homes, encouraging large numbers of Mexican children to broaden their horizons beyond their native language. In addition, it should be noted that many Mexican families have a custom of regular story telling to young children rather than reading to them from books. Story telling by American parents in earlier generations has been largely replaced by reading from children's books. Consequently, one would expect the oral language facility and associated interpersonal relations to be more highly developed among Mexican children, other things being equal, than for the American counterparts.

Other aspects of child rearing are especially signficant for personality development in the two cultures. Fewer Mexican fathers, particularly from the lower-class group, share activities with their sons. Mexican children are given less responsibility in their home and are more likely to have their friends chosen by their parents. Mexican mothers are more likely to admit to problems in child rearing, to be less accepting and more controlling of their children. They are also more likely to press their children toward socially favored goals and to place a higher value on strict obedience in their children.

Mexican mothers tended to rate in their children the personal trait "desire to make a name in the world" much more highly than did the American mothers. At the same time, the Mexican mothers gave less priority than their American counterparts to such traits as art appreciation, independence, tolerance, or curiosity. These cross-cultural differences are present for the mothers of young children as well as old, for the mothers of boys as well as girls, and regardless of socioeconomic level. Some of these differences are striking. For example, the desire to make a name in the world was the most important of the 15 traits in the

**Table 11–3** *Cross-Cultural Comparisons in Which Uniformly Significant Differences Were Obtained from Mothers*

| ITEMS FROM MOTHERS' INTERVIEW | MEXICAN | AMERICAN |
|---|---|---|
| SOCIAL CLASS AND FAMILY LIFE/STYLE | | |
| Mother's education | some secondary | some college |
| Number of siblings | 3.7 | 2.0 |
| Other relatives present in home | 18% | 3% |
| Religious preference | Catholic | Protestant |
| Attendance at church once a week | 85% | 63% |
| Club activity of mother | low | high |
| Hours/week father watches TV | 7.0 | 9.7 |
| Mother works outside home | 9% | 41% |
| SOCIALIZATION OF CHILD | | |
| Special family recreation | 52% | 67% |
| Parents helping child choose friends | 56% | 32% |
| Child has home chores | 64% | 88% |
| INTELLECTUAL STIMULATION OF CHILD | | |
| No magazines in home | 45% | 20% |
| Dictionary and encyclopedia in home | 30% | 79% |
| Parents read regularly to child as preschooler | 13% | 60% |
| Preschool child unable to read, count, or write | 59% | 22% |
| Child now regularly encouraged to read | 30% | 15% |
| Foreign language spoken in home | 49% | 25% |
| Father who has had teaching experience | 8% | 16% |
| PARENTAL ASPIRATIONS FOR CHILD | | |
| Minimum educational level most desired | high school | college |
| No preference stated for child's future occupation | 35% | 63% |
| PARENTAL INTEREST IN ACADEMIC PROGRESS OF CHILD | | |
| Only mother talks to child about school progress | 50% | 29% |
| Both parents talk to child about school progress | 40% | 66% |
| Child has regular homework | 98% | 58% |
| Parent sometimes helps child with homework | 45% | 69% |
| MOTHER'S ASSESSMENT OF CHILD | | |
| Judgment of child's rank in class | medium | high |
| Child reads unassigned books | 69% | 93% |

**Table 11–3 (cont.)**

| ITEMS FROM MOTHERS' INTERVIEW | MEXICAN | AMERICAN |
|---|---|---|
| PARENT ATTITUDE SURVEY | | |
| Factor 1: Internal Determinism | low | high |
| Factor 2: Sophisticated Acceptance | low | high |
| Factor 3: Confidence | low | high |
| Factor 4: Authoritarian Discipline | high | low |
| VALUE PLACED ON PERSONAL TRAITS OF CHILD | | |
| Desire to make a name in the world | 2.45 | 0.68 |
| Appreciation of art, music, and poetry | 1.16 | 1.56 |
| Independence | 1.38 | 2.03 |
| Tolerance | 1.48 | 2.31 |
| Curiosity | 0.71 | 1.60 |

(From W. H. Holtzman, R. Diaz-Guerrero, and J. D. Swartz, *Personality development in two cultures, a cross-cultural longitudinal study of school children in Mexico and the United States.* University of Texas Press, Austin, 1975. Copyright © 1975 by the Hogg Foundation for Mental Health.)

eyes of the Mexican mothers, while it was the least important for the Americans.

Getting very good grades in school was ranked least important by the most affluent group, the upper-class American mothers, and most important by the lower-class Mexican mothers, with the other two groups arrayed consistently in between. This negative relationship between the importance of getting very good grades in school and actual recognized attainment and affluence is consistent with the general idea that deprived people value the unattained goal much more highly than those who have achieved it. It may also indicate that education is still perceived by many lower-class mothers as a means to a better life for their children.

## Direct Personality and Attitudinal Measures

Three personality and attitudinal questionnaires were given to all the children in Mexico City and Austin. The Personality Research Form (PRF) is a comprehensive paper-and-pencil questionnaire consisting of 300 items divided into fifteen 20-item scales. It measures broadly relevant personality traits among adolescents and adults. The PRF was administered in the last year of the study when the children were in the sixth, ninth, and twelfth grades. Sarason's Test Anxiety Scale for Children with its several subscales is a specialized form of personality questionnaire that was given to all children in both cultures for five consecutive years beginning in year 2. A third questionnaire, the Occupational Values Inventory, had been used successfully in an earlier cross-cultural study of adolescents. In the last year of the study, each child was asked to rank 15 different career value phrases from the most important to the least important value from a personal point of view.

A number of highly significant cross-cultural differences were obtained for many of the scales in the PRF. The frequent presence of a major interaction between culture and either age, sex, or socioeconomic status provides deeper insight into the meaning of these cross-cultural differences. Only some of the more important findings can be noted here. On the scale of Dominance, for example, the interaction involving culture and socioeconomic status proved to be highly significant. Among upper-class children, no differences were apparent between Mexican and American children. But among lower-class children, the Mexicans received a higher mean score than did the Americans. As expected, boys received higher mean scores than girls in both cultures. High scorers on Dominance are those who attempt to control their environments and to influence and direct other people. They generally enjoy the role of leader and may assume it spontaneously.

A highly significant interaction between culture and sex was found for Aggression in the PRF. No sex differences on Aggression were found among the Mexican boys and girls, as contrasted to the marked difference obtained for the American teenagers, where the boys attained higher scores. It should also be noted that children from lower-class families received higher scores than did those from upper-class families, regardless of sex, age, or culture, a finding consistent with the common observation that children of working-class families tend to be more openly aggressive than upper-class children.

On the scale for Understanding, a significant interaction between culture and age was discovered. Among the sixth graders, the American children expressed a higher drive to understand many areas of knowledge than did the Mexicans, while in the two older groups this difference was reversed, the Mexican teenagers obtaining higher scores than the American.

Regardless of sex, age, or socioeconomic status, Mexican children were significantly higher scorers on the PRF scale for Order as well as the scale for Autonomy, indicating a greater need for neatness and order as well as a greater need for independence among the Mexican adolescents. On four other scales—Play, Social Recognition, Affiliation, and Impulsive-ness—the American children scored higher than the Mexicans. Play and Social Recognition are two scales that help define a factor or broad di-mension in the PRF often referred to as extraversion. While in general the Americans were higher on Affiliation than the Mexicans, this differ-ence was much more pronounced among the girls than among the boys, producing a significant interaction between culture and sex.

In all of these findings for the Personality Research Form scales, it is important to keep in mind that the scales measure perceived needs rather than actual behavior. Thus, for example, one should not be surprised that the Mexican child shows a greater need for independence than the American, even though other information from parental interviews and actual observation reveals that the American child enjoys considerably more autonomy than does the Mexican child of the same age, sex, and socioeconomic status.

On the Test Anxiety Scale for Children, Mexican children received higher mean scores than the American, revealing that they have consid-erably more specific anxiety about taking tests and are likely to be slightly more defensive about test taking than are American children. The mean test anxiety score for all the Mexican children was 16.8, compared to only 9.8 for the Americans. While subtle irregularities in translation from Eng-lish to Spanish could account for a slight dissimilarity in responses, a difference of this magnitude points to a rather fundamental divergence in the conscious way in which school experiences are viewed in the two cultures. Further insight into the nature of this cross-cultural difference can be obtained by examining the Lie Scale and the Defensiveness Scale for the same children. These two smaller scales in Sarason's anxiety in-ventory are designed to see how truthfully and consistently the child is revealing anxieties about being tested. Although the Mexicans obtained slightly higher scores on both scales than did the American children, the differences, while statistically significant, fall far short of explaining the striking cross-cultural differences obtained in test anxiety scores. The most anxious of all about taking tests in school are the lower-class young-er Mexican girls, and the least anxious of all are the upper-class older American boys.

The Occupational Values Inventory also proved to be highly significant in differentiating the two cultures. "Work in which you can help other people" was valued as highly by both boys and girls among the Mexican children, while among the Americans, girls valued this trait much more highly than did boys. "Work where you can get ahead" was valued more highly by boys than girls among the American children, while the reverse was true for the Mexicans. "Work in which you can be with people you like" was valued more highly by American children than by Mexican, regardless of age, socioeconomic status, or sex.

## Tests of Perceptual or Cognitive Style

One approach to the study of personality involves measures that are indirect, which have been termed by others as performance tests of personality or objective approaches to personality (Cattell and Warburton, 1967). The characteristic manner in which a person carries out a perceptual or cognitive task is commonly referred to as perceptual style or cognitive style, and several tests have been developed to measure reliably such individual differences, although little is known with any confidence about the relationship of such performance-based stylistic traits and other aspects of personality.

The Time Estimation Test is a measure of time perception under different circumstances. The Embedded Figures Test has a stylistic component as well as a direct cognitive one. The Perceptual Maturity Scale is designed specifically as a developmental measure of perceptual style. The Object Sorting Test yields a measure of equivalence range, a cognitive style variable. Kagan's Conceptual Styles Test was designed specifically to get at certain cognitive style variables underlying the formation of concepts. And Moran's Word Association Test can also be thought of as a cognitive style test providing an indirect measure of certain personality variables.

On the cognitive style tests taken as a whole, the Mexicans showed more restrictiveness in classifying concepts (Object Sorting Test), showed greater field dependency on the Embedded Figures Test, and perceived time as passing more slowly (Time Estimation Test). At the same time, the Mexican children showed faster associative learning than did the Americans (Visual Fractionation Test). When considered together with the greater number of analytic responses by Mexican children to the Conceptual Styles Test, this more rapid associative learning suggests a higher motivation to do well and a stronger wish to avoid error on the part of the Mexican children. Of these cognitive style measures, the most extensively investigated in other cross-cultural studies is the concept of field dependence as measured by Witkin's Embedded Figures Test.

The field dependence–independence dimension has been broadened to embrace the concept of differentiation (Witkin et al., 1962). Evidence has accumulated from a number of studies that such personality attributes as self-concept, articulateness of body image (degree of detailed clarity and boundaries), and method of impulse regulation (self-control) form an interrelated cluster that includes field independence as measured by Witkin's test. Such psychological differentiation is closely tied to developmental change from undifferentiated early states to more highly differentiated adult states.

Witkin's Embedded Figures Test was given initially only to the nine- and twelve-year-olds in age groups II and III respectively, since the test is too difficult for six-year-olds. The test was given repeatedly for five years, and in the fourth and fifth year of the study, the youngest children were sufficiently old to take the test for two years in a row. For the first three years of repeated testing, highly significant mean differences were discovered between the Mexican and American children. Scores of the Mexican children tended to be more field dependent, regardless of age, socioeconomic status, or sex of the child. It is interesting to note, however, that in the fourth and fifth year of repeated testing, the differences between the Mexican and American children diminished to the point where they were no longer significant. Further analysis indicated that this convergence for the older children was due largely to the fact that Mexican boys caught up with the Americans by the age of 13 and thereafter were indistinguishable from them. By contrast, the Mexican girls regardless of age were generally the slowest in finding the hidden figures. Similar results were obtained for psychological differentiation as measured by the Human Figure Drawing Test, where boys in both cultures received nearly identical scores, and American girls received higher scores than Mexican girls.

Findings presented earlier concerning attitudes, values, family lifestyle, and socialization practices, as summarized in Table 11–3, show a greater emphasis on social conformity, passive–obedient behavior, and traditional values with respect to child rearing by Mexican mothers and a greater emphasis upon independence, curiosity, and freedom for the American mothers. These many differences in family life-styles and socialization practices of Mexicans and Americans would lead one to expect that Mexicans should be more field dependent and Americans more field independent. It should be noted that the actual cross-cultural differences, though highly significant in a statistical sense, are not large. Indeed, with increasing age in the longitudinal study, the cross-cultural differences disappeared for Mexican boys but not girls. Another word of caution that should be injected in any interpretation of these results concerns the lack of any appreciable relationships between scores on the Embedded Figures Test and specific items from the parent interview within each of the two cultures. Admittedly, few of the items within the parent interview proved to be sufficiently sensitive and robust to permit their inclusion in the correlational studies. It is regrettable that more information regarding socialization practices was not obtained in a standardized fashion in each culture so that investigation of these other important points could be fully carried out.

Still another personality difference, revealed by performance on the Human Figure Drawing Test, is consistent with the above pattern of findings. Each drawing of a man or woman was rated on a five-point scale, using a score of 5 to indicate a most feminine-appearing drawing and a score of 1 to indicate a very masculine-appearing drawing. The Mexican children drew more masculine men than did the Americans, with boys generally drawing more masculine men than girls. The most feminine males were drawn by the American girls. A highly significant interaction between culture and sex also appears when the female figures are analyzed for degree of masculinity–femininity. American boys tended to draw much more masculine female figures. Further analysis revealed that the greatest amount of sex differentiation is present among the Mexican girls, followed closely by Mexican boys. The American boys show the poorest degree of differentiation in masculinity–femininity, with American girls not far behind. These marked cultural differences, linked with the sex of the child, probably arise in part from the greater stress in Mexican culture upon differentiating the two sexes.

## The Holtzman Inkblot Technique

As an approach to personality through traditional inkblot tests, the Holtzman Inkblot Technique (HIT) yields 22 standardized scores, many of which can be properly thought of as perceptual style variables, since they measure reliable individual differences in perception. Others are more directly related to personality. It is very difficult to make meaningful distinctions between perceptual–cognitive style variables in inkblot perception, which are often employed as indirect measures of personality, and the more content-oriented inkblot variables, where the personality inference is more easily recognized.

Comparison of Mexican and American children revealed strikingly significant differences for seven of the HIT scores, regardless of age, sex, or socioeconomic status of the child. The means for all Mexican and American children in the first year of testing are given in Table 11–4 for these seven HIT scores, together with a brief interpretation of the meaning of the differences. Three additional inkblot variables—Barrier, Color, and Shading—also showed highly significant differences between Mexican and American children, but the differences have to be qualified since

Table 11–4   *Cross Cultural Mean Scores on the Holtzman Inkblot Technique for Which Uniformly Significant Differences were Obtained in the First Year of Testing*

| SCORE | MEXICAN | AMERICAN | INTERPRETATION FOR MEXICAN |
|---|---|---|---|
| Reaction Time | 21.7 | 17.9 | Slower response time to inkblots |
| Pathognomic verbalization | 3.1 | 6.4 | Less pathology in fantasy |
| Location | 43.3 | 33.3 | More small details |
| Movement | 14.1 | 25.7 | Less movement in fantasy |
| Integration | 2.0 | 3.3 | Lower integration of parts into whole |
| Anxiety | 5.6 | 9.1 | Less anxiety in fantasy |
| Hostility | 6.3 | 10.1 | Less hostility in fantasy |

(From W. H. Holtzman, R. Diaz-Guerrero, and J. D. Swartz, *Personality development in two cultures, a cross-cultural longitudinal study of school children in Mexico and the United States.* University of Texas Press, Austin, 1975. Copyright © 1975 by the Hogg Foundation for Mental Health.)

they are not uniformly present regardless of age, socioeconomic status, or sex.

A brief definition of these ten HIT scores is necessary to understand the results that follow. *Reaction Time* is the average time in seconds from the presentation of an inkblot to the beginning of the response. *Pathognomic Verbalization* is a score reflecting the degree of autistic, bizarre thinking evident in responses to inkblots. *Location* is a score measuring the tendency to break down the inkblot into smaller fragments when reporting a percept. *Movement* reflects the energy level of movement or potential movement ascribed to the percept regardless of content. *Integration* is scored when two or more adequately perceived blot elements are organized into a larger whole. *Anxiety* is based on signs of anxiety in fantasy content as indicated by emotions and attitudes, expressive behavior, symbolism, or cultural stereotypes of fear. *Hostility* is based on signs of hostility in the fantasy content. *Barrier* is a score based on references to any protective covering, membrane, shell, or skin that might be symbolically related to the perception of body-image boundaries in inkblot responses. *Color* measures the apparent primacy of color (including black, gray, or white) as a determinant of a person's responses to inkblots. *Shading* is a similar score dealing with the apparent primacy of shading as a determinant of texture, depth, or vista in a person's inkblot responses.

The Mexican children got significantly lower Barrier scores, with the exception of the six-year-olds from upper-class families, where no differences were found between Mexican and American children. When taken together with the Movement and Integration scores, Barrier defines a major factor in the HIT. Previous studies have indicated that this factor is a measure of well-organized ideational activity, good imaginative capacity, well-differentiated ego boundaries, and awareness of conventional concepts. With the exception of the youngest group of upper-class Mexicans, who tend to be more like their American counterparts in cognitive performance as well, the Mexican children show a considerably lower score on the Factor 1 variables of Movement, Integration, and Barrier. Given this striking difference, it is all the more significant that no cross-cultural differences were found for the Human score, the fourth variable defining Factor 1 in the HIT. *Human* measures the degree of human quality in the content of inkblot responses. While upper-class children in both cultures gave more Human responses than their lower-class counterparts, and the older children gave more Human content than the younger ones, no differences between Mexicans and Americans were apparent. A high degree of Human content in inkblot perception is indicative of a high level of interpersonal socialization.

The extent to which Color entered in as a determinant of the percept also differed markedly in the two cultures. The American children obtained an average score nearly twice as high as the Mexican children. Among the youngest upper-class children in Group I, however, the means were the same for both Mexicans and Americans. The youngest lower-class Americans obtained the highest mean score on Color, indicating an unusually high degree of responsiveness to the color in the inkblot. An emphasis on Color is not present in the Mexican sample at any age. Only the young, lower-class American children showed unusually high scores indicative of impulsive reactive behavior.

Shading also proved much higher for the American Children in general than for the Mexican. This cultural difference was accentuated among the youngest children, diminishing somewhat in Group II and disappearing entirely among the oldest children in Group III.

The HIT was given repeatedly to all children in both cultures for the six years of the longitudinal study, making it possible to employ a repeated-measures analysis-of-variance design to determine the components of variation arising from changes in an individual through time. A general finding emerging from this analysis is that American and Mexican children become more alike with increasing age. It is almost as though socialization in the two cultures and the influences of society, peer groups, and the school, as contrasted to the family, bring the two populations of children closer together on some perceptual and personality characteristics as measured by the Holtzman Inkblot Technique.

Most of the differences between the Mexican and American children on the HIT can be understood better in terms of coping style than any other concept. The American children reacted faster, used larger portions of the inkblots in giving responses, gave more definite form to their responses, and were still able to integrate more parts of the inkblots while doing so. In addition, they incorporated other stimulus properties of the inkblots, such as Color and Shading, into their responses more often than did the Mexican children and elaborated their responses by ascribing more movement to their percepts. In attempting to deal with all aspects of the inkblots in such an active fashion, however, they failed more often than the Mexican children; that is, the Mexican children gave responses with better form and less often produced responses that showed deviant thinking and anxious and hostile content. In general, the American children tried to deal with the testing situation in a much more active fashion than the Mexican children, even when they were unable to do so successfully.

## GENERAL DISCUSSION

A basic value in Mexico is represented by the saying "As long as our family stays together, we are strong." According to the work of Maslow and Diaz-Guerrero (1960), the Mexican family in its solidarity tends to shut itself off from the outer world. The children are brought up in the bosom of the family, playing with their siblings rather than with schoolmates or neighborhood children, as American children usually do. Unlike the father in most American families, the Mexican father is the undisputed authority on all family matters and is usually obeyed without question. The mother, though she may frequently suffer in silence, is revered as the primary source of affection and care. This emphasis on family affiliation leads the Mexican to say, "I will achieve mainly because of my family, and for my family, rather than myself." By contrast, the self-reliant American would say, "I will achieve mainly because of my ability and initiative and for myself rather than my family."

An active style of coping, with all of its cognitive and behavioral implications, involves perceiving problems as existing in the physical and social environment. The best way to resolve such problems is to modify the environment. A passive style of coping assumes that, while problems may be posed by the environment, the best way to cope with them is to change oneself to adapt to circumstances. Many of the cross-cultural differences in the present study can be understood in terms of this general dimension of active versus passive coping style. American children tend to be more actively independent and to struggle for a mastery of problems and challenges in their environment, whereas Mexican children are more passively obedient and adapt to stresses in the environment rather than try to change them.

Obedience, as portrayed in this analysis, refers to clearly defined types of figures in authority, the parents and teachers of the child, who not only are highly respected but also play a major role in providing the interdependent affiliation that is a major feature of the Mexican culture. Any fear or anxiety on the part of the Mexican child concerning the taking of examinations in school is not so much a fear of individual failure as it is a fear of failing to support the interdependent system in which the family plays a central role.

Unlike most Americans, families in Mexico tend to stretch out in a network of relatives that often runs into scores of individuals. Mexicans tend to see themselves achieving by standing on the shoulders of their fathers and mothers or other family members, while Americans see themselves as achieving primarily by virtue of their own independent efforts. Some of the most striking evidence favoring this hypothesis comes from Diaz-Guerrero's studies. He found, for example, that one bipolar item consists of the following pair of statements: (a) One must fight when the rights of the family are threatened, or (b) One must fight when the rights of the individual are threatened. The great majority of Mexicans selected the family-centered alternative, while just the reverse occurred for the Americans.

A primary scale from the Parent-Attitude Survey deals with internal versus external locus of control. In general, Mexican mothers tended to appear more pessimistic, while the Americans were more optimistic in their general outlook on life. These differences are understandable in terms of the general tendency of American society to be viewed as full of hope for the future (at least until very recently), while the social milieu in Mexico would be more likely to induce a pessimistic-fatalistic outlook on life, especially among the lower class.

In spite of the many precautions taken in this cross-cultural, longitudinal study of Mexican and American school children, there may still be some minor differences in test results across the two cultures that arise from the conditions of testing. One can never be sure that one has eliminated all potentially confounding variables in any comparative study of two cultures. That there are strikingly significant cross-cultural similarities and differences in the present study of personality development cannot be denied. Indeed, most of the results reported as significant are based on large numbers of cases with sufficient replication and sufficiently conservative criteria for judging significance to be reasonably certain that the results are highly accurate. Interpretation of the obtained results is another matter. While potentially confounding variables have been reduced to a minimum, other conceivable interpretations of the meaning of the cross-cultural results cannot be definitively rejected. Nevertheless, it is our belief that the above interpretations are plausible and are of considerable value in explaining differences in the modal personalities of the two societies, while recognizing the great range and variety of individual personality configurations found in any culture.

It is also important to emphasize that, in spite of statistically significant differences across the two cultures, the degree of overlap in distribution of personal characteristics of both Mexican and American children, regardless of the trait measured, is far greater than the mean differences attributable to culture. A substantial number of Americans share the characteristics of the Mexican modal personality described above. Similarly, many Mexicans, especially among the better-educated families, exhibit highly active coping styles more characteristic of the modal American personality.

Both societies have gone through major changes during the past decade. Whether the Mexican elite will gradually take on the characteristics of the modal American personality, or whether the American personality will shift closer to the Mexican, cannot be predicted with any reliability at this time. More likely than not, the cultures of both societies will move on to a new order more in keeping with future demands, retaining some common features of the old while establishing new priorities and values. Whatever the specific outcome of these trends in Mexican and American societies, it is clear from the above studies, as well as from the findings of many other investigators, that culture has a profound influence on personality development in children, an influence that can be specifically isolated and measured by properly designed cross-cultural research.

# 12

# Moral Development in Comparative Cultural Perspective

*Carolyn Pope Edwards*

Teaching children right from wrong is a task facing all human societies. Everywhere, parent generations have the explicit task of moral socialization, of arranging the learning environment of their children so that the upcoming generation develops modes of thought and reasoning, and styles of behavior and feeling, that make people "good" or "virtuous" in the culturally desired way. This is one educational task that no society leaves completely to happenstance. The adults are consciously aware that some "teaching" or "managing" must be done to help their children recognize right from wrong and act accordingly.

The universal consciousness of parents that they must take responsibility for making their children into moral beings is a well-known, obvious fact, yet it represents a different state of affairs from what prevails

In certain other prominent domains of children's development. For example, there often seems to be much less agreement among cultural groups about whether it is necessary to plan, intervene, and "educate" to ensure optimal physical growth and development than about whether it is necessary to train and socialize in the moral area.

This broad agreement across societies about moral socialization and the need to intervene and educate would seem to suggest that moral development would constitute an exceptionally accessible subject for cross-cultural study. Yet moral development has proved to be a difficult and controversial research area in comparative child development.

There are at least two reasons for this difficulty. First, methodology remains a major subject of dispute. Havighurst and Neugarten (1955), in a classic cross-cultural study of moral development among native American and white children, commented that methods for investigating moral development were much less advanced than those available for studying mental development. Today, more than 25 years later, that comparison still holds true. No general consensus exists about the validity of any one methodology in the study of moral development. Rather, "stage" and "social-learning" views represent two competing theoretical perspectives that offer alternative methods of studying moral development. The stage perspective is also called the "cognitive-developmental" approach (Kohlberg, 1958, 1969, 1971a), to indicate a focus on the cognitive, or reasoning, component of moral development, and to emphasize the central concern with changes in the child's thought due to normal growth processes. These processes are considered to take the form of a stepwise sequence of stages of reasoning about moral issues. The stage approach originally derived from Piaget's classic (1932) study of children's moral judgments, and has recently inspired much cross-cultural research. This approach will be the focus of the present paper. In contrast, the social-learning perspective (Hoffman, 1970; Bandura, 1973; Sieber, 1980), takes as its task the defining of major dimensions of moral behavior—such as "altruism," "obedience," "cooperation," and "aggression"—and discovering what situational factors and learning experiences influence these behaviors. The social learning perspective once served as the guiding rationale for most cross-cultural study of moral development, but it is less prominent today.

The second reason why cross-cultural study of moral development has proved controversial concerns the problem of comparing cultures without making ethnocentric or invidious comparisons. This is a problem that arises in all comparative work. For example, when ethnic or societal differences on tests of intellectual performance are published, resentment understandably tends to be aroused in the group that scores "poorly" relative to another group. In the area of moral development, comparing cultures may involve (or seem to involve) ranking groups along a dimension of "virtue" or "goodness." Those who study moral development cannot avoid facing this problem. They must educate themselves in philosophical issues of ethics much more than most social scientists, because they must adequately address the question of whether there are any absolutes or universals in the ethical area—moral feelings or ideas that all societies *should* hold regardless of whether or not they *do*.

To illustrate, during the 1940s and 1950s, a group of anthropologists and psychologists discussed whether cultures could be said to rely differentially on "guilt" as the major emotion conditioning people's avoidance of culturally disapproved behavior. Ruth Benedict (1946) and Margaret Mead (1950), for instance, tried to specify cultures that relied more heavily on "guilt" (conceptualized as a self-critical emotion related to a violation of internalized standards) versus those that relied more on "shame" (conceptualized as a concern for the disapproval of others). That is, they distinguished guilt as the discomfort people experience when they disobey the dictates of their conscience, and shame as the discomfort people experience when others they care about find fault with them. The anthropologists' central purpose was not to label societies as "guilt" versus "shame" cultures, but rather to elucidate the cultural patterns, such as family structure or child-rearing practices, that varied in the different types of societies and led to the formation of personalities guided by one or the other type of moral motivation. Taking the argument further, John Whiting (1959), Whiting and Child (1953), and Beatrice Whiting (1963), arguing from a social-learning perspective, examined the systems of social control prevailing in different societies. Three such systems were, in John Whiting's (1959) vivid terms, "sorcery," "sin," and the "superego." The Whitings produced evidence to show that these social control systems were related to particular family forms and child-rearing practices that resulted in personalities suited to function in the different kinds of systems. Thus cross-cultural methods were used to gain an understanding of the forces that might produce different outcomes in terms of moral development.

The question raised by these cross-cultural studies is whether they involved ethnocentric judgments, or violated principles of cultural relativism (Brandt, 1959). That is, did the fact that the work involved comparisons between cultures contradict the notion that the morals and value systems of all cultures should be considered on an equal plane, because

there is no objective basis for judging the system of one society superior
or inferior to another? Some might say yes, the work did violate cultural
relativism because it involved evaluating whether particular cultures were
more or less characterized by "good" development defined in terms of
internalized conscience. However, the researchers did not operate from
an explicit or implicit assumption that guilt was a "better" type of moral
motivation than other motives, such as shame or fear of punishment.
Only if they had taken the position that guilt was a better moral motivation than the others could the cross-cultural comparisons be said to
have involved ranking societies as more or less moral. Such a perspective,
the Whitings would and did argue, is ethnocentric and unfounded.

It can be seen that the cross-cultural study of moral development en-
tails the problem of potentially ethnocentric ranking of cultures only
when the researchers use a moral dimension that involves a "good" or
"higher" end, and a "bad" or "lower" end. Otherwise, it concerns comparisons of a neutral or value-free type. Returning to our earlier distinction between social-learning versus stage approaches, we can say that
research in the social-learning tradition has explicitly been morally neutral, but research in the stage tradition has purposefully involved a
scheme of moral judgment stages for which higher reasoning is necessarily better reasoning—more mature, complex, and differentiated.
Kohlberg, the leading moral stage theorist, has repudiated and argued
against the doctrine of cultural relativism with respect to the ranking of
cultures on moral development. (Kohlberg, 1971a). Whether such a position by Kohlberg and his followers is justified shall be discussed later.
First, however, we shall describe the stage perspective on moral development.

## THE STAGE PERSPECTIVE: FURTHER DESCRIPTION

The stage perspective describes moral judging or reasoning as a construction by the individual. The focus of study is on the reasoning structures,
actively constructed by the thinking person, that underlie moral judging
and guide moral action. Piaget originated the stage approach to moral
development in his 1932 classic, *The Moral Judgment of the Child*, a study
of 5- to 13-year-old Swiss children of the Genevan working class. Piaget
described two childhood stages of moral reasoning. He characterized the
earlier stage, called *heteronomous morality*, or *morality of constraint*, by the
naive assumption (on the part of the child) that moral rules are external,
absolute, and unchanging. For children at this stage, a rule defines what

is forbidden and punished, and its rightness derives simply from the power of those people who do the forbidding and punishing. The later stage (generally found in children over age 7 or 8) Piaget called *autonomous morality*, or *morality of cooperation*. This stage he characterized by an understanding that "ought" in the moral realm is different from "cause" in the physical realm. Furthermore, at the later stage, moral rules are not just accepted as true without any justification. Rather, rules are understood as defensible by some broad justification having to do with such factors as tradition, legality, utility, fairness, or consensus. Piaget did not believe that all cultural groups would show the same extent of development. Rather, he expected that "primitive" or "traditional" societies would likely contain people who do *not* develop beyond the earlier, heteronomous stage (Piaget, 1932, Chapter 4). This result would follow from two features of primitive societies (as Piaget saw them): the high within-group homogeneity of traditional societies, and their heavy regulation by the elders of the group. Both features would tend to prevent the child from discovering that moral rules have an arbitrary element (that is, the rules may vary across human societies and change over time); hence, the child would not be impelled to seek rational justification of moral rules. Cross-cultural research has not substantially supported hypotheses derived from Piaget's contentions, however. Nor has research gone far in establishing what are actual cultural group variations and constancies along Piaget's dimensions (Edwards, 1980; Lickona, 1976).

## Kohlberg's System of Stages

Kohlberg's (1958, 1969, 1971a, 1978) approach to moral development is an elaboration of Piaget's with respect to both theory and method. Kohlberg's theory posits a culturally universal sequence of six developmental stages. Each of the moral stages has internal coherence; a stage is a "structure," or unified whole. The stages are arranged in ascending order of complexity, with each representing a more stable and logically powerful framework for resolving conflicts than the one before.

The testing procedure developed by Kohlberg involves a standard set of moral dilemmas and probing questions that require the subject to think as deeply as he or she can about the issues posed. For example, one dilemma developed for East African research (Edwards, 1974), concerns a man named Daniel whose secondary school fees have been paid by his older brother. Later, at the time that Daniel's first son is about to enter school, the older brother has an incapacitating accident. Daniel, who is very poor, is torn between either paying the school fees of the brother's child (as his parents urge him to do) or paying those of his own son (as his wife insists).

Such dilemmas have been found to be challenging and interesting. Scoring an interview involves ascertaining what moral stage, or combination of stages, is reflected in the subject's reasoning; Colby (1978) describes the evolution of the scoring system of procedures. The six stages are summarized in Table 12–1.

## The Social Perspectives Underlying Kohlberg's Stages

In recent years, Kohlberg and his colleagues have become more interested in different social perspectives that underlie the various stages (Kohlberg, 1976; Gibbs et al., 1976; Colby et al., 1979). These theorists have attempted to delineate how each moral judgment stage is actually predicated on a specifiable and coherent set of assumptions about the nature of social relations and society.

Developmental change in social perspectives occurs because as children mature, they become capable of more and more complex cognitive tasks. Hence they are able to conceptualize social relations in progressively more differentiated and systematic ways. For example, at Stage 1 (see Table 12–1, right-hand column), children do not yet have a social perspective, due to their cognitive egocentrism. At Stage 2, children know that another person has his or her own subjective self, and they consistently try to assume that person's perspective when they talk about what he or she wants. In resolving moral dilemmas, Stage 2 children tend to be rigid and take the point of view of one actor in the dilemma, or they vacillate from one person's perspective to another's. They cannot yet coordinate two or more people's perspectives, and so they cannot resolve the dilemma by surveying with the mind's eye the whole scene and deciding what is best "from everyone's point of view."

At Stage 3, people conceptualize society as a group of individuals in relationship with one another, and they try to rise above the point of view of the concrete individual and take a general group perspective. In resolving moral dilemmas, they identify with society and its rules and attempt to decide what meets "everybody's *best* interests." To do this, they take as guidelines the shared wisdom of their group, its rules, norms, customary role expectations. For example, when Stage 3 people hear a story of a 2-year-old giving his new birthday doll to a 12-year-old in exchange for a piece of gum, they say that the older child's behavior is "unfair" because he is taking advantage of the 2-year-old. However, the Stage 3 perspective is limited in that it assumes that there is *one* right

**Table 12–1**  *The Six Moral Judgement Stages*

| LEVEL AND STAGE | WHAT IS RIGHT? | REASONS FOR DOING RIGHT | SOCIAL PERSPECTIVE OF STAGE |
|---|---|---|---|
| LEVEL I: PRECONVENTIONAL | | | |
| Stage 1: Heteronomous Morality | To avoid breaking rules that are backed by punishment. Obedience for its own sake. Avoiding physical damage to persons and property. | Avoidance of punishment; the superior power of authorities. | Egocentric point of view. Does not consider the interests of others or recognize that they differ from the actor's; does not relate two points of view. Actions are considered physically rather than in terms of psychological interests of others. Confusion of authority's perspective with one's own. |
| Stage 2: Individualism, instrumental purpose, and exchange | Following rules only when it is to one's immediate interest; acting to meet one's own interests and needs and letting others do the same. Right is also what is fair, what is an equal exchange, a deal, an agreement. | To serve one's own needs or interests in a world where it is recognized that other people have their own interests too. | Concrete individualistic perspective. Awareness that each person has interests to pursue, and that these interests may conflict, so that right is relative (in the concrete individualistic sense). |

LEVEL II:
CONVENTIONAL

**Stage 3:**
Mutual interpersonal expectations, relationships, and interpersonal conformity

Living up to what is expected by significant others or what is generally expected of people in the role of daughter, brother, friend, and so on. "Being good" is important and means having good motives, showing concern about others. It also means keeping mutual relationships, such as trust, loyalty, respect and gratitude.

The need to be a good person in one's own eyes and those of others. Caring for others. Belief in the Golden Rule. Desire to maintain rules and authority that support stereotypical good behavior.

Perspective of the individual in relationship with other individuals.
Aware of shared feelings, agreements, and expectations that take primacy over individual interests. Relates points of view through the concrete Golden Rule, "putting yourself in the other guy's shoes." Does not yet consider generalized system perspective.

**Stage 4:**
Social system and conscience

Fulfilling duties to which one has agreed. Laws are to be upheld except in extreme cases where they conflict with other fixed social duties. Right also means contributing to society, the group, or institution.

To maintain the institution as a whole; to avoid the breakdown in the system that would happen "if everyone did it"; or the imperative of conscience to meet one's defined obligations. (Easily confused with Stage 3 belief in rules and authority.)

Societal point of view is differentiated from interpersonal agreement of motives.
Takes the point of view of the system that defines roles and rules. Considers individual relations in terms of place in the system.

**Table 12–1** *The Six Moral Judgement Stages*

| LEVEL AND STAGE | WHAT IS RIGHT? | REASONS FOR DOING RIGHT | SOCIAL PERSPECTIVE OF STAGE |
|---|---|---|---|
| LEVEL III: POSTCONVENTIONAL, OR PRINCIPLED | | | |
| Stage 5: Social contract or utility and individual rights | Being aware that people hold a variety of values and opinions, that most values and rules are relative to the group. However, these rules should usually be upheld, in the interest of impartiality and because they form the social contract. Some nonrelative values and rights such as life and liberty, however, must be upheld in any society and regardless of majority opinion. | A Sense of obligation to law because of the social contract to make and abide by laws for the welfare of all and for the protection of all people's rights. A feeling of contractual commitment, freely entered upon, to family, friendship, trust, and work obligations. Concern that laws and duties be based on rational calculation of overall utility. "The greatest good for the greatest number." | Prior-to-society perspective. Perspective of a rational individual aware of values and rights prior to social attachments and contracts. Integrates perspectives by formal mechanisms of agreement, contract, objective impartiality, and due process. Considers moral and legal points of view; recognizes that they sometimes conflict and finds it difficult to integrate them. |

| Stage 6: Universal ethical principles | Following self-chosen ethical principles. Particular laws or social agreements are usually valid because they rest on such principles. When laws violate these principles, one acts in accordance with the universal principles of justice: the equality of human rights and respect for the dignity of human beings as individual persons. | The belief as a rational person in the validity of universal moral principles, and a sense of personal commitment to them. | Perspective of a moral point of view from which social arrangements derive. Perspective is that of a rational individual recognizing the nature of morality or the fact that persons are ends in themselves and must be treated as such. |

*Source:* From L. Kohlberg, "Moral stages and moralization: The cognitive developmental approach," in T. Lickona (ed.), *Moral development and behavior.* New York: Holt, Rinehart & Winston, 1976.

set of rules and expectations. The Stage 3 perspective presumes that society is a sort of homogeneous, harmonious "we" composed of people who share moral values (Selman, 1976).

At Stage 4, society is explicitly conceived of as a complex whole composed of competing groups with conflicting values and interests. Conflicts and preferences must be mediated through formal institutions such as courts and legislatures. Stage 4 is thus more abstract than Stage 3 in its underlying assumptions about the nature of society. Stage 4 represents what Kohlberg calls a "systems perspective," because it posits the solution to social conflicts in terms of political and legal institutions. For example, Stage 3 people respect authority out of a personal feeling of affection for a leader or out of belief in the leader's personal goodness— the idea that a leader must be a "good person" is assumed without reflection. At Stage 4, with a perspective appropriate for an institution that is bureaucratically organized, people respect authority out of "respect for the *role*," for the powers formally delegated to the leader by society. The leader is not necessarily thought of as a good person but rather conceived as one who occupies a role whose duties and powers derive from the social group. Finally, at Stages 5 and 6, the individual comes to take a social perspective that is highly philosophical and detached—the individual constructs a view of someone "who has made the moral commitments or holds the standards on which a good or just society must be based" (see Colby et al., 1979).

To illustrate the thinking typical of the moral stages most frequently used by adolescents and adults, excerpts are provided below from interviews of East African university students (Edwards, 1974). The excerpts come from answers by the students to the dilemma of Daniel and the school fees. The interviews suggest the concrete flavor of Stage 2 (with its focus on instrumental exchange), the "good person" emphasis of Stage 3 (with its focus on stereotyped role expectation such as those of the good parent or good son), and the "systems perspective" of Stage 4.

*Excerpt from Interview Scored as Stage 2*

> *Interviewer:*  What should Daniel do?
> *Respondent:*  He should pay his son's school fees. When you get a child, you imagine what the child will do for you in the future, and so you have to prepare him for the future so that he can take care of you when you are old. . . .
> *Interviewer:*  Why should someone give that help to his parents?
> *Respondent:*  If your parents took care of you when you were young,

why can't you do that at least when you are grown up? Let them feel that they are gaining from what they did.

*Excerpt from Interview Scored as Stage 3*

*Interviewer:*   Why did you say Daniel should put his own son first?
*Respondent:*   You stand a chance of being blamed or kind of despised by the community because they would say, "Well, this man is failing in his duty as a father and he's depending on someone else to give help. He's leaving his own children to suffer or to fail to get an education. . . . " So it's actually you're thinking of what the community is going to say about you that makes you know you must put your son first. . . .
*Interviewer:*   Why should a grown-up person help his parents?
*Respondent:*   In most cases you just feel that your parents having loved you all the time when you were young and having helped you with what you need, it would only be right and just for you also to support them in their old age.

*Excerpt from Interview Scored as Stage 4*

*Interviewer:*   What should Daniel do?
*Respondent:*   In this case I think Daniel should help his brother's son because it is clear that he has been helped by his brother. . . . Personally, I feel he has an obligation or a duty to help his brother's son. He must also help the brother's family if he is able, at least give them something to keep them going. . . .
*Interviewer:*   What should a grown-up son do for his parents?
*Respondent:*   According to our people, there is a feeling of dependency, that you should support your parents and support your brothers and sisters. . . . You depend on one another for survival. . . . Even if the father has been unkind or cruel to you, maybe he was actually trying to put you in the right way. Say, in a polygynous household, the father has to exercise some authority or be cruel to some people so as to manage that large homestead. So in that case I think you shouldn't feel the father was punishing you. You shouldn't retaliate.

## Cultural Universality and Kohlberg's Theory

Kohlberg proposed that the sequence of stages is culturally universal and based this claim on three assumptions. First, there is a necessary order to the sequence derived from the progressive logical complexity of the six stages. Second, the moral dilemmas center on universal issues, such as life, property, authority, and trust. Thus, with suitable modifications, they (or new dilemmas constructed on similar principles) should represent real moral conflicts to anyone anywhere. Third, because all cultural groups share the same basic problems of social control, they have evolved value systems that possess certain formal and functional properties in common, such as categories of right and wrong, obligation, moral responsibility, and blame.

Although Kohlberg believes that all groups display reasoning that could be scored using the stage system, he does not see all cultural groups as typically advancing at the same rate or to the same ultimate extent. Rather, like Piaget, he believes that people in traditional, family-oriented societies lack certain social experiences that are available in many societies and that are necessary for attainment of the higher moral stages. Moreover, and more importantly, he thinks that these cultural differences have *moral* significance. As he puts it, variations between cultures "are not morally arbitrary . . . . [because] there is a sense in which we can characterize moral differences between groups or individuals as being more or less adequate morally" ( Kohlberg, 1971a, pp. 176–177).

To arrive at this conclusion, Kohlberg has started from a statement that has wide agreement: namely, that as the normal individual's moral judgment develops with age and experience, his or her thinking becomes more complex and differentiated, hence (in a formal sense) more adequate and mature. Another way of saying this is that the adults in a society, relative to the children, are capable of more adequate and mature moral judgment. Kohlberg has then extended this comparison to cultural group differences. He has asserted that cultural groups whose members display reasoning at a higher stage can be said to be more adequate with respect to their moral reasoning. Thus Kohlberg has taken the position that the stage sequence is culturally universal and so is the yardstick of increasing adequacy which accompanies that sequence. The latter point—the universality of the standard of adequacy—has proved extremely controversial. Kohlberg has been charged with cultural ethnocentrism because he claims that there is one most desirable end point to the developmental process for moral judgment (see Simpson, 1974; Aron, 1977). However, as the final section of this chapter will argue, Kohlberg's assertion about a culturally universal standard of adequacy of moral judgment (higher stages being necessarily better) is improper and invalid. But first there is a less controversial topic to consider, one in which work with stage theory has made a more generally accepted contribution to the comparative study of moral development. This topic concerns how social experiences might stimulate or facilitate development.

# EXPERIENTIAL INFLUENCES
# ON MORAL DEVELOPMENT

Experiential influences on moral stage development is one area of cross-cultural work that is extremely important. We expect cross-cultural research to prove successful for generating and testing hypotheses about sources of developmental change. Taking advantage of the natural range of variation in social life worldwide, cross-cultural research can offer an understanding of experiential influences that would be inaccessible by relying only on American studies. Cross-cultural research can be used to perform two roles; (1) to check generalizations that have been made on the basis of American studies, and (2) to investigate new hypotheses suggested by ethnographic accounts of other cultures.

Cross-cultural work on the role of experience in moral stage development could also help to fill a major gap in the literature. One major criticism of the work of the stage theorists has been their general lack of attention to the topic of experiential influences. Rather, say their critics, stage theorists have been so interested in understanding the structure and sequence of stages that they have neglected the question of what environmental events help stimulate the individual to development through those stages. In fact, few studies from a stage theoretical perspective have been designed to discover which real-life, naturally occurring experiences are most stimulating. Only a few investigations have used Kohlberg's stages (see review in Edwards, 1978) to study the facilitative influences in the normal lives of American children. This paucity stands in striking contrast to the work by the social-learning school on moral development. There, the study of "socialization" experiences has certainly always represented one of the most prominent lines of research. For example, Bandura and his colleages have studied intensively the influence of models on aggressive behavior in children (Bandura, 1973). Saltzstein and other workers have examined parent behaviors conducive to the internalization of moral norms (see Saltzstein, 1976, and review in Hoffman, 1970). Mischel and colleagues have looked for the roots of the capacity to delay gratification—that is, to withstand temptation when appropriate (Mischel and Mischel, 1976).

For those interested in natural causes of moral stage change, writings by major stage theorists (Piaget, 1932; Kohlberg, 1963, 1969; Turiel, 1974) offer a rich supply of theoretical speculations about ways in which parents, peers, and secondary reference groups might foster moral development. Because these effects are proposed to be culturally universal, they should be testable in any cultural setting. As I shall try to show, non-Western cultures in some cases offer better settings for testing certain hypotheses than can be found here at home. Naturally occurring social experiences in those cultures provide opportunities to focus on different antecedent variables. Strategic "within-culture" studies conducted in non-Western settings can expand in a crucial way our evidence on moral development.

## Social Experience and Early Moral Development

As a stage theorist, Kohlberg conceptualizes environmental influences in terms of experiences that stimulate individuals to successively restructure their moral categories. As described earlier, each stage has a different underlying social perspective. Thus experiences that stimulate individuals toward more advanced concepts of society and social relations tend to facilitate moral development. These "critical" experiences may vary according to individuals' levels of moral judging. For example, theoretical writings suggest that experiences with groups emotionally close to the self, such as one's family or circle of friends, are facilitative of early moral development, while for later moral development experiences involving distant social groups, such as the wider community or nation, play a more significant part.

Positive experiences with primary institutions or reference groups, such as the childhood peer group and the family, are considered sufficient to enable the individual to pass through the first three stages of moral judgment. In these social contexts, for example in the family, the individual first becomes able to consider the perspective of another person in a concrete situation (simple role taking), and then learns a more abstract form of role taking (for instance, by thinking in terms of culturally defined roles and stereotyped normal of good behavior). These two achievements form the foundation for transitions from moral Stages 1 to 2 and 2 to 3, respectively (Selman, 1976). Participation in neither a family nor a peer group is considered by the theory to be absolutely necessary, however. For early moral development to occur, the individual must simply have ongoing personal relationships to provide enough warmth and caring so that the person is encouraged to empathize and take another person's perspective.

To test the facilitating effect of naturally occurring family and peer relations, American psychologists have designed studies capitalizing on psychological differences between groups of people. The problem with such an approach is that it is difficult to determine cause and effect for the resulting correlations. For example, do parents who are authoritarian about family discussions create children whose moral judgment develops slowly, or does having children with low moral-judgment levels discourage parents from using democratic decision-making? It is, of course, never possible to prove causation on the basis of correlations. In the above studies, however, it is difficult even to argue which is the more reasonable direction for the causation to be going. Both the independent and the dependent variables in the correlations refer to behavioral or personality attributes that could be either causes or effects of each other. In contrast, when the *independent* variable relates to something that happens to the person "from outside" for reasons that can have nothing to do with the dependent variable, then it is possible to argue that the postulated cause–effect relationship is the more likely direction of causation.

Cross-cultural research has provided the opportunity to conduct studies with independent variables that capitalize on sources of individual variation that are not related to behavioral and personality differences between groups of people. Rather, it has been possible to locate variations in social experience that are due to institutions or due to cultural change at the societal level. Certainly, this could have been done without resorting to cross-cultural work, but the cultural perspective stimulates such an approach.

## Kenyan Studies of the Moral Development of Students

In a recent study conducted with secondary and university students in the East African nation of Kenya (Edwards, 1974, 1978), I was able to test three hypotheses about the effect of family and peer experiences on moral development. First, students from more "modernized" backgrounds were predicted to show higher levels of moral judgment than students from more "traditional" backgrounds, even when both groups had had comparable schooling. (Schooling was considered to be a different source of influence on moral development and was controlled for, rather than investigated, in my research). The first hypothesis was based on consideration of changes in child rearing practices that are occurring in Kenya today under the impact of economic development. More modernized parents (generally those with more education are likely to negotiate conflicts with their children and to allow them to "talk back" and question their authority (B. B. Whiting, 1973, 1974, 1977). Modernized parents foster the self-assertiveness and verbal facility that will help their offspring succeed at school. Traditionally in Kenya, adults have tended to expect overt forms of respect between old and young—obedience without prolonged discussion or negotiation. Therefore the dimension of modernization allowed an indirect test for a hypothesis about the stimulating experiences that are provided when parents allow or encourage abstract discussions with their children. The same hypothesis was addressed by studies of U.S. parents who handled discussions with their children in a "democratic" versus "authoritarian" style (Shoffeit, 1971; Holstein, 1972; White, 1973; Denney and Duffy, 1974). Although these studies found the expected relationships, difficulties arose in interpreting the results and distinguishing cause from effect. In the case of the African studies, in contrast, it seems clear that modernization is the cause, and differences found in children's moral judgment are the effects.

The second hypothesis concerned students who had lived on their own away from home. Such students were predicted to show higher levels of moral judgment than students who lived relatively longer at home under the authority of parenting figures. The former students were expected to have had more need to think about moral and other issues because they could not rely on their parents to make decisions for them. Their parents and other adult relatives were not near at hand to protect them from the unsettling effects of exposure to all sorts of temptation. Thus students living on their own were expected to have moved more quickly, compared to their peers living at home, to the more abstract understandings of morality embodied by the conventional stages. This second hypothesis could readily be tested in Kenya due to the fact that many rural secondary students must leave their home communities to go to boarding school or to attend an urban school while living in a youth hostel. Interviews with students at the University of Nairobi (Edwards, 1974) suggested that independent living was, in fact, experienced as a dramatic cause of personal value change. The following two quotations illustrate the students' expressed feelings:

> It's up to you to think what you should be doing, and you have to sit down and decide exactly what you want to do. And I think in this way you sort of come to the conclusion—you actually find what you are like. Sometimes when you are in secondary school you don't bother. You just think you are like everyone else.

> Coming here was a great change in that I think I was much more free, and I did not have to account to anybody what I was doing. . . . It made me, I think, grow up really.

Thus length of time away from home was predicted to related to moral judgment because it represented increased opportunity for peer interaction and moral discussion.

Third, students who attended culturally pluralistic schools were predicted to show higher levels of moral judgment than students who attended schools that contained people of only one cultural group (even when schools were fully equal in terms of academic performance of students). The last hypothesis could readily be tested in Kenya because the British colonizers set up a number of secondary schools, presently called "national" schools, that now draw students from all of the major racial (African, Indo-Pakistani, and Euro-American) and ethnic groups in the country. Thus the national schools are racially as well as tribally diverse. Other Kenyan schools, founded since independence, draw students from one ethnic region only and thus tend to be culturally homogeneous. Interviews with university students were the source of suggestions that attending the pluralistic schools might facilitate the development of moral judgment.

> I used not to have high regard for the Luo community. And then I learned they were not actually very bad people from a friend of mine, a Catholic. After living with them in Homobay I knew they were not all that bad. You knew, you were biased from childhood. We had sayings you shouldn't eat with one.

> I started questioning my previous instruction very much, and consequently I think I lost a lot of my traditionally African moral values through the interaction with these white boys.

> The Africans coming from the rural area, they tell me [an urban Indian] how they live, what sort of things they go through, what is their daily life and such, and that makes me realize how differently I have been living all this time. I have not been aware of how they have been living until quite recently, and how it affects their everyday life even at the University—how they think and the sort of ideas they come up with. . . . It has made me much more objective, really.

In the pluralistic schools, students are exposed to the perspectives of many different kinds of people. They exchange information about their cultural traditions and gain a more comprehensive view of their own value system. Sometimes they come to question childhood authorities who have taught them rules without providing any underlying justifications. Thus, attending the pluralistic schools can be an intense role-taking experience that may lead to restructuring of moral values, to moral development.

All three hypotheses predict accelerated moral development. The hypotheses were tested using as the dependent variable, Moral Maturity Quotients, a measure of level of moral judgment based on the Kohlberg interview. The subjects for the study included one sample of 52 University of Nairobi students and a second sample of 40 secondary school students from the cities of Nairobi and Nyeri. (The samples and procedures are described in full in Edwards, 1974, 1975, 1978). Each subject was individually interviewed. The taped interviews were later transcribed and rated to ascertain which one of the six stages, or which adjoining two stages, best represented the overall level of the subject's arguments (see Colby, 1978, for Global Method of rating). The stage ratings were converted into numerical scores (Moral Maturity Quotients) by obtaining weighted averages.

With both samples, the hypotheses were tested by performing correlations between Moral Maturity Quotients and independent variables based on the three experiences described above. *Family modernization* was measured by parental education, the best single measure of parents' knowledge of and orientation to the national government and the modern sector of the economy. *Independent living* was measured by the number of years that a student had spent away from home. *Attending pluralistic school* was measured by number of years that a student had spent in racially or tribally mixed schools.

Family modernization correlated positively and significantly with Moral Maturity Quotients for the younger, secondary sample. Negative results, however, were obtained from these variables with the older, university group. Significant results were also obtained for the relationship between Moral Maturity Quotients and attending pluralistic school, again for the younger sample only. These two results were not confounded by students' age, sex, facility with English (as measured by a national standardized test), or overall academic performance. Finally, amount of independent living was found to correlate significantly and positively for the university—but not the secondary school—sample.

Thus the three hypotheses were partially confirmed. Moreover, the positive findings are supported by the significant correlations that Maqsud (1976, 1977a, 1977b) found for Nigerian secondary students on his measures of Moral Maturity and the variables of independent living and attending culturally pluralistic schools. Besides providing some support for the specific hypotheses, both sets of African studies show how cross-cultural studies can stimulate thought about sociological variables and their relationship to psychological development.

Maqsud and I have not argued *how* the experiences facilitate moral development. On the one hand, the experiences might promote general cognitive growth (concrete and formal operations, in Piaget's terms) that has as a by-product the development of reasoning in a specific area, moral judgment. On the other hand, the experiences might promote moral development directly, without having any measurable effect on general cognitive growth. Which of these two alternative explanations is correct could be determined by investigating moral and cognitive development in conjunction with social experience.

## Social Experience and Later Moral Development

According to stage theory, different kinds of social experiences may promote early versus later moral development. As described above, caregivers, siblings, and friends provide the attachment experiences and small-group interaction that are valuable for facilitating the early moral stages. The social role taking that underlies the early stages is facilitated by close and warm relations with other persons. In those relations, the child learns to take the perspective of another and becomes motivated to use role-taking skills in solving moral problems. Further, interpersonal relations in family and peer group provide knowledge of social roles (for example, authority roles) as well as the problems of group living.

In contrast, to facilitate the development of the higher moral stages, experiences would be required that help a person to conceptualize the social system in abstract ways, especially to think about problems of social control and conflicts between groups or individuals. Working for an organization, studying government or sociology, and performing community leadership are a few examples of the types of experiences that might be important to an adolescent or adult in the process of developing moral reasoning. The experiences would provide the individual with the social-knowledge base needed to construct the abstract concepts of morality found at Stages 4 and above.

One type of evidence that Kohlberg has put forward to support the role of social experience in later moral development concerns social class differences in performance on the moral judgment test. Middle-class groups have consistently been found to score higher than working-class groups in all societies tested (for example, Turiel, Edwards, and Kohlberg, 1978). Kohlberg (1969) has interpreted these differences in terms of the exclusion of working-class groups from participation in the decision-making institutions of society. Thus, working-class persons have less incentive to take the perspective on morality that underlies moral reasoning beyond Stage 3. However, because members of social classes differ in so many ways other than participation in secondary institutions, further supporting evidence for the theory would be extremely valuable.

The cross-cultural literature may provide such support, in that many studies reveal a difference in performance on the moral judgment test between members of small-scale versus large-scale societies. Large-scale societies are those diversified, complex, "modern" societies characterized by large and heterogeneous populations, social classes, occupational specialization, and formal institutions such as legislatures, welfare agencies, police, and courts of law. Small-scale societies are those relatively simpler, homogeneous, "traditional" societies characterized by a small population, face-to-face relations among people, and an absence of social classes, occupational specialization, or formal institutions (Whiting and Whiting, 1975). Findings from a number of studies suggest that moral judgment Stages 4, 5, and 6 are not generally found in interviews with traditional adults who live in small-scale societies such as isolated peasant or tribal communities. (See Kenyan studies by Edwards, 1974, 1975; Turkish studies by Turiel, Edwards, and Kohlberg, 1978; Bahamian studies by White, 1975, 1977, White et al., 1978; British Honduran studies by Gorsuch and Barnes, 1973).* Rather, only Stages 1 to 3 seem to dominate among such groups of people. For such people, the frame of reference is their village, their immediate face-to-face community. Stage 4 as a predominant stage may be absent from these samples of people because the "systems" perspective underlying Stage 4 does not correspond to the social organization of peasant or tribal communities (Edwards, 1975). For example, as we discussed earlier, the definition of authority at Stage 4 is appropriate for a bureaucracy, and bureaucratic organizations are not found in traditional tribal communities.

Stage 4 as a predominant mode of reasoning does appear in interviews with the secondary- or college-educated adults from a large number of Western and non-Western societies, such as Britain, Canada, India, Israel, Kenya, Nigeria, Turkey, and Thailand (Batt, 1975a, 1975b;

---

*The merit of this generalization depends, of course, on whether the moral judgment test was actually administered and scored validly in the various studies. Regarding methodology, the following three criteria are important: (1) the dilemma must be designed or adapted to be appropriate for the cultural setting involved; (2) dilemmas and probing questions must be translated correctly into the language of the subjects, and subjects' answers must be translated without distortion back into English for scoring; and (3) interviews must be conducted so as to elicit subjects' "best," highest reasoning (this usually means oral rather than written interviews). The studies listed above can be judged to be adequate according to these criteria. However, with respect to the issue of translating, much more explicit attention needs to be paid in the future, to determine whether problems of translation could significantly alter moral judgment scores obtained.

Edwards, 1974, 1975, 1978; Kohlberg, 1971b; Maqsud, 1977a, 1977b, 1977c; Parikh, 1980; Sullivan, 1975; Turiel et al., 1978; Weinreich, 1977). The subjects in all of these studies have had experiences that could provide the knowledge base needed for abstract conceptualization of social systems. For instance, they have worked in large organizations, learned in school about the structure of their national government, and experienced conflicts in values and interests between different ethnic groups and social classes.

## Kenyan Studies of Adult Moral Reasoning

My findings from Kenya (Edwards, 1974, 1975) indicate more fully how knowledge and experiences derived from education or occupational roles might relate to moral judgment. In one study, the moral judgment of University of Nairobi students was compared to that of local community leaders from four ethnic groups, the Kikuyu, Luhia, Kipsigis, and Ismaeli. The leaders were selected by university students who went back to their home towns or villages and interviewed the men or women locally most respected for their honesty and moral leadership. The students selected as "moral leaders" those individuals generally believed to be thoughtful interpreters of community values, good advisers during community disputes, and people who could be counted on to work responsibly on behalf of the group. While the university students exceeded most of the community leaders in education and were much more identified with the modern institutions of government and politics, they did not surpass the community leaders in moral and personal reputation. The moral judgment scores of the two groups are shown in Table 12–2. It can be seen that Stage 4 is found in only 11 percent of the community leaders as opposed to 31 percent of the university students.

All four of the leaders who showed Stage 4 reasoning possessed either secondary or higher levels of education and occupations in the modern sector of the economy (teacher, business manager, bank officer, executive secretary). In contrast, the leaders who were traditional village farmers or laborers were scored as Stage 3, or Stages 2 and 3 mixed.

Moreover, in a second study of community leaders and nonleaders in a Kenyan Kipsigis agricultural community, again only Stages 2, 3, and 4 were found. The leaders were significantly more likely to be Stage 3, or 3 mixed with 4, and the nonleaders to be Stage 2, or 2 mixed with 3 (Harkness, Edwards, and Super, 1980). The two men in this latter study who showed moral reasoning at the Stage 4 level were the two most educated leaders (with 6 and 8 years of school respectively). They were

**Table 12–2**  *Frequency Distribution of Moral Judgment Scores, for Two Samples of East African Adults*

FREQUENCIES (AND PERCENTAGES) OF SUBJECTS, BY SAMPLE, RECEIVING DIFFERENT MORAL JUDGMENT STAGE SCORES

| SAMPLE | STAGE 1 | STAGES 1 AND 2 MIXED | STAGE 2 | STAGES 2 AND 3 MIXED | STAGE 3 | STAGES 3 AND 4 MIXED | STAGE 4 | STAGES 4 AND 5 MIXED | TOTAL |
|---|---|---|---|---|---|---|---|---|---|
| University students | 0 | 0 | 2 (4%) | 21 (40%) | 13 (25%) | 11 (21%) | 3 (6%) | 2 (4%) | 52 (100%) |
| Community leaders | 0 | 0 | 6 (17%) | 14 (39%) | 12 (33%) | 4 (11%) | 0 | 0 | 36 (100%) |

*Source:* Table adapted from C. P. Edwards, "Societal complexity and moral development: A Kenyan study," *Ethos,* 1975, 3, 505–527.

relatively young men (32 and 40 years of age), and were considered to be modern rather than traditional in their outlook and values.

The following two quotations illustrate how a traditional community leader, scored as Stage 3, approached questions about the value of human life in a different way than a university student with a modern orientation, scored as Stage 4. The community leader's answers were judged to be Stage 3 because they defined the value of life in terms of affectional ties, social sharing, and community. The university student's responses were judged to be Stage 4 because they conceived of life as sacred in terms of its place in categorical moral or religious order of rights and obligations. The first quotation suggests the appropriateness of Stage 3 for talking about moral relations in a tribal village, while the second quotation illustrates the usefulness of Stage 4 modes for discussing morality from a larger societal perspective.

### Quotation from a Leader in a Kipsigis Community from Western Kenya

*Interviewer:*  Should Daniel steal a drug to save the life of a friend, if he cannot obtain the drug by any legal means?

*Respondent:*  If it is his true friend, he should steal. With my great friend, we eat together, we drink together, we walk together. Then he will be willing to defend me when we meet an enemy. He will kill my enemy on my behalf, and also I in turn can steal the drug for him—because he is my friend.

*Interviewer:*  Why is human life important?

*Respondent:*  Human life is very important because human actions are good. It is intended that people should multiply, and nobody wants another person to die. In any community you find that when a person is sick, one villager may visit him everyday. Another may suggest that he should be given herbs to make him vomit. Another may suggest that a goat be slaughtered. Through these suggestions a person can recover.

### Quotation from a Student at the University of Nairobi

*Interviewer:*  What is important about human life?

*Respondent:*  Life is the only thing that matters. Human life is even sacred and above all other primitive forms of life. . . . Any form of life anywhere needs some preservation and should only perish where the laws of nature dictate. . . . Life is sacred in the sense that if we bring in the concept of God or the right of living, then you see that it is worth preserving. I mean, you would even find that all constitutions will cherish individual life; it's not something to be tampered with, nobody can take it away unless it is settled in court, because you robbed another one of his life.

*Interviewer:*  When you say all constitutions, what do you mean?

**Figure 12–1**    *In a rural Kipsigis community in western Kenya, men were asked to reason aloud about a series of moral dilemmas. Some of them, like the elder pictured here, were frequently called upon to mediate local disputes. (Photo courtesy of S. Harkness and C. Super.)*

*Respondent:*    You know, in every society people have to organize
themselves, whether it is a modern state or a nonmodern state. You
would find that the laws governing people would try to preserve life,
and also individual rights, for that matter.

Thus the findings suggest that Stage 4 as a predominant mode of moral
reasoning is linked to educational experiences, leadership and occupational roles that promote a certain kind of conceptualization of society as
a complex system. What might it be about education in particular that
facilitates the development of higher-stage moral reasoning?

On the one hand, does education promote abstract logical thinking
that indirectly makes possible abstract thinking about morality? Or, on
the other hand, can education more directly facilitate higher-level moral
reasoning by helping the individual to conceptualize society and morality
more systematically? Put another way, does schooling facilitate moral
development by promoting the type of general cognitive growth that
might be measured on a cognitive test of formal operations, or does it
more specifically facilitate conceptualization in the moral–social domain—thinking that might not be tapped by a cognitive test but is measured by the moral judgment test?

We have no final evidence on this question, but suggestive evidence
comes from breaking down the sample of 52 university students in my
Kenyan study (Edwards, 1974) into those whose major field of concentration might be directly relevant to social–moral thinking versus those
in other areas of concentration. Nineteen (37 percent) of the students
were majoring in the following fields that are rather closely involved in
the study of society, politics, and morality: sociology, political science,
law, economics, history, and religious studies. The remaining 33 were in
the professional fields of engineering, medicine, commerce, education,
and science. The latter fields (except for education) were actually more
selective and difficult to enter at the University of Nairobi because they
were considered to lead to greater job opportunities. Thus those latter
fields generally drew students who came to the university with higher
test scores and grade point averages. This differential selectivity was
reflected by the students' university grades too: as a group, students in
the first group had a lower grade point average than students in the
second group. Still, the students in the first group had significantly
higher moral judgment scores than students in the professional fields
(mean moral maturity score of 334.2 versus 284.7).

It may be that schooling promotes moral development in a direct and
specific way. Schooling at the secondary or college level, insofar as it
involves transmission of knowledge of government, sociology, ethical

systems, and the like, may help a student to acquire the more complex social perspective that underlies the higher moral stages. Excerpts from interviews with four university students illustrate how the students themselves felt such studies were important sources of value change:

> I would say that through the study of sociology, I've sort of identified the behavior of certain societies, when I learned about their value systems and began to argue them logically. At least I've added some new dimensions to my thinking.

> When I was in lower school, I could say such sweet things about the Christian religion, let's say, "Picture Moses going to get some of the Ten Commandments, or Jesus going to Heaven." But by the time I was leaving I couldn't say Christianity was best, because I had read about other religions and I couldn't think whether this is the right religion or that is the right religion.

> The educational system helps you to have some more understanding of the society. Someone who has taken something like sociology will learn . . . that there are some tribal differences but they should not be so much emphasized.

> What I was doing was just history, but it had an effect on me. . . . It started me thinking that, you know, people should be free.

From the students' own perspective, then, the study of certain academic subjects may lead to a new conceptualization of society and morality. This new conceptualization is peculiarly appropriate for an individual whose morals or political frame of reference is a large-scale society. The rather bureaucratic "systems" perspective of Stage 4 seems inappropriate for people in certain other types of societies, perhaps especially small-scale, traditional tribal ones. Therefore, as we shall presently argue in further detail, a lesser presence of Stage 4 in the thinking of people in small-scale societies should not be taken as a reflection on the adequacy of their moral judging relative to people in large-scale, diversified, modern societies. The two types of social systems are very different (though of course both are valid working types of systems), and thus everyday social life in them calls forth different modes of moral problem solving whose adequacy must be judged relative to their particular contexts.

What about moral judgment Stages 5 and 6? We have said little about these stages so far, because they appear to be very rarefied. They are virtually absent from most of the cross-cultural materials and are found in interviews with only the most educated and morally articulate subjects in countries like the United States, Britain, and Israel. In fact, Gibbs (1977, 1979), in what he calls a "constructive critique of Kohlberg," has suggested that only the first four of Kohlberg's stages constitute a true developmental sequence. Stages 5 and 6, he argues, are really something other than developmental stages. They are "metaethical reflections on morality" and should be eliminated from the system. The cross-cultural data lead us to a position friendly to the Gibbs proposal. A four-stage sequence—three stages being found in all forms of human society and a fourth stage becoming a predominant mode for some adults in large-scale societies with formal institutions—appears to best represent the current evidence on moral judgment in comparative cultural perspective.

## THE CROSS-CULTURAL UNIVERSALITY AND VALIDITY OF THE MORAL JUDGMENT STAGES

Discussion of the experiential precursors of Kohlberg's higher stages thus brings us to the final issue, the cultural universality of the moral judgment theory. The beginning of this chapter discussed the ethical problems and potential ethnocentrism of asserting differences in moral development between cultural groups. Yet the best current evidence appears to suggest a difference between small-scale and large-scale societies involving the likelihood of Stage 4 (and 5 and 6). What could be the meaning of such a difference? Is it true, as Kohlberg (1971a) asserts, that cultural environments differ substantially in the "quality" of the social stimulation that they provide? That, as a result, the moral reasoning of some groups is more "adequate" than that of others?

Such conclusions would assume that higher moral judgment stages are better or morally more adequate modes of judgment than lower ones. If we wish to reject those assumptions, we can use the findings on cultural differences as a basis for criticizing the theory. In that case, we can correct that portion of the theory that leads to a false and ethnocentric judgment about other cultures.

To begin the argument, why is it important for stage theory that "higher" stages be considered morally "better" (rather than simply "later" in the developmental sequence)? The answer has to do with the basis of the theory in the Piagetian concept of equilibration. According to the concept, internal structures are continually reorganized throughout an individual's development as a response to disequilibrium between the internal structures and the organization of information in the environment. For example, according to Piaget (1932), peer interaction helps children to develop morally by encouraging a more mature "morality of cooperation" to overcome the "morality of constraint" that is the legacy of early parent–child relations.

Development proceeds so as to lead to less and less fragile states of equilibrium or homeostasis. Thus development makes the individual able to respond to challenges to thinking from outside without having to "accommodate" or change inside to meet them. The theoretical "end point" of development is given by the state of perfect equilibrium between the mentally active person's structures of reasoning and the environment. Thus, development involves the progressive transformation of less complex into more complex and adequate structures.

In the case of moral development, Kohlberg asserts that the higher stages represent more complex and powerful cognitive structures that provide better equilibrium between the individual and the social environment. For instance, individuals at the higher moral stages would be less likely to encounter moral problems that would cause them to feel inadequacies in their current predominant mode of moral reasoning.* However, it is clear that what moral stage provides optimal equilibrium for a person would depend on the exact nature of the moral and social environment with which the person is in interaction.

In an earlier study (Harkness, et al., 1980), my colleagues and I attempted to illustrate this point in a semitraditional, rural Kipsigis village in western Kenya. We found that a sample of six men who were judged by their community to be honest and respected elders in the village were significantly higher in moral judgment level than a matched sample of six men not so judged. The elders were more likely to be Stage 3 (with some 4) and the nonelders Stage 2 (with some 3). The study included an analysis of reasoning by elders and nonelders on key moral issues of authority, reciprocity, and conscience. It was concluded that Stage 3 was more typical of a small, face-to-face society, whose members are bound together by ties of cooperation and reciprocal obligations within a hierarchical structure of authority relationships. Stage 3 appeared to constitute a well-equilibrated structure for this rural Kipsigis group, whereas Stage 2 did to a lesser extent. Of the two moral judgment stages that predominated in the responses of the men, it was the higher one that seemed more adequate, in the sense that it would provide a better framework for solving the moral disputes that might arise in that society.

For any society, there may be a stage of moral judgment that best corresponds to the principles of social organization, forms of social in-

---

*For documentation of how a personal moral crisis, an abortion decision, can lead people to a moral judgment stage change, see Gilligan (1977) and Gilligan and Belenky (1980).

teraction, and processes of conflict resolution that underlie it. It has been suggested here that Stage 3 may generally represent the best framework for judging in the face-to-face or small-scale type of community. Moral judgment development would be optimal for persons in a particular society insofar as their thinking comes to achieve the equilibrated state, and development would not be expected to typically occur beyond that point.

Thus, *within* a given society, people with higher stages of moral judgment may be said to have more adequate structures for judging moral problems than people with lower stages. However, comparing *across* societies, higher stages may not necessarily be more adequate because the societies may be different in ways that make alternative stages of moral judging more appropriate for each. To state that the moral judgments of one group are more adequate than those of another, without reference to fundamental societal differences, would represent an invalid comparison. Therefore, rather than have one ethnocentric standard of adequacy for moral judgment development, it is more in line with equilibration theory to consider adequacy with reference to a particular case of a relation between person (or group of people) and environment. For example, if members of a given cultural group are typically found to advance from Stage 1 to Stage 4 as they go from childhood to full adulthood, it probably could be determined that Stage 4 represents a more adequate "end point" for that setting than Stages 1, 2 or 3. Stage 4 contains a systems perspective on society that probably could be discovered to be more appropriate for that setting than any of the preceding stages. However, the Stage 4 "end point" for that particular setting could not be asserted to be more adequate than a Stage 3 end point for another cultural setting, without further proof of why people in the second setting *should* advance to Stage 4.

By remembering that equilibration theory has reference to interaction between organism *and* environment, it is possible to avoid making the mistake of comparing the adequacy of the structures of people who are adapted to different types of environments. Thus, we can refute Kohlberg's (1971a) claim that "there is a sense in which we can characterize moral differences between individuals and groups as being more or less adequate morally," when the individuals or groups are from different cultures. The stage theory of moral judgment development must be revised in the light of cross-cultural evidence. The "universality" of the system must be considered limited to stages and their sequence, and not to the universality of a single standard of moral adequacy in which higher is necessarily better. Moral judgment stages should not be viewed as "achievements." Rather, they should be thought of as adaptive structures developed by people to handle important problems of social living. Insofar as we come to better understand what those problems are for people in different kinds of societies, we shall better be able to construct in detail an equilibration model for moral judgment that is valid for understanding human development.

## SUMMARY AND CONCLUSIONS

Cross-cultural research using Kohlberg's stage approach to moral development has gone further than research using Piaget's approach with respect to two issues. The first involves experiential sources of development, that is, antecedent variables for moral judgment change. The second issue concerns the universality and validity of the developmental sequence in both traditional and modern societies.

The research on experiential influences has pointed to the importance of parents and peers during the first three stages of moral development in the growing child and adolescent. For example, in East African studies, antecedent variables such as family modernization, contact with other cultural groups, and living independently from parents have been related to moral development during the years of adolescence and young adulthood. Additional research has considered the role of experience on moral development above Stage 3. Together, studies from a variety of cultural settings suggest the importance of education, work, and leadership roles on the later moral development.

The studies on experiential influences have been designed to check generalizations derived from American data and to test new hypotheses about the particular ways that development normally proceeds in different cultures. This is a wide area for study, and although the research to date is promising, it is still just beginning on all the above topics. Nevertheless, studies using the technique described have proved that they can provide new insight about socialization.

Research on the cultural universality of the moral judgment sequence has provided some confirming evidence and a basis for criticizing the theory. On the confirming side, Kohlberg's moral-dilemma interview process has proved itself to be a robust cross-cultural instrument. In contrast to most other Western psychological tests, the dilemma interview poses problems that people in a wide variety of traditional and modern societies find intrinsically provocative and engaging. The oral interview is not unlike the kinds of talking aloud they often need to do about social problems in everyday community life, and young and old alike typically respond enthusiastically and thoughtfully to the interview. Well-conducted interviews are easily scored by trained interviewers, and the comparative evidence so far upholds Kohlberg's claims about the universality of a developmental sequence of moral judgment stages (at least through the first three stages). However, cultural group differences that have been found with respect to the highest stage achieved indicate the need for revising certain central claims of the theory. The claim that each judgment stage is "morally more adequate" than the one before it must be understood to have reference only to *within*-setting comparisons. Because the notion of "adequacy" should refer to the relation between an active subject and the environment, it cannot be used to interpret differences in moral judgment scores of various cultural groups, leaving aside facts about how those groups live their lives. This mistaken cross-cultural application of the adequacy notion not only leads to potentially invidious comparisons but also invites upon the theory the charge of ethnocentrism. Cultural group differences in the distribution of scores on the moral reasoning test can be understood only if the claim that "higher developed reasoning is more adequate reasoning" is drastically limited. Then and only then can we hope to begin to accumulate solid information about moral reasoning and how it is shaped by sociocultural forces.

# References

## PREFACE

Dasen, P., *Piagetian psychology: Cross-cultural contributions.* New York: Gardner, 1977.

Munroe, R. L., and R. H. Munroe, *Cross-cultural human development.* Belmont, Calif.: Wadsworth, 1975.

Munroe, R. L., R. H. Munroe, and B. B. Whiting (eds.), *Handbook of cross-cultural human development.* New York: Garland, 1981.

Triandis, H. (ed.), *Handbook of cross-cultural psychology,* Vols. I–VI. Boston: Allyn and Bacon, 1980 *et seq.*

Werner, E. E., *Cross-cultural child development.* Belmont, Calif.: Wadsworth, 1979.

## CHAPTER 1

Brazelton, T. B., J. S. Robey, and G. A. Collier, "Infant development in the Zin-acanteco Indians of southern Mexico." *Pediatrics,* 1969, 44, 274–290.

Caudill, W., and L. A. Frost, "A comparison of maternal care and infant behavior in Japanese-American, American, and Japanese families." In W. Lebra (ed.), *Youth, socialization, and mental health (Vol. 3 of Mental health research in Asia and the Pacific).* Honolulu: University Press of Hawaii, 1973.

Caudill, W., and H. Weinstein, "Maternal care and infant behavior in Japan and America." *Psychiatry,* 1969, 32, 12–43.

Clarke, A. M., and A. D. B. Clarke, *Early experience: Myth and evidence.* New York: Free Press, 1976.

Freedman, D. G., "Smiling in blind infants and the issue of innate vs. acquired." *Journal of Psychology and Psychiatry,* 1964, 5, 17–184,

Harkness, S., "The cultural context of child development." In C. M. Super and S. Harkness (eds.), "Anthropological perspectives on child development," *New Directions for Child Development,* 1980, 8, 7–13.

Harkness, S., C. P. Edwards, and C. M. Super, "Social roles and moral reasoning: A case study in rural Africa." *Developmental Psychology,* 1981.

Harkness, S., and C. M. Super, "Why African children are so hard to test." In L. L. Adler (ed.), "Issues in cross-cultural research," *Annals of the New York Academy of Sciences,* 1977, 285, 326–331. Reprinted in L. L. Adler (ed.), *Issues in cross-cultural research.* New York: Academic Press, forthcoming.

Harkness, S., and C. M. Super, "Child development theory in anthropological perspective." In C. M. Super and S. Harkness (eds.), "Anthropological perspectives on child development," *New Directions for Child Development*, 1980, *8*, 1–5.

Kagan, J., "Emergent themes in human development." *American Scientist*, 1976, *64*, 186–196.

Kagan, J., R. B. Kearsley, and P. R. Zelazo, *Infancy: Its place in human development*. Cambridge, Mass.: Harvard University Press, 1978.

Kilbride, J. E., and P. L. Kilbride, "Sitting and smiling behavior of Baganda infants: The influence of culturally constituted experience." *Journal of Cross-Cultural Psychology*, 1975, *6*, 88–107.

Kilbride, P. L., and J. E. Kilbride, "Sociocultural factors and the early manifestation of sociability behavior among Baganda infants." *Ethos*, 1974, *2*, 296–314.

Landau, R., "Spontaneous and elicited smiles and vocalizations of infants in four Israeli environments." *Developmental Psychology*, 1977, *13*, 389–400.

LeVine, R. A., "Anthropology and child development." In C. M. Super and S. Harkness (eds.), "Anthropological perspectives on child development," *New Directions for Child Development*, 1980, *8*, 71–86.

Manners, R. A., "The Kipsigis of Kenya: Culture change in a 'model' East African tribe." In J. H. Steward (ed.), *Three African tribes in transition*. Urbana, Ill.: University of Illinois Press, 1967.

McGraw, M. B., "Maturation of behavior." In L. Carmichael (ed.), *Manual of child psychology*. New York: Wiley, 1946.

Nash, J., *Developmental psychology: A psychobiological approach*. Englewood Cliffs, N. J.: Prentice-Hall, 1970.

Parmalee, A. H., Jr., "The developmental evaluation of the blind premature infant." *Journal of Diseases of Children*, 1955, *90*, 135–140.

Piaget, J., *The origins of intelligence in children*. New York: International University Press, 1952.

Spitz, R. A., R. N. Emde, and D. R. Metcalf, "Further prototypes of ego formation: A working paper from a research project on early development." *Psychoanalytic Study of the Child*, 1970, *25*, 417–441.

Spock, B., *Baby and child care*. New York: Pocket Books, 1968.

Super, C. M., "Environmental influences on motor development: The case of 'African infant precocity.' " *Developmental Medicine and Child Neurology*, 1976, *18*, 561–567.

Super, C. M., "Behavioral development in infancy." In R. L. Munroe, R. H Munroe, and B. B. Whiting (eds.), *Handbook of cross-cultural human development*. New York: Garland Press, 1981.

Super, C. M., and S. Harkness, "The infant's niche in rural Kenya and metropolitan America." In L. L. Adler (ed.), *Issues in cross-cultural research*. New York: Academic Press, forthcoming.

Sutton, J. E. G., "The settlement of East Africa." In B. A. Ogot (ed.), *Zamani: A survey of East African History*. Nairobi, Kenya: East African Publishing House and Longman Group, 1968.

Thomas, A., and S. Chess, *Temperament and development*. New York: Brunner Mazel, 1977.

Weisner, T. S., and R. Gallimore, "My brother's keeper: Child and sibling caretaking." *Current Anthropology*, 1977, *18*, 169–180.

Whiting, B. B., "Culture and social behavior: A model for the development of social behavior." *Ethos*, 1980, *8*, 95–116.

Whiting, B. B., and J. W. M. Whiting, *Children of six cultures: A psycho-cultural analysis*. Cambridge, Mass.: Harvard University Press, 1975.

Whiting, J. W. M., "Causes and consequences of the amount of body contact between mother and infant." Paper presented at meeting of the American Anthropological Association, New York, November 18, 1971.

Yakovlev, P. I., and A. Lecours, "The myelogenetic cycles of regional maturation of the brain." In A. Minkowski (ed.), *Regional development of the brain in early life*. Oxford: Blackwell, 1967.

## CHAPTER 2

Als, H., "Assessing an assessment: Conceptual considerations, methodological issues, and a perspective on the future of the Brazelton Neonatal Behavioral Assessment Scale." In A. Sameroff (ed.), "Organization and stability of newborn behavior: A commentary on the Brazelton Neonatal Behavioral Assessment Scale." *Monographs of the Society for Research in Child Development*, 1978, Serial No. 177.

Als, H., E. Tronick, B. M. Lester and T. B. Brazelton, "The Brazelton Neonatal Behavioral Assessment Scale (BNBAS)." In J. Osofsky (ed.), *Handbook of infant development*. New York: J. Wiley, 1979.

Anastasi, A., "Heredity, Environment, and the Question 'How?'" *Psychological Review*, July 1958, *65*, 197–208.

Brazelton, T. B., "Neonatal Behavioral Assessment Scale." *Clinics in Developmental Medicine, No. 50*. London: William Heinemann Medical Books; Philadelphia: J. P. Lippincott, Philadelphia, 1973.

Brazelton, T. B., B. Koslowski, and E. Tronick, "Neonatal behavior among urban Zambians and Americans." *Journal of the American Academy of Child Psychiatry*, 1976, *15*, 97–107.

Brazelton, T. B., J. S. Robey, and G. A. Collier. "Infant development in the Zinacanteco Indians of Southern Mexico." *Pediatrics*, 1969, *44*, 274–290.

Brazelton, T. B., E. Tronick, A. Lechtig, R. E. Lasky, and R. E. Kelin, "The behavior of nutritionally deprived Guatemalan infants." *Developmental Medicine and Child Neurology*, 1977, *19*, 364–372.

Brazelton, T. B., Y. Tryphonopoulou, and B. M. Lester, "A comparative study of Greek neonatal behavior," *Pediatrics*, 1979, *3*, 279–285.

Cole, M., J. Gay, J. A. Glick, and D. W. Sharp, *The cultural context of learning and thinking: An exploration in experimental anthropology*. New York: Basic Books, 1971.

Coll, C., C. Sepkoski, and B. M. Lester, "Differences in Brazelton scale performance between Puerto Rican and mainland Black and Caucasian infants." *Developmental Psychobiology*, 1981, *14*, 147–154.

DeVries, M. and C. M. Super, "Contextual influences on the Brazelton Neonatal Behavioral Assessment Scale and implications for its cross-cultural use." In A. Sameroff (ed.), "Organization and stability of newborn behavior: A commentary on the Brazelton Neonatal Behavioral Assessment Scale." *Monographs of the Society for Research in Child Development*, 1978, Serial No. 177.

Freedman, D. G., "Genetic influences on development of behavior." In G. B. A. Stoelinga and J. J. Van Der Werff Ten Bosch (eds.), *Normal and abnormal development of behavior*. Leiden: Leiden University Press, 1971.

Freedman, D. G., and N. Freedman, "Behavioral differences between Chinese-American and European-American newborns." *Nature*, 1969, *224*, 1127.

Hebb, D. O., "Heredity and environment in mammalian behavior." *British Journal of Animal Behavior*, 1953, *1*, 319.

Keefer, C., S. Dixon, E. Tronick and T. B. Brazelton, "Gusii infants' neuromotor behavior: Use of the neonatal behavioral assessment scale in cross-cultural studies." Paper presented at the International Conference on Infant Studies, Providence, R.I., March 12, 1978.

Kluckhohn, C. and D. Leighton, *The Navajo*. Cambridge, Mass.: Harvard University Press, 1946.

Lester, B. M., "A synergistic process approach to the study of prenatal malnutrition." *International Journal of Behavioral Development*, 1979, 377–393.

Lester, B. M., "Behavioral assessment of the neonate." In E. S. Sell (ed.), *Follow-up of the high-risk newborn: A practical approach*. Springfield, Ill. Charles C Thomas, 1980.

Lester, B. M., H. Als, and T. B. Brazelton, "Regional obstetric anesthesia and newborn behavior: A reanalysis towards synergistic effects." *Child Development*, 1982.

Lester, B. M., H. Als and T. B. Brazelton, "Scoring criteria for seven clusters of the Brazelton scale." Unpublished manuscript, Child Development Unit, Children's Hospital Medical Center, Boston, Mass. 1978.

Prechtl, H. F. R., "Neurological findings in newborn infants after pre- and paranatal complications. In J. Jonix, H. Visser and J. Troelsta (eds.), *Aspects of prematurity and dysmaturity: A Nutricia symposium*. Leiden: Stenfelt Kroese, 1968, 303–321.

Prechtl, H. F. R. and D. Beintema, "The neurological examination of the full-term newborn infant." *Little Club Clinics in Developmental Medicine, No. 12*. Suffolk, England: Spastics International Medical Publications, 1974.

Scrimshaw, N. S., C. E. Taylor, and J. E. Golden, "Interactions of nutrition and infection." *World Health Organization monograph*, Series No. 57, 1968.

Super, C. M. "Environmental effects on motor development: The case of 'African Infant Precocity.'" *Developmental Medicine and Child Neurology*, 1976, *18*, 561–567.

Super, C. M., "Behavioral development in infancy." In R. H. Munroe, R. L. Munroe, and B. B. Whiting (eds.), *Handbook of cross-cultural human development*. New York: Garland Press, 1981.

Werner, H., "The concept of development from a comparative and organismic point of view." In D. B. Harris (ed.), *The concept of development: An issue in the study of human behavior*. Minneapolis: University of Minnesota Press, 1957, 125–148.

Werner, H., *Comparative psychology of mental development*. Chicago: Follett, 1980.

Yang, R. K., A. R. Zweig, T. C. Douthitt, and E. J. Federman, "Successive relationships between attitudes during pregnancy, maternal analgesic medication during labor and delivery and newborn behavior." *Developmental Psychology*, 1976, *12*, 204–210.

# CHAPTER 3

Addington, D. W., "The relationship of selected characteristics to personality perception." *Speech Monographs*, 1968, *35*, 492–503.

Berko-Gleason, J., "Fathers and other strangers: Men's speech to young children." In D. P. Dato (ed.), *Developmental psycholinguistics: Theory and applications*. Washington, D.C.: Georgetown University Press, 1975.

Blount, B. G., "Aspects of Luo socialization." *Language in Society*, 1972, *1*, 236–248.

Blount, B. G., and W. Kempton, "Child language socialization: Parental speech and dimensions of interaction." *Sign Language Studies*, 1976, *12*, 251–277.

Blount, B. G., and E. Padgug, "Mother and father speech: Distribution of parental speech features in English and Spanish." *Papers and Reports on Child Language Acquisition*, 1976, *12*, 47–59.

Blount, B. G., and E. Padgug, "Prosodic, paralinguistic, and interactional features in parental speech: English and Spanish." *Journal of Child Language*, 1977, *4*, 67–86.

Bruner, J. S., "From communication to language: A psychological perspective." *Cognition*, 1975, *3*, 255–287.

Culp, R., and E. Boyd, "Visual fixation and the effect of voice quality and content differences in two-month-old infants." In F. D. Horowitz (ed.), "Visual attention, auditory stimulation, and language discrimination in young infants." *Monographs of the Society for Research in Child Development*, 1975, *39*, Serial No. 158.

Ferguson, C., "Baby talk in six languages." *American Anthropologist*, 1964, *66* (part 2), 103–114.

Ferguson, C., "Baby talk as a simplified speech register." In C. Snow and C. Ferguson (eds.), *Talking to children: Language input and acquisition*. Cambridge, England: Cambridge University Press, 1977.

Fraiberg, S., "Blind infants and their mothers: An examination of the sign system." In M. Lewis and L. A. Rosenblum (eds.)., *The effect of the infant on its caregiver.* New York: Wiley, 1974.

Freedle, R., and M. Lewis, "Pre-linguistic conversations." In M. Lewis and L. A. Rosenblum (eds.), *Interaction, conversation, and the development of language.* New York: Wiley, 1977.

Goodenough, W., "Cultural anthropology and linguistics." In P. Garvin (ed.), *Report of the Seventh Annual Round Table Meeting on Linguistics and Language Study.* Washington, D. C.: Georgetown University Press, 1957.

Klaus, M. H., and J. H. Kennell, *Maternal-infant bonding.* St. Louis, Mo.: Mosby, 1976.

Kramer, C., "Women's speech: Separate and unequal." *Quarterly Journal of Speech,* 1974, *60,* 14–24.

Mendelson, M. J., and M. M. Haith, "The relation between audition and vision in the human newborn." *Monographs of the Society for Research in Child Development,* 1976, *41,* Serial No. 167.

Ninio, A., and J. Bruner, "The achievement and antecedents of labelling." *Journal of Child Language,* 1978, *5,* 1–16.

Spitz, R. A. "Hospitalism: An inquiry into the genesis of psychiatric conditions in early childhood." In A. Freud (ed.), *The Psychoanalytic Study of the Child,* vol. 1. New York: International Universities Press, 1945.

Spitz, R. A., "Hospitalism: A follow-up report on investigations described in Volume 1, 1945." In A. Freud (ed.), *The Psychoanalytic Study of the Child,* vol. 2. New York: International Universities Press, 1946.

Stern, D. N., "Mother and infant at play: The dyadic interaction involving facial, vocal, and gaze behaviors." In M. Lewis and L. A. Rosenblum (eds.), *The effect of the infant on its caregiver.* New York: Wiley 1974.

Stern, D. N., *The first relationship: Infant and mother.* London: Fontana Open Books, 1977.

Tylor, E. B., *Primitive culture.* London: John Murray, 1871.

# CHAPTER 4

Biesheuvel, S., "The study of African ability." *African Studies,* 1952, *11,* 45–57.

Bower, T. G. R., "Stimulus variables determining space perception in infancy." *Science,* 1965, *149,* 88–89.

Bower, T. G. R., "The visual world of infants." *Scientific American,* 1966, *215,* 80–92.

Brimble, A. R., "The construction of a non-verbal intelligence test in Northern Rhodesia." *Rhodes-Livingstone Journal,* 1963, *34,* 23–35.

Brown, L. B., "The 3D reconstruction of a 2D visual display." *The Journal of Genetic Psychology,* 1969, *115,* 257–262.

Dawson, J. L. M., B. M. Young, and P. P. C. Choi, "Developmental influences in pictorial depth perception among Hong Kong Chinese children." *Journal of Cross-Cultural Psychology*, 1974, *1*, 3–22.

Deregowski, J. B., "Pictorial recognition in subjects from a relatively pictureless environment." *African Social Research*, 1968, *5*, 356–364.

Deregowski, J. B., E. S. Muldrow, and W. F. Muldrow, "Pictorial recognition in a remote Ethiopian population." *Perception*, 1972, *1*, 417–425.

Donaldson, M, and G. Balfour, "Less is more: A study of language comprehension in children." *British Journal of Psychology*, 1968, *59*, 461–471.

Doob, L. W., *Communication in Africa*, New Haven: Yale University Press, 1961.

Forge, A., "Learning to see in New Guinea." In P. Mayer (ed.), *Socialization*. London: Tavistock, 1970.

Gibson, E. J., *Principles of perceptual learning and development*. New York: Meredith Corporation, 1969.

Gibson, J. J., "Pictures, perspective and perception." *Daedalus*, 1960, *89*, 216–227.

Gibson, J. J., *The senses considered as perceptual systems*. Boston: Houghton Mifflin, 1966.

Gibson, J. J., "The information available in pictures." *Leonardo*, 1971, *4*, 27–35.

Goodman, N., *Language of art: An approach to the theory of symbols*. Indianapolis: Bobbs-Merrill, 1968.

Hagen, M. A., "Picture perception: Toward a theoretical model," *Psychological Bulletin*, 1974, *81*, 471–497.

Hagen, M. A., and R. Glick. "Pictorial perspective: perception of size, linear, and texture perspective in children and adults." *Perception*, 1977, *6*, 675–684.

Hagen, M. A. and R. K. Jones, "Cultural effects on pictorial perception," In H. Pick and R. Walk (eds.), *Perception and experience*. New York: Plenum Press, 1978.

Herskovits, M. J., *Man and his works*. New York: Knopf, 1950.

Hochberg, J., and V. Brooks, "Pictorial recognition as an unlearned ability: A study of one child's performance." *American Journal of Psychology*, 1962, *75*, 624–628.

Holmes, A. C., *A study of understanding of visual symbols in Kenya*. London: The Overseas Visual Aids Centre, 1963.

Hudson, W., "Pictorial depth perception in sub-cultural groups in Africa." *Journal of Social Psychology*, 1960, *52*, 183–208.

Hudson, W., "Problems in pictorial perception." *South African Journal of Science*, 1962, *58*, 189–195. (a)

Hudson, W., "Pictorial perception and educational adaptation in Africa." *Psychologia Africana*, 1962, *9*, 226–239. (b)

Hudson, W., "The study of the problem of pictorial perception among unacculturated groups." *International Journal of Psychology*, 1967, *2*, 90–107.

Jahoda, G., H. McGurk, "Pictorial depth perception: A developmental study." *British Journal of Psychology*, 1974, *65*, 141–149. (a).

Jahoda, G., and H. McGurk, "The development of pictorial depth perception: Cross-cultural replications. *Child Development*, 1974, 45, 1042–1047. (b)

Jahoda, G., and H. McGurk, "Pictorial depth perception in Scottish and Ghanaian children: A critique of some findings with the Hudson test." *International Journal of Psychology*, 1974, 9, 255–267. (c)

Jahoda, G., W. M. Cheyne, J. B. Deregowski, D. Sinha, and R. Collingbourne, "Utilization of pictorial information in classroom learning: A cross-cultural study." *Audio-Visual Communications Review*, 1976, 24, 295–315.

Jahoda, G., J. B., Deregowski, B. Ampene and N. Williams, "Pictorial recognition as an unlearned ability." In G. E. Butterworth (ed.), *The Child's Representation of the World*. London: Plenum, 1977.

Kennedy, J. M., and A. S. Ross, "Outline picture perception by the Songe of Papua." *Perception*, 1975, 4, 391–406.

Kidd, D., *The essential Kafir*. London: A. & C. Black, 1904.

Kilbride, P. L., M. C. Robbins, and R. B. Freeman, "Pictorial depth perception and education among Baganda school children." *Perceptual and Motor Skills*, 1968, 26, 1116–1118.

Laurendeau, M. and A. Pinard. *The development of the concept of space in the child*. New York: International Universities Press, 1970.

Laws, R., in H. P. Beach (ed.), *Geography and atlas of Protestant missions*. New York: Student Volunteer Movement for Foreign Missions, 1901. Quoted in Deregowski, Muldrow, and Muldrow, 1972.

Leach, L. M., "Pictorial depth perception: Task levels imposed by testing instruments" *International Journal of Psychology*, 1977, 12, 1, 51–56.

Leibowitz, H. W., and H. L. Pick, "Cross-cultural and educational aspects of the Ponzo perspective illusion." *Perception and Psychophysics*, 1972, 12, 430–432.

McGurk, H., and G. Jahoda, "The development of pictorial depth perception: The role of figural elevation." *British Journal of Psychology*, 1974, 65, 367–376.

McGurk, H., and G. Jahoda, "Pictorial depth perception by children in Scotland and Ghana." *Journal of Cross-cultural Psychology*, 1975, 6, 279–296.

Miller, R. J., "Cross-cultural research in the perception of pictorial materials." *Psychological Bulletin*, 1973, 80, 135–150.

Mundy-Castle, A. C., "Pictorial depth perception in Ghanaian children." *International Journal of Psychology*, 1966, 1, 290–300.

Olson, R. K., "Children's sensitivity to pictorial depth information." *Perception and Psychophysics*, 1975, 17, 59–64.

Olson, R. K., and S. C. Boswell, "Pictorial depth responses in very young children." *Report No. 6, Institute for the Study of Intellectual Behaviour*. Boulder: University of Colorado, 1975.

Olson, R. K., and S. L. Boswell, "Pictorial depth sensitivity in two-year-old children." *Child Development*, 1976, 47, 1175–1178.

Omari, I. M., and H. Cook, "Differential cognitive cues in pictorial depth perception." *Journal of Cross-Cultural Psychology*, 1972, 3, 321–325.

Omari, I. M., and W. H. MacGinitie, "Some pictorial artifacts in studies of African children's pictorial depth perception." *Child Development*, 1974, *45*, 535–539.

Piaget, J., and B. Inhelder, *The child's conception of space*. London: Routledge and Kegan Paul, 1956.

Pirenne, M. *Optics, painting and photography*, Cambridge: Cambridge University Press, 1970.

Segall, M. H., D. T. Campbell, and M. J. Herskovits, *The influence of culture on visual perception*. Indianapolis, Ind.: Bobbs-Merrill, 1966.

Vernon, P. E., "Environmental handicaps of intellectual development: Parts I and II." *British Journal of Educational Psychology*, 1965, *35*, 9–20, 117–126.

Winter, W., "The perception of safety posters by Bantu industrial workers." *Psychologia Africana*, 1963, *10*, 127–135.

Yonas, A., and M. Hagen, "Effects of static and motion parallax depth information on perception of size in children and adults." *Journal of Experimental Child Psychology*, 1973, *15*, 254–265.

Yonas, A., W. Cleaves, and L. Pettersen, "Sensitivity to pictorial depth in infants." Paper presented at biennial meeting of the Society for Research in Child Development. New Orleans, April 1977.

## CHAPTER 5

Atkinson, R. C., and R. M. Shiffrin, "Human memory: A proposed system and its control processes." In K. W. Spence and J. T. Spence (eds.), *The psychology of learning and motivation: Advances in theory and research*, vol. 2. New York: Academic Press, 1968.

Bartlett, F. C., *Remembering*. London: Cambridge University Press, 1967 (1932).

Brown, A. L., "The development of memory: Knowing, knowing about knowing, and knowing how to know." In H. W. Reese (ed.), *Advances in Child Development and Behavior*, vol. 10. New York: Academic Press, 1975.

Campbell, D. T., "The mutual methodological relevance of anthropology and psychology." In F. L. K. Hsu (ed.), *Psychological anthropology*. Homewood, Ill.: Dorsey Press, 1961.

Cole, M., J. Gay, J. Glick, and D. Sharp, *The cultural context of learning and thinking*. New York: Basic Books, 1971.

Cole, M., and S. Scribner, *Culture and thought*. New York: Wiley, 1974.

Dirks, J., and U. Neisser, "Memory for objects in real scenes: The development of recognition and recall." *Journal of Experimental Child Psychology*, 1977, *23*, 315–328.

Feldman, D. H., *Beyond universals in cognitive development*. Norwood, N. J.: Ablex, 1980.

Gregory, R. L., *Eye and brain: The psychology of seeing*. New York: McGraw-Hill, 1966.

Hagen, J. W., R. H. Jongeward, and R. V. Kail, Jr., "Cognitive perspectives on the development of memory." In H. W. Reese (ed.), *Advances in child devel opment and behavior,* vol. 10. New York: Academic press, 1975.

Lane, H., *The wild boy of Aveyron.* Cambridge, Mass.: Harvard, 1976.

Leibowitz, H. W., R. Brislin, L. Perlmutter, and R. Hennessey, "Ponzo perspective illusion as a manifestation of space perception." *Science,* 1969, *166,* 1174–1176.

Luria, A. R., *Cognitive development.* Cambridge, Mass.: Harvard, 1975.

Rivers, W. H. R., "Observation on the senses of the Todas." *British Journal of Psychology, 1905, 1,* 321–396.

Schweder, R. A., "The between and within of cross-cultural research." *Ethos,* 1973, *1,* 531–545.

Segall, M. H., *Cross-cultural psychology: An introduction.* Monterey, Calif.: Brooks-Cole, 1980.

Segall, M. H., and D. T. Campbell, *A cross-cultural study of perception.* Indianapolis, Ind.: Bobbs-Merrill, 1969.

Segall, M. H., D. T. Campbell, and M. J. Herskovits, *The influence of culture on visual perception.* Indianapolis, Ind.: Bobbs-Merrill, 1966.

Vygotsky, L. S., *Mind in Society,* M. Cole, V. John-Steiner, S. Scribner, and E. Souberman (eds.), Cambridge, Massachusetts: Harvard, 1978.

Wagner, D. A., "The development of short-term and incidental memory: A cross-cultural study." *Child Development,* 1974, *45,* 389–396.

Wagner, D. A., "The effects of verbal labeling on short-term and incidental memory: A cross-cultural and developmental study." *Memory and Cognition,* 1975, *3,* 595–598.

Wagner, D. A., "Ontogeny of the Ponzo illusion." *International Journal of Psychology,* 1977, *12,* 161–176.

Wagner, D. A., "Memories of Morocco: The influence of age, schooling, and environment on memory." *Cognitive Psychology,* 1978, *10,* 1–28. (a)

Wagner, D. A., "The effects of formal schooling on cognitive style." *Journal of Social Psychology,* 1978, *106,* 145–151. (b)

Wagner, D. A., "Culture and memory development." In H. Triandis and A. Heron (eds.), *Handbook of cross-cultural psychology,* Vol. 4. Boston: Allyn & Bacon, 1981.

Wagner, D. A. and K. Heald, " 'Carpentered world' vs. Piaget: Revisiting the illusions of Segall, Campbell and Herskovits." In L. H. Eckensberger, W. J. Lonner, and Y. H. Poortinga (eds.), *Cross-cultural contributions to psychology.* Lisse, The Netherlands: Swets & Zeitlinger, 1979.

Wagner, D. A., and A. Lotfi, "Traditional Islamic education in Morocco: Socio-historical and psychological perspectives." *Comparative Education Review,* 1980, *24,* 238–251.

Wagner, D. A., and S. G. Paris, "Problems and prospects in the comparative studies of memory." *Human Development,* 1981.

290 References

Wickelgren, W. A., "Age and storage dynamics in continuous recognition memory." *Developmental Psychology*, 1975, *11*, 165–169.
Witkin, H. A., P. K. Oltman, E. Raskin, and S. A. Karp. *A manual for the embedded figures tests.* Palo Alto, Calif.: Consulting Psychologists Press, 1971.

## CHAPTER 6

Béhar, M, "Prevalence of malnutrition among preschool children in developing countries. In N.S. Schrimshaw and J. E. Gordon (eds.), *Malnutrition, Learning and Behavior.* Cambridge, Mass.: M.I.T. Press, 1968.
Belkings, R. C., and D. M. Hegsted, "Consequences of early protein and energy malnutrition in monkeys." Paper presented at the International Conference on Behavioral Effects of Energy and Protein Deficits, Washington, D. C., November 30–December 2, 1977.
Brožek, J, "Nutrition, malnutrition and behavior." *Annual Review of Psychology,* 1978, *29*, 157–177.
Champakan, S., S. G. Srikantia, and C. Gopalan, "Kwashiorkor and mental development," *American Journal of Clinical Nutrition, 1968, 21,* 844–852.
Chase, H. P., and H. P. Martin, "Undernutrition and child development." *New England Journal of Medicine,* 1970, *282,* 933–939.
Chávez, A., C. Martínez, and H. Bourges, "Nutritional level and physical activity." *Nutrition Reports International,* 1972, *5,* 139–144.
Chávez, A., C. Martínez, and T. Yaschine, "The importance of nutrition and stimuli on child mental and social development." In *Swedish Nutrition Foundation Symposia XII.* Uppsala, Sweden: Almqvist and Wiksell, 1974.
Chávez, A., and C. Martínez, "Effects of nutrition on child behavior." In J. Brožek (ed.), *Behavioral effects of energy and protein deficits.* International Conference, Washington, D. C., November 30–December 2, 1977.
Edwards, A. J., "Using vocabulary as a measure of general ability." *Personnel and Guidance Journal,* 1963, *42,* 153–154.
Elardo, R., R. H. Bradley, and B. M. Caldwell, "The relationship of infants' home environments to mental test performance from 6–36 months: A longitudinal analysis." *Child Development,* 1975, *46,* 71–76.
Evans, D. E., A. D. Moodie, and J. D. L. Hansen, "Kwashiorkor and intellectual development." *South African Medical Journal,* 1971, *45,* 1413–1426.
Frankóva, S., "Interaction between early nutrition and stimulation in animals. In J. Cravioto, L. Hambraeus, and B. Vahlquist (eds.), *Early malnutrition and mental development,* Swedish Nutrition Foundation Symposia XII. Uppsala, Sweden: Almqvist and Wiksell, 1974.
Honzik, M. P., "Developmental studies of parent–child resemblance in intelligence." In M. Jones, N. Bayley, J. MacFarlane, and M. P. Honzik, (eds.); *The course of human development,* Waltham, Mass.: Xerox College Publishing, 1971.

Inkeles, A., and D. H. Smith, *Becoming modern: Individual change in six developing Countries.* Cambridge, Mass.: Harvard University Press, 1974.

Irwin, M., P. Engle, C. Yarbrough, R. E. Klein, and J. Townsend, "The relationship of prior ability and family characteristics to school attendance and school performance in rural Guatemala." *Child Development*, 1978, *49*, 415–427.

Klein, R. E., "Some considerations in the measurement of the effects of food supplementation on the intellectual development and social adequacy." In N. S. Scrimshaw and M. Altschul (eds.), *Amino acid fortification protein foods.* Cambridge, Mass.: M.I.T. Press, 1971.

Klein, R. E., H. E. Freeman, B. Spring, S. B. Nerlove, and C. Yarbrough, "Cognitive test performance and indigenous conception of intelligence." *Journal of Psychology*, 1976, *93*, 273–279.

Klein, R. E., M. Irwin, P. L. Engle, and C. Yarbrough, "Malnutrition and mental development in rural Guatemala." In N. Warren (ed.), *Advances in cross-cultural psychology.* New York, Academic Press, 1977.

Levitsky, D. A., and R. H. Barnes, "Nutritional and environmental interactions in the behavioral development of the rat: Long-term effects." *Science*, 1972, *176*, 63–71.

Lloyd-Still, M. B., I. Hurwitz, P. H. Wolff, and H. Schwachman, "Intellectual development after severe malnutrition in infancy. *Pediatrics*, 1974, *54*, 306–311.

Martorell, R., A. Lechtig, C. Yarbrough, H. Delgado, and R. E. Klein, "Protein-calorie supplementation and postnatal physical growth: A review of findings from developing countries." *Archivos Latinoamericanos de Nutrición*, 1976, *26*, 115–128.

McKay, H., L. Sinisterra, A. McKay, H. Gómez, and P. Lloreda, "Improving cognitive ability in chronically deprived children." *Science*, 1978, *200*, 270–278.

McNemar, Q., *The revision of the Stanford-Binet Scale: An analysis of the standardization data.* Boston: Houghton Mifflin, 1942.

Mejía-Pivaral, V., "Características económicas y socio-culturales de cuatro aldeas Ladinas de Guatemala." *Guatemala Indígena (Monografía)*, vol. 8, no. 3, 1972.

Mora, J. O., J. Clement, N. Christiansen, N. Ortíz, L. Vuori, M. Wagner, and M. G. Herrera, "Nutritional supplementation, early home stimulation and child development." In J. Brožek (ed.), *Behavioral effects of energy and protein deficits.* International Conference, Washington, D.C., November 30–December 2, 1977.

Nerlove, S. B., J. M. Roberts, R. E. Klein, C. Yarbrough, and J.-P. Habicht, "Natural indicators of cognitive development: An observational study of rural Guatemalan children." *Ethos*, 1974, *2*, 265–295.

Pollitt, E., and C. Thompson, "Protein-calorie malnutrition and behavior: A view from psychology." In R. J. Wurtman and J. J. Wurtman (eds.), *Nutrition and the Brain*, vol. 2. New York: Raven, 1977.

Scrimshaw, N. A., "Through a glass darkly." *Nutrition Today,* Jan.-Feb. 1978.

Snedecor, G. W. and W. G. Cochran, *Statistical methods,* 6th edition. Ames: Iowa State Unviersity Press, 1967.

Stoch, M. B., and P. M. Smythe, "The effect of undernutrition during infancy and subsequent brain growth and intellectual development." *South African Medical Journal,* 1967, *41,* 1027–1030.

Warren, N., "Malnutrition and mental development." *Psychological Bulletin,* 1973, *80,* 324–328.

Winick, M., K. K. Meyer, and R. C. Harris, "Malnutrition and environmental enrichment by adoption." *Science,* 1975, *190,* 1173–1175.

Wu, L. and T. Woo, with the cooperation of M. Flores, "Food composition table for use in Latin America." Research project sponsored jointly by the Institute of Nutrition of Central America and Panama and the Interdepartmental Committee on Nutrition for National Defense, National Institute of Health. Washington, D. C.: U. S. Government Printing Office, 1961.

Zimmerman, R. R., C. R. Geist, D. A. Stroebel, and T. J. Cleveland, "Attention deficiencies in malnourished monkeys." In J. Cravioto, L. Hambraeus, and B. Vahlquist (eds.), *Early malnutrition and mental development.* Swedish Nutrition Foundation Symposia XII. Uppsala, Sweden: Amqvist and Wiksell, 1974.

# CHAPTER 7

Beth, E. W., and J. Piaget. *Mathematical epistemology and psychology.* Dordrecht, The Netherlands: Reidel, 1966.

Brislin, R. W., "Methodology of cognitive studies." In G. E. Kearney and D. W. McElwain (eds.), *Aboriginal cognition: Retrospect and prospect.* Atlantic Highlands, N. J.: Humanities Press, 1976.

Cole, M., J. Gay, J. Glick and D. Sharp, *The cultural context of learning and thinking.* New York: Basic Books, 1971.

Dasen, P. R., "Cross-cultural Piagetian research: A summary." *Journal of Cross-Cultural Psychology, 1972, 3,* 23–29. (a)

Dasen, P. R., "The development of conservation in Aboriginal children: A replication." *International Journal of Psychology, 1972, 7,* 75–85. (b)

Dasen, P. R., "The influence of ecology, culture and European contact on cognitive development in Australian Aborigines." In J. W. Berry and P. R. Dasen (eds.), *Culture and cognition: Readings in cross-cultural psychology.* London: Methuen, 1974.

Dasen, P. R., *Piagetian psychology: Cross-cultural contributions.* New York: Gardner Press, 1977.

de Lemos, M. M., "The development of conservation in Aboriginal children." *International Journal of Psychology.* 1969, *4,* 255–269.

Elkind, D., "Children's discovery of the conservation of mass, weight, and volume: Piaget replication study II." *Journal of Genetic Psychology*, 1961, *98*, 219–227.

Flavell, J. H., "Cognitive changes in adulthood." In L. R. Goulet and P. P. Baltes (eds.), *Life-span developmental psychology: Research and theory*. New York: Academic Press, 1970.

Furth, H. G., *Piaget for teachers*. Englewood Cliffs, N.J.: Prentice-Hall, 1970.

Heron, A., and W. Dowel, "Weight conservation and matrix-solving ability in Papuan children." *Journal of Cross-Cultural Psychology*, 1973, *4*, 207–219.

Heron, A., and M. Simonsson, "Weight conservation in Zambian children: A non-verbal approach." *International Journal of Psychology*, 1969, *4*, 281–292.

Kamara, A. I., and J. A. Easley, Jr., "Is the rate of cognitive development uniform across cultures? A methodological critique with new evidence from Themne children." In P. R. Dasen (ed.), *Piagetian psychology*. New York: Gardner Press, 1977.

Kiminyo, D. M., "A cross-cultural study of the development of conservation of mass, weight, and volume among Kamba children." In P. R. Dasen (ed.), *Piagetian psychology: Cross-cultural contributions*. New York: Gardner Press, 1977.

Laurendeau, M. and A. Pinard, *Causal thinking in the child*. New York: International Universities Press, 1972.

Lloyd, B. B., "Studies of conservation with Yoruba children of differing ages and experience." *Child Development*, 1971, *42*, 415–428. (a)

Lloyd, B. B., "The intellectual development of Yoruba children: A reexamination. *Journal of Cross-Cultural Psychology*, 1971, *2*, 29–38. (b)

Lovell, K. and E. Ogilvie, "A study of the conservation of substance in the junior school child." *British Journal of Educational Psychology*, 1960, *30*, 109–118.

Lovell, K. and E. Ogilvie, "A study of the conservation of weight in the junior school child." *British Journal of Educational Psychology*, 1961, *31*, 138–144. (a)

Lovell, K., and E. Ogilvie, "The growth of the concept of volume in junior school children." *Journal of Child Psychology and Psychiatry*, 1961, *2*, 118–126. (b)

Mangan, J., "Piaget's theory and cultural differences: The case for value-based modes of cognition." *Human Development*, 1978, *21*, 170–189,

Nyiti, R. M., "The development of conservation in the Meru children of Tanzania." *Child Development*, 1976, *47*, 1122–1129.

Nyiti, R. M., "Schooling and conservation in Tanzania. A lack of effects." Paper presented at biennial meeting of Society for Research in Child Development, New Orleans, March 1977.

Piaget, J., *The child's conception of the world*. London: Routledge and Kegan Paul, 1929.

Piaget, J., *The psychology of the child*. New York: Basic Books, 1969.

Piaget, J., *The child and reality*. New York: Grossman, 1972.

Piaget, J., "Need and significance of cross-cultural research in genetic psychology." In B. Inhelder and H. H. Chipman (eds.), *Piaget and his school: A reader in developmental psychology*. New York: Springer-Verlag, 1976.

Piaget, J., and B. Inhelder, "Intellectual operations and their development." In P. Fraisse and J. Piaget (eds.), *Experimental psychology: Its scope and methods*, Vol.7. London: Routledge and Kegan Paul, 1969.

Piaget, J., and B. Inhelder, "Diagnosis of mental operations and theory of intelligence." *American Journal of Mental Deficiency*, 1947, *51*, 401–406.

Poole, H. E., "The effect of urbanization upon scientific concept attainment among Hausa children of northern Nigeria." *British Journal of Educational Psychology*, 1968, *38*, 57–63.

Price-Williams, D. R., "A study concerning concepts of conservation of quantities among primitive children." In D. R. Price-Williams (ed.), *Cross-cultural studies*. Harmondsworth, Middlesex: Penguin, 1969.

Vernon, P. E., "Abilities and educational attainments in an East African environment." In D. R. Price-Williams (ed.), *Cross-cultural studies*. Harmondsworth, Middlesex: Penguin, 1969.

## CHAPTER 8

Beckwith, M., *Hawaiian mythology*. Honolulu: University of Hawaii Press, 1970.

Berzonsky, M.D., "A factor-analytic investigation of child animism." *Journal of Genetic Psychology*, 1973, *122*, 287–295.

Carr, E., *Da kine talk*. Honolulu: University of Hawaii Press, 1972.

Dasen, P. *Piagetian psychology: Cross-cultural contributions*. New York: Gardner Press, 1977.

Dennis, W. "Animism and related tendencies in Hopi children." *Journal of Abnormal and Social Psychology*, 1943, *38*, 21–36.

Gould, J. and W. Kolb, *A dictionary of the social sciences*. London: Tavistock Publications, 1964.

Huang, I., and H. W. Lee, "Experimental analysis of child animism." *Journal of Genetic Psychology*, 1945, *66*, 69–74.

Jahoda, G., "Child animism: I. A critical survey of cross-cultural research: II. A study in West Africa." *Journal of Social Psychology*, 1958, *47*, 197–212, 213–222.

Kalakaua, D., *The legends and myths of Hawaii*. Edited by R. M. Daggett. Rutland, Vermont, and Tokyo: Charles E. Tuttle, 1972.

Kastenbaum, R., and R. Aisenberg, *The psychology of death*. New York: Springer, 1972.

Klingberg, G., "The distinction between living and not living among 7–10 year old children, with some remarks concerning the so-called animism controversy." *Journal of Genetic Psychology*, 1957, *90*, 227–238.

Klingensmith, S. W., "Child animism: What the child means by 'alive'." *Child Development*, 1953, *42*, 51–61.

Laurendeau-Bendavid, M., "Culture, schooling, and cognitive development: A comparative study of children in French Canada and Rwanda." In P. Dasen (ed.), *Piagetian psychology: Cross-cultural contributions*. New York: Gardner Press, 1977.

Looft, W. R., "Animistic thought in children: Understanding of 'living' across its associated attributes." *Journal of Genetic Psychology*, 1974, *124*, 235–240.

Mead, M., "An investigation of the thought of primitive children with special reference to animism." *Journal of the Royal Anthropological Institute*, 1932, *62*, 173–190.

Nagy, M., "The child's view of death." In H. Feifel (ed.), *The meaning of death*. New York: McGraw-Hill, 1959.

Piaget, J., "Need and significance of cross-cultural research in genetic psychology." *International Journal of Psychology*, 1966, *1*, 3–13.

Piaget, J., *The origins of intelligence in children*. New York: Norton, 1952.

Piaget, J., *The child's conception of the world*. Totowa, N.J.: Littlefield, Adams, 1972 (1929).

Piaget, J., *The child's conception of physical causality*. Totowa, N.J.: Littlefield, Adams, 1972.

Pukui, M., and S. Elberg, *Hawaiian Dictionary*. Honolulu: University of Hawaii Press, 1971.

Pukui, M., E. W. Haertig, and C. Lee, *Nana I Ke Kumu* (Look to the Source). Honolulu: Queen Liliuokalani Children's Center, 1972.

Westervelt, W. D., *Hawaiian legends of ghosts and ghost-gods*. Rutland, VT.: Charles E. Tuttle, 1963.

# CHAPTER 9

Adjei, K., "Influence of specific maternal occupation and behavior on Piagetian cognitive development." In P. Dasen (ed.), *Piagetian psychology: Cross-cultural contributions*. New York: Gardner Press, 1977.

Bartlett, F. C., "Psychological methods and anthropological problems." *Africa*, 1937, *10*, 401–420.

Bateson, G., *Naven*. Stanford, Calif.: Stanford University Press, 1958.

Bateson, G., *Steps to an ecology of the mind*. New York: Ballantine Books, 1972.

Blanco, M. H., and N. J. Chodorow, "Children's work and obedience in Zinacantan." Unpublished paper, Harvard Chiapas Project, Harvard University, 1964.

Bruner, J., "The course of cognitive growth." *American Psychologist*, 1964, *19*, 1–15.

Cancian, F., *Another place: Photographs of a Maya community*. San Francisco: Scrimshaw Press, 1974.

Cazden, C. B., and V. B. John, "Learning in American Indian children." In M. L. Wax, S. Diamond, and F. O. Gearing (eds.), *Anthropological perspectives in education*. New York: Basic Books, 1971.

Childs, C. P. and P. M. Greenfield, "Informal modes of learning and teaching:

The case of Zinacanteco weaving." In N. Warren (ed.), *Studies in cross-cultural psychology*, vol. 2. New York: Academic Press, 1980.

Cohen, Y. A., "The shaping of men's minds: Adaptations to imperatives of culture." In M. L. Wax, S. Diamond, and F. O. Gearing (eds.), *Anthropological perspectives in education*. New York: Basic Books, 1971.

Cole, M., J. Gay, J. Glick, and D. W. Sharp, *The cultural context of learning and thinking*. New York: Basic Books, 1971.

Cole, M., and S. Scribner, *Culture and thought: A psychological introduction*. New York: Wiley, 1974.

Cole, M., D. Sharp, and C. Lave, "The cognitive consequences of education: Some empirical evidence and theoretical misgivings." *Urban Review*, 1976, *9* (4), 218–233.

Durojaiye, M., "Conservation in six cultures." Papers presented at the meeting of the Twentieth International Congress of Psychology, Tokyo, August 1972.

Eggan, D., "Instruction and affect in Hopi cultural continuity." *Southwestern Journal of Anthropology*, 1956, *12* (4), 347–370.

Erchak, G. M., *Full respect: Kpelle children in adaption*. HRA Flex Books, No. FDG-001. New Haven, Conn. Human Relations Area Files, 1977.

Fortes, M., "Social and psychological aspects of education in Taleland." *Africa*, 1938, *11*. Reprinted in J. Middleton (ed.), *From child to adult: Studies in the anthropology of education*. Garden City, N. Y.: Natural History Press, 1970.

Gay, J. and M. Cole, *The new mathematics and an old culture: A study of learning among the Kpelle of Liberia*. New York: Holt, Rinehart, & Winston, 1967.

Gladwin, T., *East is a big bird*. Cambridge, Mass.: Harvard University Press, 1970.

Goody, E., *Questions and politeness: Strategies in social interaction*. Cambridge: Cambridge University Press, 1980.

Graves, N. B., "City, country, and child rearing in three cultures." Unpublished manuscript, 1968, University of Colorado.

Greenfield, P. M., "Comparing dimensional categorization in natural and artificial context: A developmental study among the Zinacantecos of Mexico." *Journal of Psychology*, 1974, *93*, 157–171.

Greenfield, P. M., "On culture and conservation." In J. S. Bruner, et al. (eds.), *Studies in cognitive growth*. New York: Wiley, 1966.

Greenfield, P. M., "Oral or written language: The consequences for cognitive development in Africa, the United States, and England." *Language and Speech*, 1972, *15*, 169–178.

Greenfield, P. M., and C. P. Childs, "Understanding sibling concepts: A developmental study of kin terms in Zinacatan." In P. Dasen (ed.), *Piagetian psychology: Cross-cultural contributions*. New York: Gardner Press, 1977.

Greenfield, P. M., and C. P. Childs, "Weaving, color terms, and pattern representation: Cultural influences and cognitive development among the Zinacantecos of Southern Mexico." Presented at the Inaugural meeting of the International Association for Cross-Cultural Psychology, Hong Kong, 1972. *Interamerican Journal of Psychology*, 1977, *11*, 23–48.

Greenfield, P. M., L. Reich, and R. R. Olver, "On culture and equivalence: II." In J. S. Bruner, et al. (eds.), *Studies in cognitive growth.* New York: Wiley, 1966.

Harkness, S., "Modernization and child language development in rural Africa." Paper presented at the meeting of the Second Pan-African Conference on Psychology, Nairobi, Kenya, October, 1975.

Harkness, S. and C. M. Super, "Why African children are so hard to test." In L. L. Adler (ed.), "Issues in cross-cultural research." *Annals of the New York Academy of Sciences,* 1977, *285,* 326–331.

Hogbin, H. I., "A New Guinea childhood: From weaning to the eighth year in Wogeo." *Oceania,* 1946, *16,* 275–296. Reprinted in J. Middleton (ed.), *From child to adult: Studies in the anthropology of education.* Garden City, N.Y.: Natural History Press, 1970.

Hunt, J. McV., *Intelligence and experience.* New York: Ronald Press, 1961.

Kaye, K. and L. G. Giannino, "Instruction by modeling can be too effective." Unpublished manuscript, University of Chicago, 1978.

Kirk, L., "Cross-cultural measurement of maternal behavior in mother-child teaching interaction." *Quality and Quantity,* 1976, *10,* 127–143.

Kneller, G. F., *Educational anthropology: An introduction.* New York: Wiley, 1965.

Lave, J., "Tailor-made experiments and evaluating the intellectual consequences of apprenticeship training." *Quarterly Newsletter of the Institute of Comparative Human Development,* 1977, *1* (2), New York: Rockefeller University. (a)

Lave, J., "Cognitive consequences of traditional apprenticeship training in West Africa." *Anthropology and Education Quarterly,* 1977, *8,* 177–180. (b)

Lave, J., "Tailored learning: Education and cognitive skills among tribal craftsmen in West Africa." Unpublished manuscript, University of California, Irvine, 1980.

LeVine, R. A., "Child rearing in sub-Saharan Africa: An interim report." *Bulletin of the Menninger Clinic,* 1963, *27,* 245–256.

Mead, M. *Coming of age in Samoa.* New York: William Morrow, 1928.

Mead, M., *Growing up in New Guinea.* New York: William Morrow, 1930.

Mead, M., "An investigation of the thought of primitive children with special reference to animism." *Journal of the Royal Anthropological Institute,* 1932, *63,* 173–190.

Mead, M., "Our educational emphasis in primitive perspective." *American Journal of Sociology,* 1943, *48,* 633–639.

Munroe, R. L., and R. H. Munroe, "Obedience among children in an East African society." *Journal of Cross-Cultural Psychology,* 1972, *3,* 395–399.

Munroe, R. L. and R. H. Munroe, "Levels of obedience among U.S. and East African children on an experimental task." *Journal of Cross-Cultural Psychology,* 1975, *6,* 498–503.

Nadel, S. F., "Experiments on cultural psychology." *Africa,* 1937, *10,* 421–435.

Nadel, S. F., *The foundations of social anthropology.* London: Cohen & West, Ltd., 1951.

Peshkin, A., *Kanuri schoolchildren: Education and social mobilization in Nigeria.* New York: Holt, Rinehart, & Winston, 1972.

Price-Williams, D. R., *Explorations in cross-cultural psychology.* San Francisco: Chandler & Sharp, 1975.

Price-Williams, D., W. Gordon, and M. Ramirez, "Manipulation and conservation: A study of children from pottery-making families in Mexico." *Memorias del XI Congresso Interamericano do Psicologia.* Mexico City, 106–126, 1967.

Price-Williams, D., W. Gordon, and M. Ramirez, "Skill and conservation: Study of pottery-making children." *Developmental Psychology,* 1969, *1,* 769.

Raum, O. F., *Chaga childhood.* Oxford: University Press, 1940.

Read, M., *Children of their fathers: Growing up among the Ngoni of Malaur.* New Haven, Conn.: Yale University Press, 1960.

Rogoff, B., "Mother's teaching style and child memory: A highland Guatemala study." Paper presented at the meeting of the Society for Research in Child Development, New Orleans, March 1977.

Scribner, S., and M. Cole, "Unpackaging literacy." *Social Science Information,* 1978, *17,* 19–40.

Scribner, S., and M. Cole, "Cognitive consequences of formal and informal education." *Science,* 1973, *182,* 553–559.

Steinberg, B. M., and L. A. Dunn, "Conservation competence and performance in Chiapas." *Human Development,* 1976, *19,* 14–25.

Vygotsky, L. S., *Mind in society.* Cambridge, Mass.: Harvard University Press, 1977.

Wagner, D., A., "Memories of Morocco: The influence of age, schooling, and environment on memory." *Cognitive Psychology,* 1978, *10,* 1–28.

Whiting, B. B., and J. W. M. Whiting, *Children of six cultures: A psychological analysis.* Cambridge, Mass.: Harvard University Press, 1975.

Wood, D. J., J. S. Bruner, and G. Ross, "The role of tutoring in problem solving." *Journal of Child Psychology and Psychiatry,* 1976, *17,* 89–100.

Wood, D., and D. Middleton, "A study of assisted problem-solving." *British Journal of Psychology,* 1975, *66,* 181–191.

Wood, D., H. Wood, and D. Middleton, "An experimental evaluation of four face-to-face teaching strategies." Unpublished manuscript, University of Nottingham (no date).

## CHAPTER 10

Irwin, M., P. L. Engle, C. Yarbrough, R. E. Klein, and J. W. Townsend, "The relationship of prior ability and family characteristics to school attendance and school achievement in rural Guatemala." *Child Development,* 1978, *49,* 415–427.

Rogoff, B., "Schooling and the development of cognitive skills." In H. C. Triandis and A. Heron (eds.), *Handbook of cross-cultural psychology,* vol. 4. Boston: Allyn and Bacon, 1981.

Stevenson, H. W., T. Parker, A. Wilkinson, B. Bonnevaux, and M. Gonzales, "Schooling, environment and cognitive development: A cross-cultural study." *Monographs of the Society for Research in Child Development*, 1978, 43, Serial No. 175.

# CHAPTER 11

Anderson, H. H. and G. L. Anderson, "Image of the teacher by adolescent children in seven countries." *American Journal of Orthopsychiatry*, 1961, *31*, 481–492.

Campbell, D. T., "The mutual methodological relevance of anthropology and psychology." In F. L. K. Hsu (ed.), *Psychological anthropology*. Homewood, Ill.: Dorsey Press, 1961, 333–352.

Cattell, R. B. and F. W. Warburton, *Objective personality and motivation tests*. Urbana: University of Illinois Press, 1967.

Diaz-Guerrero, R., "Socio-cultural and psychodynamic processes in adolescent transition and mental health." In M. Sherif and C. W. Sherif (eds.), *Problems of youth*. Chicago: Aldine, 1965, pp. 129–152.

Diaz-Guerrero, R., "Sociocultural premises, attitudes, and cross-cultural research." *International Journal of Psychology*, 1967, *2*, 79–87. Also in *Psychology of the Mexican: Culture and personality*. Austin: University of Texas Press, 1975.

Havighurst, R. J., M. E. Dubois, M. Csikszentmihalyi, and R. Doll, *A cross-national study of Buenos Aires and Chicago adolescents*. Basel: S. Karger, 1955.

Holtzman, W. H., J. S. Thorpe, J. D. Swartz, and E. W. Herron, *Inkblot perception and personality*. Austin: University of Texas Press, 1961.

Holtzman, W. H., R. Diaz-Guerrero, and J. D. Swartz, *Personality development in two cultures, a cross-cultural longitudinal study of school children in Mexico and the United States*. Austin: University of Texas Press, 1975.

Kagan, S., and M. C. Madsen, "Cooperation and competition of Mexican, Mexican-American, and Anglo-American children of two ages under four instructional sets." *Developmental Psychology*, 1971, *5*, 32–39.

Lynd, R. S., and H. M. Lynd, *Middletown*. New York: Harcourt, Brace, 1937.

Malinowski, B., *Sex and repression in savage society*. New York: Harcourt, Brace, 1927.

Maslow, A. H., and R. Diaz-Guerrero, "Delinquency as a value disturbance." In J. Peatman and E. L. Hartley (eds.), *Festschrift for Gardner Murphy*. New York: Harper & Row, 1960, 228–240.

Mead, M., *Coming of age in Samoa*. New York: Morrow, 1928.

Murphy, L. B., and A. E. Moriarty, *Vulnerability, coping, and growth*. New Haven, Conn.: Yale University Press, 1976.

Sapir, E., "The unconscious patterning of behavior in society." In E. S. Dummer (ed.), *The unconscious: A symposium*. Chicago: University of Chicago Press, 1927, 114–142.

Whiting, B. B. (ed.), *Six cultures: Studies in child rearing*. New York: Wiley, 1963.

Whiting, J. W. M., and I. L. Child, *Child training and personality.* New Haven, Conn.: Yale University Press, 1953.

Witkin, H. A., R. B. Dyk, H. F. Faterson, D. R. Godenough, and S. A. Karp, *Psychological differentiation.* New York: Wiley, 1962.

Witkin, H. A., D. Price-Williams, M. Bertini, B. Christiansen, P. K. Oltman, M. Ramirez, and J. van Meel, "Social conformity and psychological differentiation." *International Journal of Psychology,* 1974, *9,* 11–29.

## CHAPTER 12

Aron, I. E., "Moral philosophy and moral education: A critique of Kohlberg's theory." *School Review,* 1977, *85,* 197–217.

Bandura, A., *Aggression: A social learning analysis.* Englewood Cliffs, N.J.: Prentice-Hall, 1973.

Batt, H., "Guilt, shame and the bureaucratic model: With specific reference to Thai public administration." Doctoral dissertation, State University of New York at Albany, 1975. Ann Arbor, Mich.: University Microfilms, 1975, 75–9462. (a)

Batt, H., "Thai conceptions of justice on Kohlberg's moral development scale." Unpublished manuscript, 1975. (b).

Benedict, R., *The Chrysanthemum and the sword.* Boston: Houghton Mifflin, 1946.

Brandt, R. B., *Ethical theory.* Englewood Cliffs, New Jersey: Prentice-Hall, 1959.

Colby, A., "Evolution of a moral-development theory." In W. Daman (ed.), *Moral development.* San Francisco: Jossey-Bass, 1978.

Colby, A. L., J. Gibbs, L. Kohlberg, B. Speicher-Dubin, and D. Candee, "Standard Form Scoring Guide." Center for Moral Education, Harvard University, 1979.

Denney, N. W., and D. M. Duffy, "Possible environmental causes of stages in moral reasoning." *Journal of Genetic Psychology,* 1974, *125,* 277–283.

Edwards, C. P., "The effect of experience on moral development: Results from Kenya." Doctoral dissertation, Harvard Graduate School of Education, 1974. Ann Arbor, Michigan: University Microfilms, 1975, 75–16860.

Edwards, C. P., "Societal complexity and moral development: A Kenyan study." *Ethos,* 1975, *3,* 505–527.

Edwards, C. P., "Social experience and moral judgment in Kenyan young adults." *Journal of Genetic Psychology,* 1978, *133,* 19–29.

Edwards, C. P., "The comparative study of the development of moral judgment and reasoning." In R. H. Munroe, R. L. Munroe, and B. B. Whiting, *Handbook of Cross Cultural Human Development.* New York: Garland Press, 1981.

Gibbs, J. C., "Kohlberg's stages of moral judgment: a constructive critique." *Harvard Educational Review,* 1977, *47,* 43–61.

Gibbs, J. C., "Kohlberg's moral stage theory: a Piagetian revision." *Human Development,* 1979, *22,* 89–112.

Gibbs, J., L. Kohlberg, A. Colby, and B. Speicher-Dubin, "The domain and development of moral judgment: A theory and a method of assessment." In J. R. Meyer (ed.), *Reflections on values education.* Waterloo, Ont.: Wilfrid Laurier University Press, 1976.

Gilligan, C., "In a different voice: Women's conceptions of the self and of morality." *Harvard Educational Review,* 1977, 47, 481–517.

Gilligan, C., and M. F. Belenky, "A naturalistic study of abortion decisions." In R. L Selman and R. Yando (eds.), *Clinical-developmental psychology.* San Francisco: Jossey-Bass, 1980.

Gorsuch, R. L., and M. L. Barnes, "Stages of ethical reasoning and moral norms of Carib youths." *Journal of Cross-Cultural Psychology,* 1973, 4, 283–301.

Harkness, S., C. P. Edwards, and C. M. Super, "Social roles and moral reasoning: A case study in a rural African community." *Developmental Psychology,* 1981.

Harris, S., P. Mussen, and E. Rutherford, "Some cognitive, behavioral, and personality correlates of maturity of moral judgment." *Journal of Genetic Psychology,* 1976, 128, 123–135.

Havighurst, R. J., and B. L. Neugarten, *American Indian and white children: A sociological investigation.* Chicago: University of Chicago Press, 1955.

Hoffman, M. L., "Moral development." In P. Mussen (ed.), *Carmichael's manual of child psychology,* Vol. 2. New York: Wiley, 1970.

Holstein, C. B., "The relation of children's moral judgment level to that of their parents and to communications patterns in the family." In R. C. Smart and M. S. Smart (eds.), *Readings in child development and relationships.* New York: Macmillan, 1972.

Keasey, C. B., "Social participation as a factor in the moral development of preadolescents." *Developmental Psychology,* 1971, 5, 216–220.

Kohlberg, L., "The development of modes of moral thinking and choice in the years ten to sixteen." Unpublished doctoral dissertation, University of Chicago, 1958.

Kohlberg, L., "Moral development and identification." In H. W Stevenson (ed.), *Yearbook of the National Society for the Study of Education.* Part 1: *Child Psychology.* Chicago: University of Chicago Press, 1963.

Kohlberg, L., "Stage and sequence: The cognitive development approach to socialization." In D. Goslin (ed.), *Handbook of socialization.* New York: Rand McNally, 1969.

Kohlberg, L., "From is to ought: How to commit the naturalistic fallacy and get away with it in the study of moral development." In T. Mischel (ed.), *Cognitive development and epistemology.* New York: Academic Press, 1971. (a)

Kohlberg, L., "Cognitive-developmental theory and the practice of collective education." In M. Wolins and M. Gottesman (eds.), *Group care: An Israeli approach.* New York: Gordon and Breach, 1971. (b)

Kohlberg, L., "Moral stages and moralization: The cognitive-developmental approach." In T. Lickona (ed.), *Moral development and behavior.* New York: Holt, Rinehart & Winston, 1976.

Kohlberg, L., "Revisions in the theory and practice of moral development." In W. Damon (ed.), *Moral development*. San Francisco: Jossey-Bass, 1978.

Lickona, T., "Research on Piaget's theory of moral development." In T. Lickona (ed.), *Moral development and behavior*. New York: Holt, Rinehart & Winston, 1976.

Maqsud, M. "The effects of different educational environments on moral development of Nigerian children belonging to various tribes." Unpublished doctoral dissertation, University of London, 1976.

Maqsud, M., "The influence of social heterogeneity and sentimental credibility on moral judgments of Nigerian Muslim adolescents." *Journal of Cross-Cultural Psychology*, 1977, *8*, 113–122. (a)

Maqsud, M., "Social interaction and moral judgment in Northern Nigerian adolescents." Unpublished manuscript, Bayero University College, Kano, Nigeria, 1977. (b)

Maqsud, M., "Moral reasoning of Nigerian and Pakistani Muslim adolescents." *Journal of Moral Education*, 1977, *7*, 40–49. (c)

Mead, M., "Some anthropological considerations concerning guilt." In M. L. Reymert (ed.), *Feelings and emotions*. New York: McGraw-Hill, 1950.

Mischel, W., and H. N. Mischel, "A cognitive social-learning approach to morality and self-regulation." In T. Lickona (ed.), *Moral development and behavior*. New York: Holt, Rinehart & Winston, 1976.

Parikh, B., "Moral judgment development and its relation to family environmental factors in Indian and American families." *Child Development*, 1980, *51*, 1030–1039.

Piaget, J., *The moral judgment of the child*. London: Routledge and Kegan Paul, 1932. New York: Free Press, 1965.

Saltzstein, H. D., "Social influence and moral development: A perspective on the role of parents and peers." In T. Lickona (ed.), *Moral development and behavior*. New York: Holt, Rinehart & Winston, 1976.

Selman, R. L., "Social-cognitive understanding: A guide to educational and clinical practice." In T. Lickona (ed.), *Moral development and behavior*, New York: Holt, Rinehart & Winston, 1976.

Shoffeitt, P. G., "The moral development of children as a function of parental moral judgments and childrearing." Unpublished doctoral dissertation, George Peabody College for Teachers, Nashville, Tenn. 1971.

Sieber, J. E., "A social learning theory approach to morality." In M. Windmiller, N. Lambert, and E. Turiel (eds.), *Moral development and socialization*. Boston: Allyn and Bacon, 1980.

Simpson, E. L., "Moral development research: A case study of scientific cultural bias." *Human Development*, 1974, *17*, 81–106.

Sullivan, E. V., *Moral learning: Some findings, issues and questions*. New York: Paulist Press, 1975.

Turiel, E., "Conflict and transition in adolescent moral development." *Child Development*, 1974, *45*, 14–29.

Turiel, E., C. P. Edwards, and L. Kohlberg, "Moral development in Turkish children, adolescents and young adults." *Journal of Cross-Cultural Psychology,* 1978, *9* (1), 75–86.

Weinreich, H., "Some consequences of replicating Kohlberg's original moral development study on a British sample." *Journal of Moral Education,* 1977, *7,* 32–39.

White, C. B., "Moral judgment in college students: The development of an objective measure and its relationship to life experience dimensions." Unpublished doctoral dissertation, University of Georgia, 1973.

White, C. B., "Moral development in Bahamian school children: A cross-cultural examination of Kohlberg's stages of moral reasoning." *Developmental Psychology,* 1975, *11,* 535–536.

White, C. B., "Moral reasoning in Bahamian and United States elders: Cross-national comparison of Kohlberg's theory of moral development." Unpublished manuscript, University of Texas at Dallas, 1977.

White, C. B., N. Bushnell, and J. L. Regnemer, "Moral development in Bahamian school children: A three-year examination of Kohlberg's stages of moral development." *Developmental Psychology,* 1978, *14,* 58–65.

Whiting, B. B., *Paiute sorcery.* New York: Harcourt Brace Jovanovich, (Johnson Reprints), 1963.

Whiting, B. B., "The Kenyan career woman: Traditional and modern." *Annals of the New York Academy of Sciences,* 1973, *208,* 71–75.

Whiting, B. B., "Folk wisdom and child rearing." *Merrill-Palmer Quarterly,* 1974, *20,* 9–19.

Whiting, B. B., "Changing life styles in Kenya." *Deadalus,* 1977, *106,* 211–225.

Whiting, J. W. M., "Sorcery, sin and the superego: A cross-cultural study of some mechanisms of social control." In M. R. Jones (ed.), *Nebraska symposium on motivation.* Lincoln: University of Nebraska Press, 1959.

Whiting, J. W. M., and I. L. Child, *Child training and personality.* New Haven, Conn.: Yale University Press, 1953.

Whiting, B. B., and J. W. M. Whiting, *Children of six cultures: A psycho-cultural analysis.* Cambridge, Mass.: Harvard University Press, 1975.

# The Contributors

**Ben G. Blount** is a professor and head of the Department of Anthropology, University of Georgia. Dr. Blount received his Ph.D. from the University of California, Berkeley, and has conducted research in Mexico, Kenya, Uganda, Belize, and the United States. His current research interests include communication and socialization on a cross-cultural basis, and nonverbal communication and attention structures in the socialization of nonhuman primates.

**T. Berry Brazelton,** is an associate professor of pediatrics at Harvard Medical School, a practicing pediatrician, and head of a post-residency training center in pediatrics at Boston's Children's Hospital Medical Center. The research center at Harvard Medical School, in which he and Barry Lester participate, is concerned with neonatal behavior and early parent–infant interaction. His cross-cultural research, again in early infancy and child-rearing practices, has been in Mexico, Guatemala, East Africa, and Greece.

**Thomas Ciborowski** received his Ph.D. in experimental psychology at the University of California, Irvine. After postdoctoral study at Rockefeller University, he joined the faculty at the University of Hawaii. His latest publication, which he co-edited, is *Perspectives on Cross-Cultural Psychology* (Academic Press, 1979).

**Carolyn Pope Edwards** received her doctorate from Harvard University. Besides studying the development of moral judgment, she has collaborated with Beatrice B. Whiting on cross-cultural studies of sex differences in children's social behavior. While a postdoctoral fellow at Educational Testing Service, she began studies concerning preschool children's concepts of age categories and social roles. These studies have been continued at the University of Massachusetts–Amherst, where Dr. Edwards directs nursery and toddler programs and teaches early childhood education.

**Patricia L. Engle** is teaching developmental psychology and conducting research at California State University in San Luis Obispo. She received her Ph.D. from Stanford University in childhood development and was at INCAP from 1973 to 1976.

**Patricia Greenfield** received her Ph.D. in social psychology from Harvard's Department of Social Relations. Her doctoral research dealt with the influence of schooling on cognitive development of children in

Senegal. Later fieldwork in Mexico was concentrated on the nature and impact of informal education. This focus on informal education is being extended to a study of language acquisition in the United States.

**Wayne Holtzman** is president of the Hogg Foundation for Mental Health and Hogg Professor of Psychology and Education, the University of Texas. Dr. Holtzman has had a long-term interest in international aspects of psychology, has served as secretary-general, International Union of Psychological Science, and received the Interamerican Psychology Award from the Interamerican Psychological Association in 1979. Dr. Holtzman is a Stanford Ph.D. in psychology and statistics.

**Marc H. Irwin** currently is working in clinical and cross-cultural psychology at the Universidad Francisco Marroquin in Guatemala. He received his Ph.D. in developmental psychology from the University of California, Berkeley, and worked at INCAP from 1974 to 1979.

**Gustav Jahoda** is a professor of psychology at the University of Strathclyde, Glasgow. A past president of the International Association of Cross-Cultural Psychology, he has carried out fieldwork over some 20 years in West Africa and, to a limited extent, in Asia. While his earlier work was chiefly concerned with social psychological issues, his more recent interests are mainly spatial–perceptual development and social cognition.

**Robert E. Klein** has been director of the Human Development Division of INCAP since 1970. During this time he has directed the large research project summarized in this volume. He is a Minnesota Ph.D. in child psychology.

**Jean Lave** received her Ph.D. in social anthropology from Harvard University. Her dissertation was based on research among a group of Indians in Central Brazil. Since then she has taught at the University of California at Irvine. Her research on Liberian tailors investigated different forms of education (apprenticeship and school) and their impact on cognitive skills. She is currently studying informal learning and use of arithmetic skills in the United States.

**Barry M. Lester** is an assistant professor of pediatrics (psychology) at Harvard Medical School and director of developmental research at the Child Development Unit, Children's Hospital Medical Center. His research interests are in the development of the organization of behavior in infancy. Dr. Lester received his Ph.D. from Michigan State University, spent two years at the Institute of Nutrition of Central America and Panama, and taught at the University of Florida.

**Harry McGurk** was a visiting research fellow at Educational Testing Service. He is currently senior lecturer in the Department of Psychology at the University of Surrey. His research interests are in perceptual, cognitive, and social development during infancy and early childhood.

**Raphael M. Nyiti** was born in Arusha, Tanzania, attended Central Philippine University, and McGill University, and received his Ph.D. from the University of Illinois, Urbana-Champaign. He is an associate professor in the Department of Psychology, College of Cape Breton, Nova Scotia, Canada. Dr. Nyiti's special areas of research are culture, cognition, and children's understanding of reality.

**William Owens** has an M.S. in mathematics from New Mexico State University. He is devoting primary attention to the reanalysis of the INCAP data on physical growth and diet.

**Douglass Price-Williams** has taught at the London School of Economics and Rice University and is presently a professor in the Departments of Psychiatry and Anthropology at the University of California, Los Angeles. He received his Ph.D. in psychology from the University of London and has conducted research in Nigeria, Mexico, Guatemala, and Hawaii. He was co-editor of *Ethos* from the time of its founding until 1979.

**Harold W. Stevenson** is a professor of psychology and a Fellow in the Center for Human Growth and Development at the University of Michigan. He and his associates have conducted research on the influence of schooling and environmental conditions on children's cognitive development in Peru for the past 6 years. Currently he is engaged in a study of the correlates of academic achievement among children in Japan, Taiwan, and the United States. He is a Stanford Ph.D. in psychology and previously taught at the Universities of Texas and Minnesota.

**Charles M. Super** is a developmental psychologist interested in both the universal and the culturally specific patterns of human development. In studying the complementary roles of biology and environment in creating these patterns, he has worked with children and families in Kenya, Guatemala, and the United States. Dr. Super holds research appointments at Harvard University in the Schools of Education, Public Health, and Medicine, and at the Judge Baker Guidance Center in Boston.

**Sara Harkness,** a psychological anthropologist, has conducted research in Kenya, Colombia, Guatemala, and the United States. Mental health of women and children is a central topic in her work, with particular attention on the role of culture in mediating sound development. Dr. Harkness holds research appointments at the Judge Baker Guidance Center in Boston and at Harvard University in the Schools of Education and Medicine.

**John W. Townsend,** a social psychologist with a Ph.D. from the University of Minnesota, is currently involved in the evaluation of an integrated program of primary health care in Guatemala.

**Daniel A. Wagner** completed his Ph.D. in psychology at the University of Michigan after serving two years in the Peace Corps. Since 1976, he has been an assistant professor in the Graduate School of Education at the University of Pennsylvania. He has been a Fulbright Lecturer at the Université Mohamed V in Rabat, Morocco, and has recently spent two years as a visiting postdoctoral fellow in the Laboratory of Human Development at Harvard University.

**Charles Yarbrough** is a statistician with a Ph.D. from the University of California, Berkeley. At present he is working on the application of computers to marketing research in the United States, and was a statistician–programmer at INCAP from 1970 to 1977.

# Index